Agnes Repplier, Ernest Clifford Peixotto

Philadelphia

The Place and the People

Agnes Repplier, Ernest Clifford Peixotto

Philadelphia
The Place and the People

ISBN/EAN: 9783337019273

Printed in Europe, USA, Canada, Australia, Japan

Cover: Foto ©Andreas Hilbeck / pixelio.de

More available books at **www.hansebooks.com**

PHILADELPHIA

THE PLACE

AND

THE PEOPLE

BY

AGNES REPPLIER

AUTHOR OF " ESSAYS IN IDLENESS," " POINTS
OF VIEW," " VARIA," ETC., ETC.

WITH ILLUSTRATIONS BY ERNEST C. PEIXOTTO

New York

THE MACMILLAN COMPANY

LONDON: MACMILLAN & CO., LTD.

1904

Norwood Press
J. S. Cushing & Co. · Berwick & Smith
Norwood Mass. U.S.A

To the Memory of

PHILADELPHIA'S FOUNDER

CONTENTS

vii

ILLUSTRATIONS

CHAPTER V

CHAPTER VI

CHAPTER VII

CHAPTER VIII

CHAPTER IX

CHAPTER X

CHAPTER XV

CHAPTER XVI

CHAPTER XVII

CHAPTER XVIII

CHAPTER XIX

To the Memory of

PHILADELPHIA'S FOUNDER

CONTENTS

CHAPTER X

THE EVE OF THE REVOLUTION.

CHAPTER XI

THE DAWN OF THE REVOLUTION.

CHAPTER XII

WAR.

CHAPTER XIII

A GAY CAPTIVITY.

CHAPTER XIV

LORDS OF MISRULE.

CHAPTER XV

CHAPTER XVI

CHAPTER XVII

CHAPTER XVIII

CHAPTER XIX

ILLUSTRATIONS

xiii

INTRODUCTION

OUT of the mists that mercifully conceal those early
school-days which, being forgotten, are unduly
praised, comes the spectre of a little American history
with green sides and a red back, an odious little history, arranged in questions and answers like a cate-
chism, and wholly destitute of anything that could
arouse childish interest or quicken childish enthusiasm.
One page and one only lingers in my memory, as a return for the many gloomy hours wasted in the companionship of this book, — a page containing a print
of West's picture, of the "Great Treaty" at Shackamaxon.

Our grandfathers loved this picture, and implicitly
believed all the details of the incident it portrays.
We have outgrown our grandfathers' narrow artistic
standards, and their broad historic credulity; and the
agreeable consciousness of such double progress en-
riches our self-esteem. Yet it is a pleasant scene that
West painted in those easy, ignorant days, when im-
pressionism had still to be invented, and people had
not begun to make a fetich of truth. The "Treaty
Elm" spreading its mighty branches, as proud and as

honoured as England's "Royal Oak." William Penn, years older than his age, dressed as he never did dress in early manhood, benignantly blessing everybody. Venerable Friends, in the loosest and longest of coats, holding a parchment deed of mighty bulk, the document which has been lost for more than two hundred years. Boxes and bales of goods scattered on the sward. Indian braves solemnly inspecting their contents. Indian squaws and pappooses grouped picturesquely in the foreground. The whole composition suggesting an entertainment midway between a church fair and an afternoon tea, placid, decorous, satisfactory, and sincere.

This was the peaceful fashion in which the little Quaker colony took her infant steps, this was the atmosphere which nurtured her tender youth. And now, after two centuries have rolled slowly by, something of the same spirit lingers in the quiet city which preserves the decorum of those early years, which does not jostle her sister cities in the race of life, nor shout loud cries of triumph in their ears, nor flaunt magnificent streamers in the breeze to bid the world take note of each pace she advances.

Every community, like every man, carries to old age the traditions of its childhood, the inheritance derived from those who bade it live. And Philadelphia, though she has suffered sorely from rude and alien hands, still bears in her tranquil streets the impress of the Founder's touch. Simplicity, dignity, reserve, characterize her now as in Colonial days. She remembers those days with silent self-respect, placing a high value upon names which then were honoured, and are honoured still. The pride of the past mingles and is one with the pride of the present. The stainless record borne by her citizens a hundred and fifty years ago flowers anew in the stainless record their great-great-grandsons bear to-day ; and the city cherishes in her cold heart the long annals of the centuries, softening the austerity of her presence for these favoured inheritors of her best traditions. She is not eager for the unknown ; she is not keen after excitement ; she is not enamoured of noise. Her least noticeable characteristic is enthusiasm. Her mental balance cannot lightly be disturbed. *Surtout pas trop de zèle*, she says with Talleyrand ; and the slow, sure process by which her persuasions harden into convictions does not leave her, like a derelict, at the mercy of wind and wave. She spares herself the arduous labour of forming new opinions every morning, by recollecting and cherishing her opinions of yesterday. It is a habit which promotes solidity of thought.

To those who by right of heritage call themselves her sons, and even to such step-children as are, by nature or grace, attuned to the chill tranquillity of their foster mother, Philadelphia has a subtle charm that endures to the end of life. In the restful atmosphere of her sincere indifference, men and women gain clearness of perspective, and the saving grace of modesty. Few pedestals are erected for their accommodation. They walk the level ground, and, in the healthy absence of local standards, have no alternative save to accept the broad disheartening standards of the world. Philadelphians are every whit as mediocre as their neighbours, but they seldom encourage each other in mediocrity by giving it a more agreeable name. Something of the old Quaker directness, something of the old Quaker candour, — a robust candour not easily subdued, — still lingers in the city founded by the "white truth-teller," whose word was not as the words of other men, — spoken to conceal his thoughts, and the secret purpose of his soul.

Deep is the debt of gratitude which the City of Peace owes to the many hands that have laboured for two hundred years in her behalf; but deepest of all is her debt to Penn who knew her little but who loved her well, whom she thrust aside from her councils, and forgot in his hour of need, but whose influence lingers to-day in that atmosphere of serenity which is the finest characteristic of Philadelphia. More impetuous towns speed like meteors on their paths, dazzling the western world by their velocity, and dazzled themselves by their own glitter and glory; but the Quaker City sees them rush by without envy, without ambition, without distaste, without emotions of any kind. She knows, and she has known for many years, what is best for her; and if this best be ever out of reach, it is not by mere swiftness of step that she can hope to overtake it. She is content to grow slowly if she can grow symmetrically, and if grace and strength keep pace with her increasing bulk. She is content to face the future if she can hold closely to the past, recalling its lessons, valuing its traditions, respecting its memory, and loving in her cold, steadfast fashion the living links which connect her with her honourable history, with her part in the great story of the nation.

PHILADELPHIA

CHAPTER I

/ 0 3 2 4

THE FOUNDER OF THE QUAKER CITY

IT is hard for us who live in an age of careless and
cheerful tolerance to understand the precise inconveniences attending religious persecution. The lamentable decline of church discipline leaves us powerless to
interfere with the erroneous convictions of our neighbours, and our own polite indifference permits them to
cherish their delusions unassailed. We are so full of
courteous phrases, pulpit bowing to pulpit, and "*Après
vous, Monsieur,*" murmured all along the line, that it is
like stepping into another world, into a bleak, clear,
atmosphere of sincere ungraciousness, when we hear
what old Robert Burton — a man of infinite good temper — has to say anent the Anabaptists; or when we
listen to the vigorous anathemas launched by Sydney
Smith against the Methodists, or even when we open
the diary of that fine old English gentleman, John
Evelyn, and read *his* opinion of Quakers. On the
eighth of July, 1656, he visits some of these innocent
offenders in prison; and, far from expressing any sym-

pathy for their sufferings, or any admiration for their fortitude, he writes them coldly down a " fanatic sect of dangerous principles, who show no respect to any man, magistrate or other, and seem a melancholy, proud sort of people, and exceedingly ignorant."

One year before this prison visit, little William Penn, a boy of eleven, enjoyed his first ghostly " manifestation." There was " an external glory in the room," and the voice of the Lord rang in his ears and in his heart, summoning him to the life of the spirit, and to the relinquishment of earthly vanities. The visionary child, with his brilliant eyes, his fluent speech, his moods of strange abstraction, must have been a sore trial to his father, that hearty sailor, Sir William Penn, who, being himself singularly unvexed by nice distinctions of creed, failed, at any time, to understand what his troublesome son was worrying about. Vice-Admiral of England's navy at thirty-one, Sir William fought as valiantly and as blithely for Cromwell as for Charles. England's foes were his foes, and England's ruler was his ruler, and England's faith was his faith ; and it was certainly not a sailor's business to inquire too closely into these things, nor to meddle with church or state. The friend and associate of Mr. Samuel Pepys, — who at heart cordially detested him, — his careless gallantry to Mrs. Pepys aroused the jealousy of her neglectful and exacting husband. It was at Penn's house that Mr. Pepys supped so gayly one Sunday night — the

Vice-Admiral's brother, "a traveller and a merry man," being of the party — that the next morning found the wretched diarist sick and befuddled, with an aching head, and a spirit steeped in woe. Then came along Sir William, in nowise the worse for his potations, and, pitying the civilian's miserable plight, advised him jovially to drink "two draughts of sack," as a sure remedy for his disorder, — which counsel Mr. Pepys promptly followed, and found the physic marvellously efficacious.

Did little William peep in upon this scandalous supper party, and listen to the merry uncle's tales, made all the merrier by his mellow mood? The boy was no youthful prig, for all his visions and manifestations. He was straight, and tall, and strong, loved athletic sports, had a fluctuating taste for cheerful company, and showed no lack of discernment anent things that were of the earth earthy. Between him and his father there existed a cordial understanding until at Oxford he began to attend the preaching of Thomas Fox, instead of going duly to the college service. This might have been passed over, but the immediate results were of a character which demanded notice. Young Penn not only refused to wear his academic gown,—as savouring vaguely of prelacy,—but he apparently refused to permit other students to wear theirs in peace ; and his attitude was so determined and annoying—the gowns being unpopular at best—that he was sent down from college for nonconformity in 1661.

Sir William, angry, distressed, and hopelessly bewildered by what seemed to him much ado about nothing, decided, like a wise old worldling, not to make a martyr of his son by showing any grave displeasure, but to despatch him at once to France, where he might be trusted to quickly forget this unimaginable folly. To Paris accordingly went the youthful Penn, was presented at the court of Louis XIV., enjoyed the new experience amazingly, and made a brave, boyish figure amid those brilliant scenes. In fact, when he returned to England, he was what Mr. Pepys termed a "modish person"; and we note in the diary a ring of amusing but very human displeasure at the admiration this "compleat young gentleman" never failed to excite. "Comes Mr. Penn to visit me," writes the unpacified Pepys. "I perceive something of learning he hath got; but a great deal, if not too much, of the vanity of the French garb, and affected manner of speech and gait."

The cure being thus happily effected, Penn began to enjoy life in earnest, and found London very little behind Paris in affording the means of entertainment. The terrible advent of the Plague oppressed him, indeed, not unnaturally, with "a deep sense of the vanity of the world"; but he shook off this heavy-heartedness in Ireland, whither his father had sent him to look after the family estates, and where we find him presently fighting with carnal weapons — and in the

gayest of spirits — to put down one of those period-
ical uprisings which for many centuries have diversi-
fied the monotony of Irish life. So well did this
brief campaign please him, that he decided with
swift incontinence to adopt the profession of arms,

which decision was,
strangely enough,
combated by the sail-
or father, who had
destined his clever
son for the civil ser-
vice, and who was
shrewd enough to
know in what field a
man's fortunes might
be most rapidly ad-
vanced. It was dur-
ing the warlike
episode of 1666 that
the charming picture
was painted which

PENN'S CREST

now seems so utterly at variance with Penn's career,
and which, for that very reason perhaps, has been
prized, and cherished, and duplicated, until it is pleasantly familiar to us all. The original still hangs, it
is said, on the walls of that stately home which John
Penn the younger built for himself on the Isle of
Portland, and which is now the seat of J. Merrick

Head, Esq.; but the Pennsylvania Historical Society in Philadelphia possesses an excellent copy, and there is another at Tempsford Hall in Bedfordshire; while Schoff's admirable engraving has found its way into hundreds of English and American homes. The half-length portrait in steel breastplate and lace cravat, with dark hair flowing loosely over the mail-clad shoulders, looks more like a cavalier than a Quaker. The brilliant eyes have the splendid confidence of youth; a lurking smile is lost in the flexible corners of the mouth. Altogether a gay and gallant young gentleman, and not unlike the portrait of the gay and gallant Admiral his father, which, painted by Sir Peter Lely, ruffles it in conscious pride on the walls of Greenwich Hospital.

At the very time, however, that the world's victory seemed securely won, it was on the eve of discomfiture. The ubiquitous and untiring Fox was preaching now in Ireland, and Penn's pietism, which had been either lulled to sleep by pleasure, or forgotten in the tumult of hard work, awoke again to vehement life under the controlling influence of a religion which satisfied all the spiritual requirements of his nature. The doctrine of renunciation, the yielding up of worldly distinctions,—this had always seemed to him God's word spoken to the soul; and once more, and for the last time, he turned resolutely away from a life filled to the brim with honourable

ambitions and rewards. In a very few weeks we
find him arrested for "riot and tumultuous assembling," — *i. e.*, listening peaceably to Quaker sermons; and — having not yet reached that point of
sanctity when persecution becomes a pleasure — we
find him also writing indignant letters to Lord
Orrery, son of the Lord-Lieutenant, demanding an
immediate release from jail. Six months later, Mr.
Pepys records in his journal, this time with malicious
satisfaction,—there is always something which does
not displease us in the misfortunes of our friends,—
that "Mr. Penn, who has lately come over from
Ireland, is a Quaker again, or some such melancholy
thing."

Sir William, exasperated beyond the limits of endurance, argued and entreated in vain. He was even then
willing to temporize with his unmanageable son, being
at heart sincerely indifferent as to what that son believed, provided he would behave like other people,
which was precisely what the ardent young convert declined to do. A compromise of the broadest kind was
finally proposed. Sir William declared himself ready
to close his eyes to all eccentricities — they were simply
eccentricities to him — if Penn in return would consent
to uncover to the King, to the Duke of York, and to
himself. Penn stanchly refused, and left his father's
roof for the troubled life of a nonconformist preacher
in London. Mrs. Oliphant, who wrote an elaborate

sketch of Philadelphia's Founder, marked by her usual anxious sense of justice, and by more than her usual lack of sympathy, intimated that, beyond some gentle ridicule, the Quakers suffered little persecution from English laws. But if any of us were called upon to endure as much to-day, I doubt not we should think it heavy enough. The Quakers were not burned, that is true, stakes and fagots being out of vogue since Mary's reign; but fines and imprisonment grow wearisome to the spirit, and so Penn probably thought when he found himself committed to the Tower for the unlicensed publication of " Sandy Foundations Shaken."

The book made a profound impression upon many minds. Mrs. Pepys read it aloud to Mr. Pepys, who grows strangely serious in discussing it. It is well written, he thinks, so very well written that he can hardly understand how the young Penn came to write it; yet it is a "serious sort of book, and not fit for everybody to read," — Mr. Pepys being of Lord Chesterfield's opinion concerning those who disturb the serene convictions of society. The authorities considered it eminently unfit for everybody, or for anybody, to read; and its author, still in the Tower, defended his principles in " No Cross, no Crown," and in " Innocency with her Open Face," a charming title that sounds as though it had come straight from the " Faerie Queene."

The good offices of the Duke of York finally procured Penn's release from prison, and Sir William, a perfect model of long-suffering paternity, took him back into favour, his contempt for Quakerism being somewhat modified by the knowledge that it had in no-wise weakened his son's natural aptitude for business. So he paid, with what serenity he could muster, the fines that followed on each new indiscretion, kept him in charge of the Irish estates, and bequeathed to him, when he died, his blessing, an annual income of sixteen hundred pounds, and a claim of sixteen thousand pounds against the crown, to which happy, though by no means unusual circumstance, we owe our Quaker town. To wring money, especially a just debt, from the Merry Monarch was something that bordered closely on the impossible. Penn realized this as fully as his father had realized it before him ; and, pondering the matter over, there came to him the first faint outlines of a plan which, if carried out, might mean not wealth alone, but such distinction as his new faith permitted him to enjoy, and, above all, a peaceful haven from the petty persecutions which assailed him. For more and more, as his convictions grew and strengthened, had he come into sharp conflict with the unyielding majesty of the law, and he was not fitted by nature for the passive rôle of sanctity. His father's blood ran hotly in his veins, and, far from suffering in silence, he lifted up his voice with remarkable fluency, and a lamentable lack of meekness, in behalf of the holy cause. A young man who would call the Vice-Chancellor of Oxford a " poor mushroom," must have studied but lamely the part of consistent and dutiful non-resistance.

So the King was entreated to pay the Old World debt with a grant of New World land, and was by no means ready to consent to even this kingly compromise. Much pleading and long waiting well-nigh wore out the pleader's patience, before Charles, urged by the friendly Duke of York, set his royal seal in 1680 to the parchment which made William Penn governor and proprietor of a province whose boundaries were to be disputed for many years to come. The land was vested in Penn in fee simple, subject to the quit-rent of two beaver skins, and a fifth part of its gold and silver ore, — at which we Pennsylvanians smile to-day, thinking of those other mines which lay with their untold wealth beneath the fertile soil. The governor was invested by the charter with executive and legislative power, subject to the control of the Privy Council, and to the "advice and consent of the freemen of the province," who were to help make the laws before they reverenced and obeyed them. Sylvania was the pretty name chosen for the forest-covered district, to which appellation Charles prefixed the Penn, and was so pleased with his royal jest that he refused to relinquish it. So "Pensilvania," as it is spelled in the original charter, like Baltimore, enshrines its founder's memory, and affords a welcome relief from the perpetual " New," — New York, New England, New Jersey, New Orleans, — which

our unimaginative ancestors were never weary of repeating with monotonous loyalty to their lost homes.

Matters having been brought to this successful issue,
Penn applied himself immediately to a threefold task.
He despatched his cousin William Markham, an officer
in the King's navy, as deputy governor, to the province,
to inspect its condition, to report upon its possibilities,
to choose a site for "a fair city," and above all to assure

"A SITE FOR 'A FAIR CITY'"

the Germans, Swedes, and English already settled along
the Delaware that there should be no infringement upon
their rights and privileges. The young Proprietor
next drew up his first prospectus, addressed to the Free
Society of Traders, in which he was exceedingly ex-
plicit and businesslike concerning the cost of the trip,
the buying and renting of land, the chances offered to
agricultural and mechanical labour ; only permitting
himself a few words of gentle allurement when describ-

ing the country he had never seen, — a country, he said, teeming with fish and game, and "six hundred miles nearer the sun than England," which truth probably impressed itself forcibly upon the colonists' minds when their first July came around. The result of this excellent advertising was the almost immediate sale of five hundred and sixty-five thousand acres of land, in lots of from two hundred and fifty to twenty thousand acres.

A still more congenial occupation to the long-harassed and persecuted Quaker was the framing of a constitution, of a code of laws which should temper justice with mercy, and restrain ill-doing, while it permitted the widest possible freedom to every citizen. In this labour of love Penn was nobly assisted by Algernon Sidney, and, between them, they produced those statutes which Montesquieu has so infelicitously compared to the laws of Lycurgus, but which in truth were far more distinguished by leniency than by Spartan rigour. At a time when every convicted thief was promptly hanged in England, Penn found no crime save murder to warrant the death sentence. The clauses which punished profane swearing, intemperance, and card playing ; and which strictly forbade the "drinking of healths," "stage plays," — of which there were none, — "masks and revels," and all "evil sports and games," — even the innocent old games of May-day, were added to the original code by the first Assembly, which met to represent the "freemen of the province" in 1682. A rather unruly Assembly this, and as troublesome as freemen and their representatives were ever wont to be. It marred Penn's beloved constitution with a number of rigid little rules and regulations to promote sanctity, or the pretence of sanctity, before it permitted his statutes to pass into the "Great Law." Yet even in this altered form he was so strenuously attached to it that, as soon as the first schoolhouses were built in Philadelphia, he ordered it should be read aloud to all the boys and girls every scholastic year.

PENN'S SEAL

In one respect alone the code remained unchanged. There was to be tolerance in the new colony for every form of Christian belief; "freedom," as Gabriel Thomas aptly phrased it, "for all persuasions in a sober and civil way." This tolerance was so far in advance of its generation, that it awoke surprise and consternation rather than universal delight. The New World had been as ready as the Old to lay a chastening hand upon every unsanctioned and unwelcome creed, and in more than one instance the colonists had thoroughly enjoyed dispensing to others the hard fare they had received at home. Only Lord Baltimore and Roger Williams, strangely indifferent to the blessed privilege of "doing as you have been done by," proclaimed in Maryland and Rhode Island the absolute liberty granted to every subject of the King to worship God as he or she thought right. Quaker, Baptist, and Roman Catholic stood side by side, the pioneers of religious freedom in America.

To Penn, at least, it all seemed so natural, so reasonable, and so right. He was but thirty-six when the King signed that memorable parchment deed, and his heart beat high with hope as the peaceful city of his dreams shaped itself slowly into a realized ambition. He had married a wife of his own faith, the daughter of Sir William Springett of Brayle Place, Ringmere, Sussex. She had a charming Italian name, Gulielma Maria, a beautiful face, and a pious disposition. She bore him children, children who were still too young to bring sorrow and heartbreak in their train. A man in his early prime, with superb health, an ample fortune, an honourable career, and, above and beyond all, a mission — a mission in which he firmly believed, and for which he ardently desired success — what wonder that Penn felt an exultant "uplifting of the spirit" when he looked westward over the great grey seas to the land of promise, to the visionary city of peace!

CHAPTER II

THE FOUNDING OF THE QUAKER CITY

IT was on a quiet afternoon in the autumn of 1681 that three ships lay in London harbour, making ready for a protracted voyage, fraught with some danger and every possible discomfort. Past these vessels came the royal barge, its silken banners fluttering in the breeze; and the King, noticing the swift bustle of departure, asked what ships they were, and whither they were bound? On being told that they bore the first Quaker emigrants to Pennsylvania, Charles had the barge rowed closer, and gravely, yet with mirthful eyes, bestowed his princely blessing on the decorous groups, who stood, their heads covered, but their hearts filled with serious emotion, to receive it. They understood clearly enough that the good-natured monarch had always wished them well, and that the persecutions they had suffered were not of his contriving. Indeed, it is little wonder that both Charles and his less affable and less tolerant brother should have sincerely liked

15

the Quakers, who seldom gave any trouble, took no part in public life, and shrank from the noisy quarrels of worldlings. With a strange indifference to science, to wit, to learning, and to literature, they combined a breadth of vision, a sane tolerance of humanity, and an instinctive knowledge of what we are apt to consider the principles of purely modern philanthropy. "Since the time of the primitive Christians," says Mr. Sydney Fisher, "there never had been such apostles of gentleness. They were a striking contrast to the Puritans, every one of whom was a restless politician, whose religion included a theory of civil government which he felt it his duty to enforce."

So Charles gave his blessing with the kindliest good-will to these innocent non-combatants, who, their hearts full of hope, their hands unstained by blood, set sail with the outgoing tide for the far-away shores of America. It would have been more picturesque had Penn accompanied them, but he remained in London, busy with the sale of land, and with schemes for the advancement of the colony. The three little ships carried with them in his place three commissioners, a plan of the proposed city, and a conciliatory letter to the Delaware Indians, who had always claimed these heavily wooded tracts as their favourite hunting-ground. Friendly Indians they were for the most part, who had been

conquered years before and reduced to subjection by
the victorious Five Nations, and who were, moreover
accustomed to the sight of white men dwelling
within their territory. There was little trouble to
be apprehended from them, unless goaded by unkindness into hostility, and the Quakers were not
settlers likely to arouse the fierce passion of resentment in the Red Man's bosom. They regarded him,
neither as an unwarranted interloper, which is our
modern point of view, nor as accursed of God, and
cut off from all mercy in Heaven or on earth, which
was the gentle conviction of the Puritan. They
made allowances for his being an Indian, since it
had pleased God to create him one ; and they conceived that he was not without some claim to the
land which Providence had granted him for his own.
These extraordinary sentiments — the strangest heresy ever yet carried from the Old World to the
New — bore lasting fruit in the good-will shown to
Pennsylvania's colony by its savage neighbours. The
early history of the Quaker City is almost ignominious in its peacefulness, monotonous in its unvarying,
uninteresting prosperity. By the side of infant Philadelphia, so quiet and so well behaved, the story of
infant New Orleans reads like some long fairy tale,
in which the picturesque, the marvellous, the sinister,
and the lawless, contend on every glowing page for
mastery.

c

Yet the decorous record of the little settlement on
the Delaware is not without its sober charm, a charm
to be sought for in minute detail and simple incident. With incredible speed, the colonists, who had
first found shelter in caves along the river's bank,
built themselves log cabins and frame houses, chilly,
capacious, strong. The emigration increased rapidly.
Twenty-three ships sailed from England to Pennsylvania in 1682, and by the close of 1683, three hundred and fifty-seven houses had been erected in
Philadelphia. Already, though but three years old,
it had become the city of homes. But the first
child of English parents was born in a cave, afterwards used as a rude tavern, and called the "Penny-
pot." To this child, John Key, Penn presented a lot
of ground, and he lived to be eighty-five years old,
and was known as the "first born" to the day of
his death, though by that time early traditions and
landmarks were rapidly disappearing from the town.
When Penn arrived in November, 1682, he found his
colony so well advanced, its surroundings so tranquil
and beautiful, that in his enthusiasm he pronounced
the country worthy of Abraham, and Isaac, and
Jacob; a land overflowing with the visible mercies
of God. "Oh! how sweet is the quiet of these
parts, freed from the anxious and troublesome solicitations, hurries, and perplexities of woeful Europe,"
he wrote joyously, and no doubt sincerely, being as

yet new to the situation, and unaware of the persistence with which "woeful Europe" tugs at the
heartstrings of an exile. The "fair mansion-house"
of Pennsbury had not yet been begun, but he built the
demure little Letitia House for his winter quarters,
promising himself, doubtless, many years of peaceful

"THE DEMURE LITTLE LETITIA HOUSE"

and congenial labour in the city which owed him
her existence. His letter of 1683, to the Free Society of Traders, gives unstinted praise to the new
province ; its game, its fruit, its abundant crops, its
oysters "six inches long," its pure and wholesome
water, (alas ! alas !) and its charming climate, which
we might imagine had altered strangely since those
halcyon days, were it not for another letter — a

private missive this time to Lord North — in which Penn ruefully confesses that "the weather often changeth without notice, and is constant almost in its inconstancy." "No climate at all," as M. Bourget wittily expresses it, — "only samples of weather."

The meeting of the first Assembly, which adopted Penn's code with many modifications, the unsuccessful attempt to settle the boundary line between Pennsylvania and Maryland, and the famous treaty with the Indians at Shackamaxon engrossed the governor's attention. The treaty is one of those historic facts or fictions, the details of which we are taught to believe as children, and to doubt as adults, with the result that we are credulous or sceptical according to our mental attitudes. Those for whom it is the sole incident that emerges from the mist of long-forgotten lessons are naturally unwilling to relinquish a single circumstance, not even the broad blue sash, Penn's only emblem of authority. If there be no evidence beyond tradition for the support of the truth, there is no shadow of improbability, and there are no conflicting statements to give tradition the lie. The loss of the original document is of scant significance, for little importance was attached to it at the time, and many papers shared its fate in those early careless days. The fact that the speech assigned to Penn was really uttered by him twenty years later, is but an instance of the way in which history is made, the natural and admirable process by which anything that will harmonize is woven into the narrative. Nothing can be clearer than the story as it has come down to us, — the story of a great treaty made and kept. The Indians cherished its memory for generations; the Quakers were justly proud of a deed that did them infinite credit; and the English have always vied with Americans in honouring a compact which, as Voltaire lucidly remarked, was "the only treaty between savages and Christians that had not been ratified by an oath, and that was never broken."

When the English army occupied Philadelphia in 1777, a guard was placed before the "Treaty Elm," to preserve it from the evil chances of war. The picture by which West has so deeply offended antiquarians has at least familiarized many of us with that famous tree, and with all that happened beneath its spreading branches. Penn was, indeed, at the time, no corpulent old man in full-skirted coat and broad-brimmed hat; but tall, athletic, well formed, and, notwithstanding his Quaker creed, extremely fastidious about dress, especially about his curled and flowing wigs; — "the handsomest, best-looking, and liveliest of gentlemen," says an old chronicler, "affable and friendly with the humblest."

Friendly with the Indians he certainly was, winning their affection by his kindness, and their respect by his activity and endurance. The undeviating policy of conciliation which he pursued for years ensured the docility of the savages, and the consequent safety of an unarmed community, which went about its daily toil as unmolested as though it lived in the heart of civilization. There have not been lacking virtuous voices to protest against Penn's inadequate payment for land of which the Indians never realized the value; but as so few colonists were in the habit of paying anything at all, or of acknowledging any claim, save their own, to provinces granted them by the crown, it seems hardly worth while to save up our resentment for the one man who gave what was demanded.

It was not from Indians that Penn suffered his keenest disappointments, but from those whose lasting gratitude he had rashly hoped to win. Already the bickerings had begun which were destined to overshadow his life. Already he found it a difficult matter to please his colonists, to control the Assembly, to have his own way about anything. " Is it not the general history of colonies," says that garrulous old chronicler, John Watson, "to whine and fret like wayward children, to give immeasurable trouble and expense to rear them to maturity, and then to reward the parental care with alienation?" If this be true, Pennsylvania was certainly no exception to the rule. Penn loved the province he had founded, the goodly city he had helped to build. He hoped to make her beautiful as

well as prosperous, and had dreamed of a noble river
front along the Delaware, of a promenade and a public
párk, with the trees of the forest primeval spreading
their mighty branches over the cooling waves. The
steady encroachment of warehouses and shipping
yards upon this river front, the inevitable triumph of

"OVER THE COOLING WAVE"

the commercial over the picturesque, chagrined him
deeply. But before ever the buildings rose frowning
and ugly on the bank, there were more urgent anxieties to mar his peace of mind. Among them was the
still unsettled boundary line, which promised endless
trouble in the future. Lord Baltimore being a man
loath to relinquish his territorial rights, and not

easily moved by arguments or solicitations. It seemed Penn's wisest course to return to England, and lay the matter once more before the Privy Council. Other questions arose which required his presence in London. He had left his wife and family in the Old World, not without serious misgivings ; for Gulielma Maria, pious and beautiful though she was, had her share of gentle feminine weaknesses, all of which are hinted at very plainly in the long letter of instruction which Penn wrote for her guidance in his absence. He entreats her, for example, to be more regular at her meals ; to have her dinner served promptly at the appointed hour ; to "guard against encroaching friendships," which lead to lamentable waste of time ; and, above all, to forbear grieving herself with careless servants ; — excellent but futile advice, easier at any time to give than to obey. So back to "woeful Europe," which seemed a little less woful after two years' absence, back to household cares and to graver issues went Penn in 1684. He intended to rejoin the colony within a twelvemonth. He remained in England nearly fifteen years.

CHAPTER III

THE QUAKER CITY'S CHILDHOOD

A COMPACT little town as level as the sands of the desert; narrow streets running evenly from east to west, and from north to south, intersecting each other with monotonous regularity like the lines which mark out the squares on a checkerboard; houses built of wood or of bright red brick, as much alike as the sea-god's daughters, — "as the faces of sisters should be." A town built between two rivers; the broad and beautiful Delaware rolling on one side to the sea, and, on the other, barely two miles away, the placid little Schuylkill, unskirted yet by human habitation, untainted by mill, or mine, or factory, winding, a sylvan stream, through woods of oak and chestnut. There was much comfort and scant luxury within the red brick houses. Not a carpet nor a rug for many years upon the sanded floors. Heavy English furniture in the low-ceilinged rooms, pewter dishes on the shelves, huge logs burning merrily in the wide fireplaces, good food, and plenty of it, in the larders. For to the game, and fish, and six-inch-long oysters, the colonists had added swiftly the Indian delicacies, — corn, and hominy,

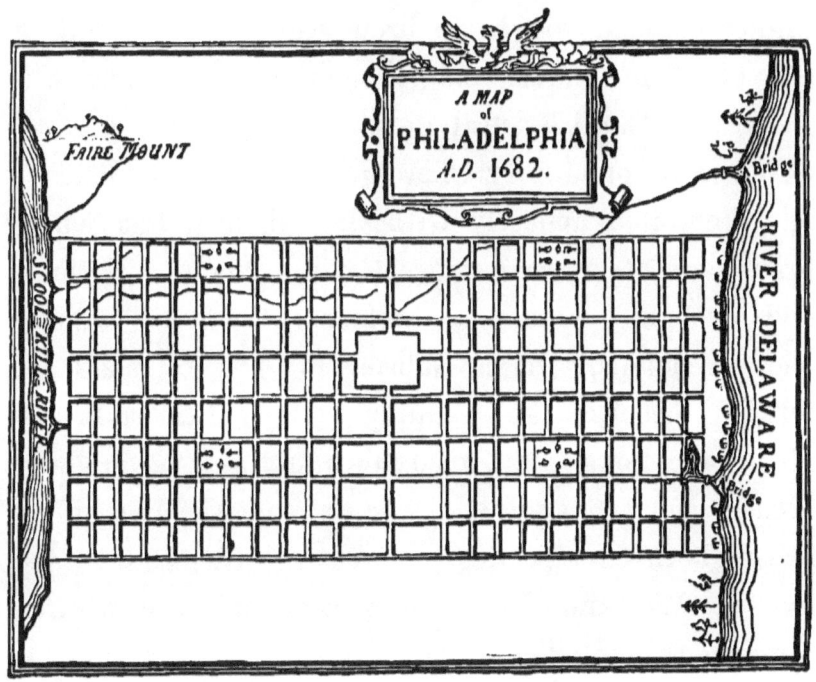

and the delicious succotash. Mighty drinkers they were, too, in their own sober fashion, consuming vast quantities of ale and spirits, and making no serious inroads on the "pure and wholesome" water; althoug we are gravely assured that particular pumps, one r i Walnut Street, and one in Norris Alley, were held in especial favour, as having the best water in the tow ' for the legitimate purpose of boiling greens. The first beer was made from molasses, and we have Penn's assurance that when "well boyled, with Sassafras or Pine infused into it, this is a very tolerable drink," — which we should never have supposed. Rum pun' was also in liberal demand; and, after a few years, tl thirsty colonists began to brew real : e, and drank it out of deep pewter mugs, such a: still adorn the shelves of English rural inns.

It was a community where good wa es were paid to all who toiled honestly with their h nds, but where brain workers were not greatly in c nand. Farmers and mechanics were made welcome; but of lawyers and physicians," writes Gabriel Th as, "I shall say nothing, because the Country is v y Peaceable and Healthy. Long may it so continue and never have occasion for the Tongue of the on' or the Pen of the other, both equally destructive to nen's estates and lives." We know, alas! how Bra ord, the printer, fared in a town where there was practically nothing to print, yet which had advanced beyo'd her sister cities in New York, Maryland, and Vir inia, by the mere possession of a press. Bradford came to Philadelphia in 1685, struggled for eight years with almanacs and 'a occasional pamphlet; and then — Satan finding mis-c ief for his idle hands to do — embroiled himself hope-lessly in religious and political dissensions, which made him an exile for the remainder of his life.

The wages paid to women in the colony were dis-proportionately h. ı, because young girls were sought so eagerly in marriage that female servants were always needed, and always hard to keep. Tomas enthusiasti-cally describes little Philadelphia — then in her seven-enth year — as a sort of terrestrial paradise, and not altogether unlike the happy village of the bucolic drama. "Here are no beggars to be seen," he writes, "nor indeed has anyone the least temptation to take up that scandalous, lazy life. Jealousy among men is very rare, nor are old maids to be met with; for all commonly marry before they are twenty years of age. The Christian children born here are generally well favoured and beautiful to behold. I never knew any with the least blemish." One is irresistibly reminded, as one reads, of Prester John, and the blameless people whom he ruled. "No vice is tolerated in our land, and, with us, no one lies."

It is but fair to record, however, that the praises of the local historian receive earnest confirmation from at least one stranger whom the perils of the sea had flung upon our hospitable shores. In 1710, Richard Castelman, having suffered shipwreck on a voyage from Bermuda, came to Philadelphia, and was so delighted with all he saw that he remained for many months, writing a minute account of his adventures, his "miraculous escape," and of the peaceful haven to which the kindly fates had led him. Castleman's eulogiums are as loving and as lavish as those of Gabriel Thomas. He does not even acknowledge that "inconstancy" of the climate which Penn lamented, but stoutly affirms the sky to be "rarely overcast," and the air "so healthy that there is no occasion for physicians, the people finding cures for their accidental diseases by simples." Even the horses

are stronger and less liable to sickness than in England.
Game of every kind is plentiful throughout the province, and he particularly admires "a creature called a
Possum, that has a false belly into which the young
retire in time of danger."

As for the town itself, it is, though not yet thirty
years old, "a noble, large, and populous city," having
houses "that cost six thousand pounds the building."
Here "all religions are tolerated, which is one means to
increase the riches of the place"; here "a journeyman
taylor has twelve shillings a week, besides his board";
and here "even the meanest single women marry well,
and, being above want, are above work." "If the distressed people of England knew the comforts of this
colony, and the easy means there is of a livelihood, they
would never stay where they are, in a continual scene
of poverty and misery."

When the days were warm, Mr. Castelman was wont
to seek recreation in walking "with some of the Town"
to Faire Mount, "a charming spot, shaded with trees,
on the river Schuylkill"; and he can find no words
glowing enough in which to describe the beautiful
country that stretched for many miles along the river's
bank. Altogether, he is plainly of the opinion that
his lines are cast in pleasant places, and it is with
keen regret that he meditates a departure from new-
found, hospitable friends. "The generosity of the
Philadelphians is rooted in their natures," he writes

warmly, "for it is the greatest crime among them not
to show the utmost civility to strangers; and if I were
obliged to live out of my native country, I should not
long be puzzled in finding a place of retirement, which
should be Philadelphia. There the oppressed in fort-

"ALONG THE RIVER'S BANK"

une or principles may find a happy Asylum, and drop
quietly to their graves without fear or want."

The "well-favoured" Christian children born in this
peaceful community had their young lives saddened by
being sent as regularly and pitilessly to school as if
merry England had been their home; for the Quaker
colonists were equally averse to extremes of ignorance
or of erudition. Before Philadelphia was five years of

age she had her first institution of learning, a very small and humble one, kept by Enoch Flower, whose modest charges varied with the amount he was expected to impart. For four shillings a quarter, the child was taught to read; for six shillings, to read and write; for eight shillings, to read, write, and cast accounts. Beyond these standard accomplishments, Master Flower wisely declined to lead his little flock. In 1689 the Friends established their grammar school, and placed George Keith, a Scotch Quaker, at its head. His salary was a good one: fifty pounds a year, with dwelling and schoolhouse provided, and twice that sum for two years, if he would consent to teach the children of the poor separately, without charge. There was no royal and smooth paved road to learning in those days. The little scholars took their first reluctant steps along the dismal pathway of the New England Primer.

> " In Adam's fall,
> We sinned all.

> " Job feels the rod,
> Yet blesses God.

> " Xerxes the great did die,
> And so must you and I."

After weary weeks spent in grappling with this theological alphabet, — during which they freely shared Job's privilege, — the reward of actually learning to read was the cheerless history of John Rogers, burned

at the stake for heresy, while the pathetic picture of his
wife with "nine small children, and one at the breast,"
added unutterable gloom to the narrative.

George Keith, waxing fat in the fulness of his salary,
proved himself a troublesome colonist. Like a true
Scottish " unco gude," he felt the piety of his neighbours
to be of an inconsistent and unsatisfactory character ;
so founded his own little sect of " Christian Quakers,"
thus relegating his former brethren into the darkness
of heathenism, an innuendo which they were not slow
to resent. The schoolmaster was accused in Meeting of
" enmity, wrath, self-exaltation, contention, and jan-
gling,"—a long indictment,—and also of making the
Friends whom he reviled "a scorn to the profane, and
the song of the drunkards," the meaning of which
words they probably understood. After much animated
quarrelling he returned to England, abandoned the
Quaker creed, took orders in the Anglican church, and
became Penn's most bitter opponent, arousing by every
means in his power that sharp animosity which led to
the Proprietor's being temporarily deprived of his province. In return, Keith has been roundly abused by
Voltaire, who condescended to pelt his insignificance
into notice. " The wretch was doubtless possessed of
the devil, for he dared to preach intolerance," said the
great Frenchman, — himself the most genuinely intolerant of mortals.

After the departure of this Scottish firebrand from

Philadelphia, the little grammar school flourished bravely under the care of less pharisaical masters, and the system of education organized by the Friends has been eminently successful for more than two hundred years. Like the Jesuits,— in this regard if in no other,— they have shown exceptional skill in teaching and controlling the young.

"THE MEETING-HOUSE"

Side by side with the schoolhouse arose the meeting-house, the church, and the prison, amply providing for the needs of all classes of society. For twelve years an ordinary frame dwelling was the only jail the town possessed, and it was oftenest empty. Indeed, the prison at Third and High streets was never finished

D

and placed at the disposal of criminals until 1723; but in the interval they found both public and private accommodation. " A cage seven foot high, seven foot long, and seven foot broad" was constructed for the evil-doer, who dwelt temporarily therein, like a monkey at the Zoo; being taken out with due formality to be " smartly whipped," —perhaps for selling drink to Indians, perhaps for watering the white man's rum, both of them offences of which the law took especial cognizance. Twenty shillings was the fine imposed for working on the Sabbath day, ten shillings for being drunk on the Sabbath day, and twelve pence for smoking upon the streets on any day of the week. In 1702 George Robinson, a butcher, was fined for "uttering two very bad curses"; and, for presenting a paper which was deemed disrespectful to the Council, Anthony Weston was whipped in the market-place three days, receiving but ten lashes each day, thus suffering as much ignominy and as little pain as could be easily held together. It is well to remember, however, that these public whippings were charged for at the exorbitant rate of six shillings each, and that the offender was compelled to pay for the unwelcome service done him, — a touch of ironical thrift which fully justifies Lamb's admiration for the latent humour of Quakers. Could Anthony Weston have taken his thirty lashes at once, he would have been far easier in his mind, and full twelve shillings richer.

As years went by, the criminal code became more severe, and the death sentence, which Penn had allotted to murderers only, was inflicted upon counterfeiters and highway robbers. Nor were the colonists disposed, like their successors to-day, to wax sentimental over female malefactors. They held women to be as accountable as men before the law, and punished their offences with impartial alacrity. In 1720 John and Martha Hunt were convicted of making counterfeit dollars, and both were promptly hanged, to the unqualified satisfaction of honest and law-abiding citizens.

If real crimes, however, were visited with careful retribution, imaginary ones created but little excitement in a community too sane for fanaticism. The Quaker colonist, indeed, devoutly believed in the possibility of witchcraft; he enacted laws against witches; but he hanged no witch. The opportunity was given him at the very outset of his career, and he passed it lightly by. In 1683 two Swedish women, Margaret Mattson and Yeshro Hendrickson, were accused of sorcery, Penn presiding as governor at the trial. The prisoners were ready, after the painful fashion of such culprits, to admit their guilt; but the unmoved Friends declined to credit them with supernatural powers. The verdict was alike in both cases; vaguely worded, but satisfactory, and a miracle of sturdy common sense. " Guilty of having the common fame of a witch, but not guilty in the manner and form as she stands indicted."

This was a heavy blow to would-be warlocks, who found it difficult to thrive in an atmosphere of calm depreciation. They made frantic efforts from time to time, but with no dramatic success. In vain a negro arrogantly announced that he had sold himself to Satan. The colonists prayed over him, and strove with reasonable perseverance to banish the evil spirit; but they declined to grant him the public honour of a hanging. In vain a white man affirmed that he was to be carried, body and soul, to hell, at six P.M. An idle crowd, foredoomed to disappointment, assembled to witness his departure; but the authorities took no notice of the circumstance, and showed a most mortifying indifference as to whether he went or stayed. Even the phantom coach, which the superstitious averred was driven by a demon at midnight through the silent Quaker streets, awoke but languid curiosity; and little wonder, when we consider how mild was the guilt of its ghostly occupant. " He was deemed," says the old narrative, " to have died with unkind feelings towards one dependent on him." If the town could boast no villain and no villany more picturesquely lurid than this, it had scant right to supernatural honours, to a cavalcade of spectres and evil spirits like the dark procession which bore with dreadful pomp and rejoicing the soul of the terrible, brave old Laird of Lag down to its final doom. The legends which cling so naturally and sympathetically to the blood-stained soil of Scotland seem trivial and pitifully incongruous in the daylight atmosphere of our peaceful and prosperous colony.

The history of Philadelphia's churches is much longer and more disturbing than the history of her crimes and prisons. It is a record of quarrelsome Christian piety, which lacked on the one side the power, and on the other side the desire, to be keenly and consistently intolerant. The Quaker settlers had, indeed, hoped to establish a community where absolute freedom of conscience should silence the voice of discord. This was the "Holy Experiment" on which their hearts were set, and in pursuance of this amiable design they forbore, as far as possible, to meddle with any man's religion. Emigrants of every persecuted creed flocked hopefully to the new Arcadia. The Mennonites settled in Germantown, and Pastorius the schoolmaster, with wise eloquence and gentle ways, held them aloof from worldlings. The Dunkards joined them after a few years, and the pretty straggling village with its substantial homes, its roomy gardens, its one long street, bordered by blossoming peach trees, possessed from the very beginning a charm which it has never wholly lost. The Moravians who founded Bethlehem made it the garden spot of Pennsylvania, and kept the best inns

—a proud distinction—in the province. Even the devout and mystic hermits, known as the "Society of the Woman of the Wilderness," came gladly over from Germany—which did not at all want them—and settled in the beautiful glades of the Wissahickon, where they awaited the coming of the Millennium, and, in the interval, dabbled unmolested in astrology, fortune-telling, and the mildest of mild magic. The Welsh wisely chose the Schuylkill's lovely banks, and built the little church of St. David, at Radnor, two hundred years ago.

ST. DAVID'S AT RADNOR

" Dim and small
Is the space that serves for the Shepherd's fold;
The narrow aisle, the bare white wall,
The pews and the pulpit quaint and tall
Whisper and say: ' Alas! we are old.' "*

* "Old St. David's." Longfellow.

The Roman Catholics, who were well outside the pale of Christian clemency at home, stole over the sea quietly, and in small numbers, to discover whether or not the City of Brotherly Love held any charity for them. Penn's tolerance extended even to the Papacy. He loved and served a Catholic king loyally for years, and he was willing enough that Catholics should practise their own rites, provided they did so secretly, and in a manner that would give no scandal, and create no disturbance. More than this he had not the power to grant, for any open concessions were met by fierce hostility, both at home, where the Anglican party protested with vehemence against such dangerous lenity, and in England, where the old maxim, "Avoid Papishers, and learn to knit," was still held to embody sound morality and wisdom. There is something truly pathetic in the anxious letter which Penn writes from London to James Logan on the subject in 1708. Angry voices are at work maligning the colony, and seeking to bring it into disfavour. "With these is a complaint against your government, that you suffer public Mass in a scandalous manner. Pray send the matter of fact, for ill-use is made of it against us here."

There can be little doubt that for many years before the building of St. Joseph's Church in Willing's Alley, 1733,—a church as carefully hidden away as a martyr's tomb in the Catacombs — the Roman

Catholics worshipped in small chapels which lay often beyond the town limits, and had the outward appearance of shops and dwelling-houses. The open apprehension with which they were regarded by all except the Quakers was destined later to assume odious and terrible proportions; and among those who helped to fan the flame of mad intolerance was the eloquent and hostile Whitefield, who preached out of doors to vast and eager crowds, — fifteen hundred people assembling at a time to hear him. He it was who succeeded in closing for a while ball-room and concert hall, and who deprived the good people of Philadelphia, not only of all amusements, but of all weak desire to be amused. And he it was who broadened and deepened the breach between Protestantism and Catholicity in the peaceful Quaker. town. " He strikes much at priestcraft, and speaks very satirically of Papists," writes Mr. James Pemberton in 1739; adding, with the exquisite serenity of the Friend and non-combatant: " His intentions are good, but he has not yet arrived at such perfection as to see so far as he yet may."

An eloquent proof of the ill-will aroused in England by the repeated protests of the Christ Church party against the tolerance of the proprietary government may be found in a letter printed in the "London Magazine," 1737, which charges the growth of Romanism in the province to the weakness and indifference of the Quakers, and which vehemently demands reform. The letter is brimful of religious wrath, and gives us a very accurate idea of how gossip travelled in those tardy days.

"As I join with you about the Quakers," writes this devout correspondent, " I shall give you a small specimen of a notable step taken towards the Propagation of Popery abroad; and as I have it from a gentleman who has lived for many years in Pennsylvania, I confide in the truth of it; let the Quakers deny it if they can. In the Town of Philadelphia, in that Colony, is a Publick Popish Chapel, where that Religion has free and open exercise; and in it all the superstitious Rites of that Church are as avowedly performed as those of the Church of England are in the Royal Chapel at St. James. And this Chapel is open, not only upon Fasts and Festivals, but it is so all day, and every day in the week, and exceedingly frequented at all Hours, either for publick or private devotion. . . . That these are Truths, (whatever use you are pleased to make of them) you may at any time be satisfied by any Trader or Gentleman who has been there within a few years, (except he be a Quaker) at the Carolina and Pennsylvania Coffee-House, near the Royal Exchange."

Little did it profit the Friends to be so peacefully inclined towards every Christian creed, when their neigh-

hours repudiated with scorn this policy of concession.
The Rev. Colin Campbell, secretary of the "London
Society for the Propagation of the Gospel in Foreign
Parts," complains bitterly in one of his reports that
Quakerism in Pennsylvania is but a "nursery of Jesuits"; and the Rev. John Talbot, who held for years
the same pious post, accuses Penn openly of being "a
greater Antichrist than Julian the Apostate, inasmuch
as instead of striving to convert the Indians to the
faith, he labours to make Christians heathens, *and
proclaims liberty and privileges to all that believe in one
God.*"

Among the hosts of emigrants who flocked from the
Old World to try their fortunes in the New, the Scotch-
Irish Presbyterians had least patience with the gentle
tolerance of the Quakers whom they regarded with un-
concealed aversion and contempt. Men of brawn and
muscle were these Scotch-Irish colonists, strong of purpose, steadfast in action, brave, thrifty, and intelligent;
but, on the other hand, quarrelsome, arrogant, and exceedingly hostile to the Indians, whom they promptly
antagonized by rough treatment, and to whom they
showed scant equity, and scantier compassion. It became, in time, a difficult matter to keep the peace with
savages, perpetually angered by encroachments and
high-handed injustice.

The two most interesting places of worship now
standing in Philadelphia are Christ Church and Gloria

GLORIA DEI

Dei, — the first because of the important part it has played in the history of the colony, and the second because of its old age and curious associations. Five years before Penn sent his first ships over the sea, the pious Swedes had established a congregation, and met for service in a rude blockhouse, built of logs, and

"THE ANTIQUE FONT"

pierced with narrow loopholes, through which attacking Indians might be spied and shot. On the site of this primitive chapel they built in 1700 a brick church, costing twenty thousand Swedish dollars, which, at the time, was deemed " a great edifice, and finest in the town." Poor and few as were these simple worshippers, they gave fifteen thousand dollars before the first stone was laid in place; and, with that laudable shrinking from debt which has ceased to harass the modern church builder, they left the belfry unfinished, "in order to see whether God will bless us so far that we may have a bell, and in what manner we can procure it." The antique marble font of Gloria Dei was once the sole adornment of the blockhouse chapel, and in the graveyard which surrounds its venerable walls are huddled close together mouldy and crumbling tomb-

stones, from many of which the wind and weather have
worn away all records of the forgotten dead. We read
on one the name of a little child who died in 1708,
nearly two centuries ago, when Anne ruled over England, and Marlborough carried the might of English
arms past the Flemish frontier into France.

A keener and more combative interest attaches itself
to Christ Church, which was for many years the sole
rallying point of the Anglican party, a church militant
in a peaceful community, and a standing peril to the
dominant Quaker power. Its congregation, small in
numbers, was strong in intelligence, in sustained hostility, and in the support of the English government.
It was natural that such men should find much to anger
them in the new province. They had expected the
Quakers to claim complete tolerance for their own worship, and they were prepared to concede as much with
a good grace; but they had never anticipated this
strange, serene, perverse colony, where all creeds were
on an absurdly equal footing, and where the time-honoured privilege of snubbing dissenters and persecuting
Papists was rigorously denied them. English clergymen, keenly alive to their distinction in representing
the great National Establishment, were little disposed
to receive poor Francis Pastorius, or Count Zinzendorf,
the Moravian bishop, or even the Rev. Henry Mel-
chior Muhlenberg, pastor of the German Lutherans, as
brothers in Christ. From the very beginning they and

their parishioners held themselves stanchly aloof, a small, compact, able, antagonistic body of men; and, as a first step towards concentration and influence, they built a church which, for the time and place, must always be regarded as a marvel of extravagance and beauty.

Now church building was no easy task in colonial days, when fortunes were few, and men were reluctant to part with hard-earned gains. The present edifice, old though it be, — as we count age in the New World, — replaced a still more ancient structure which for thirty-five years harboured the little congregation. Perhaps the second church would never have seen completion, had it not been for the ever popular device of lottery tickets, by help of which our unscrupulous ancestors reared most of their important public buildings. Two lotteries were projected by the vestry of Christ Church, the tickets for each selling at four dollars apiece. One of them, known as the "Philadelphia Steeple Lottery," was drawn as late as March, 1753, and paid for the steeple, nearly twenty years after the body of the church was built. Within its walls generations of Philadelphians knelt to pray; and from its vestry and congregation issued those endless petitions to the Privy Council which kept the colony in a state of perpetual agitation and alarm. Four times in seventy years the crown was urged to compel the Quaker Assembly to place the province in a state of defence

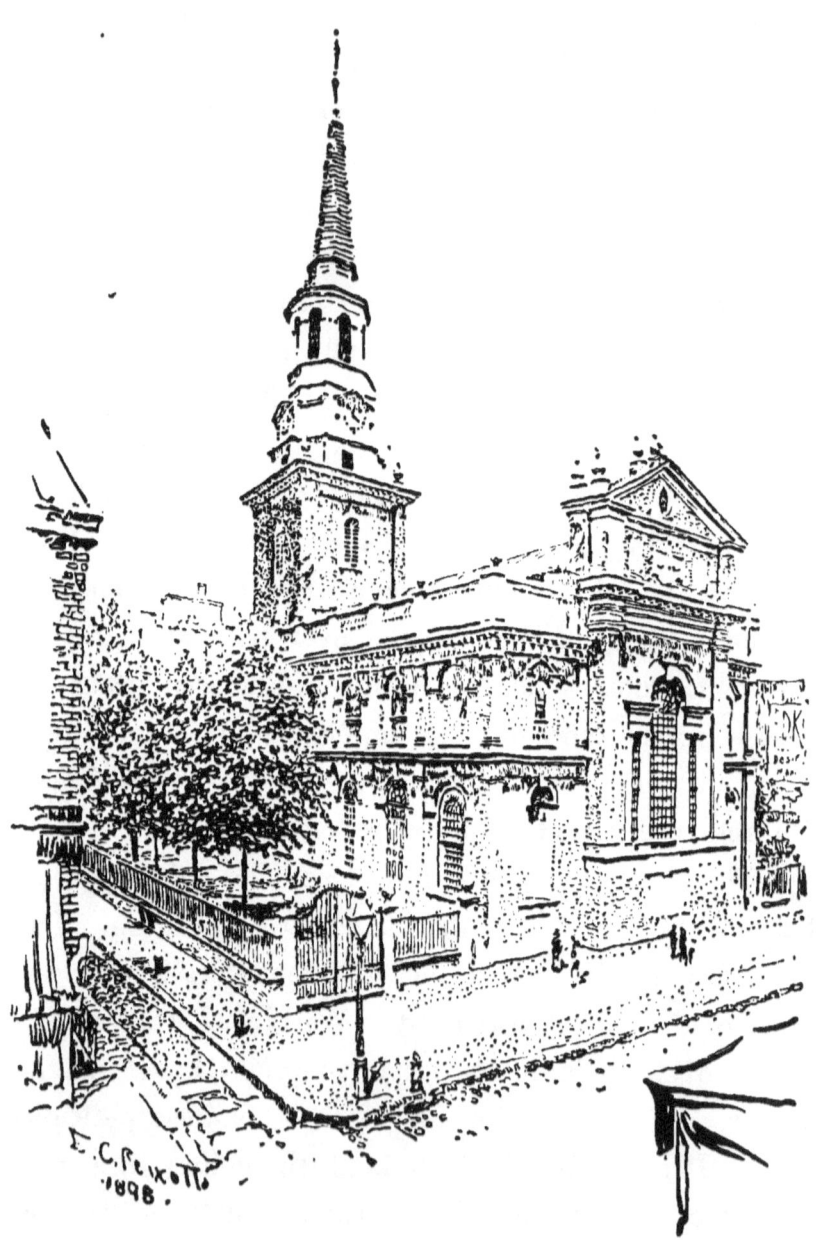

CHRIST CHURCH

against pirates and Indians, — a reasonable request; and four times in seventy years it was urged to force upon the Quaker magistrates such oaths of office as were customary and obligatory in England, — an utterly unreasonable request, having for its aim and object nothing less than the exclusion of Friends from the Assembly, and from all positions of trust in a colony which owed to them its existence, its prosperity and peace. The Anglicans in the heat of their resentment did not hesitate to petition the King to dispossess the Proprietor, to dissolve the existing government, and to rule Pennsylvania as a royal province. In fact, they were as willing at one time to relinquish their charter, and with it their colonial rights, as they were determined a few years later to protect and cherish both. The ardent churchman felt no sacrifice too great for the coveted privilege of correcting his neighbour's misdemeanours.

An occasional success crowned these untiring efforts. After the accession of William and Mary, and the passing of what, by an exquisite stroke of irony, was called the Toleration Act, the vestry of Christ Church petitioned the Privy Council, through Colonel Quarry, to impose the "Test" upon all who wished to hold office, or worship publicly in Pennsylvania. The Council yielded to this demand, and a congregation of five hundred souls succeeded for a time in saddling the whole province with one of those petty exactions, harmless enough in itself, — as the only class it really injured were the Roman Catholics, and they were too few for consideration, — but opposed to the broad-minded, tolerant spirit of the colony, and sufficiently annoying to keep a peace-loving population in a state of ill-humour and disquiet.

It must be frankly admitted, however, that this combative little church held within itself a large proportion of Philadelphia's ability, energy, and learning. As time went on, both the proprietors and governors of Pennsylvania added the weight of their influence to the Anglican party, in a ceaseless conflict with the Quaker Assembly, which held its own for nearly a hundred years by the simple and time-honoured device, dear to the Anglo-Saxon heart, of granting or withholding supplies. Nothing could wrench from it the power of the purse, and nothing could long survive the closing of the purse-strings. Even the governors who came over from England with sovereignty in their hearts, and sealed letters of instruction in their pockets, found it more or less difficult to maintain the dignity of their position when the Assembly paid them no salaries; and, after a year or two of high-handed autocracy, they were glad to temporize with the imperturbable Friends for the sake of a necessary income.

No such humiliation as this befell the Christ Church rectors. Their stout-hearted congregations supported them liberally, and found money to spare for intel-

E

lectual, as well as for spiritual and political requisitions.
When Franklin conceived his plan for organizing
the "College and Academy of Philadelphia," he found
the assistance he needed in the Anglican party; four-
fifths of the college trustees were church members;
and the Rev. William Smith—one of the most able,
irascible, and contentious men in the community, with
whom Franklin was destined to have many a quarrel
—was elected the first head-master. When the hostile
French and Indians threatened the safety of the
province, it was Christ Church again which maintained the duty of a defensive—which rapidly became an offensive—warfare; and Dr. Smith preached
from its pulpit eight rousing military sermons, well
calculated to increase the general discontent at the
moderate measures of the Assembly. As usual, too,
the Christ Church vestry, aided and abetted by the
vestry of St. Peter's, which by this time had taken up
its share of the dispute, petitioned the crown to exclude
all non-resident Quakers from the legislative body,—a
petition which was wisely ignored.

Finally, when the coming Revolution cast its signifi-
cant shadow on the colony, the Anglicans, while always
hoping for peace, remonstrated clearly against the injustice of the Stamp Act, and the impolicy of concessions to England. If they paused on the brink of
open rebellion, it was through conservatism and not
cowardice. Three of the signers of the Declaration

of Independence, — Franklin, Robert Morris, and Hopkinson, — were Christ Church pew-holders; and it was immediately determined to drop from the service the long familiar prayer for the King and the Royal Family. With the departure of that prayer, the political importance of the church ceased forever. Severed from the great English Establishment, it stood politically on a par with every sectarian chapel in the land. The old order had passed away, and the new order concerned itself but little with doctrines and dogmas. No more Tests! No more petitions to the Privy Council! Only an intellectual supremacy remained, and that was soon to be disputed by rival creeds. The clergy, the vestry, the congregation of Christ Church recognized clearly what the Revolution was to cost them. They did not long hesitate to sacrifice their own interests to the wider, greater, nobler needs of a country which demanded to be free.

GLORIA DEI

IN 1699 Penn returned to Philadelphia, and was welcomed with enthusiasm by the city, now nineteen years old, and rapidly outgrowing her pretty primitive simplicity. Much had happened to her Quaker Founder in the last fifteen years, much that has no place in this New World chronicle, though it may be read with interest by those who love to follow a brave man through the intricacies and fatal fortunes of life. The accession of James II. placed Penn in a position of trust and influence at court, for the King had always regarded him and his sober followers with favour; and one of the first acts of the new reign was the remission of the penalties imposed upon all who had refused to take the oath of allegiance, by which royal clemency more than twelve hundred Quakers were immediately released from prison. The faithful service rendered by Penn to the monarch who had befriended him from boyhood has been made the subject of much invidious and foolish criticism. Macaulay, whose attitude towards any adherent of the Stuarts resembles Voltaire's attitude towards Habak-

kuk, has not hesitated to accuse the courtly Quaker
of more than one harsh deed; and though none of
these accusations rest upon convincing authority, and
most of them rest upon no authority whatever, there
lingers in many minds a vague impression that Penn
was at heart a time-server and a worldling. Even
Mrs. Oliphant wonders with pious scorn, how a man
who professed sanctity could obey a master so palpably
imperfect as James, as though it were possible, under
any form of government, to make character the condition of our obedience and our service to those who
rule the land.

More dispassionate minds will find in the strange incongruous friendship something equally creditable to
king and subject. James held this gentle yet outspoken
follower at his true worth, and many gracious deeds
were the result of his influence and intercession.
Penn's loyal heart found little to forgive. The King's
Catholicity troubled him not at all, for in his serene
breadth of mind he saw no reason why even a monarch
should not cherish his own faith, an idea which had not
then dawned upon the civilized world, and which has
made but little headway in the intervening years. He
believed James to be sincere — albeit sincerity was not
a Stuart failing — and he had a grateful affection for
the morose man who won so little love. The revolution of 1689 brought him serious disaster, and was full
of evil omens for the Quakers who clung to him as

their leader and support. He found himself an object of deep suspicion at court, was accused before the Privy Council of treasonable correspondence with the exiled King, and was promptly deprived of his proprietary rights. Disgraced, poor, well-nigh friendless, separated from his wife, who died before his restoration to favour, he bore this sharp reversal of fortune with unalterable patience and composure. It was not until England had grown calm again, and had reconciled herself sagaciously, though with no lively satisfaction, to the great and wise and disagreeable prince whom she had invited to her throne, that Penn was able to prove his absolute innocence. He had loved and served James. He neither loved nor wished to serve William. But his creed forced him to play a passive part in these strange shifting scenes which changed the destinies of nations, and made even his own little life the sport and plaything of conflicting fates.

When, after years of trouble and disrepute, the sun of royal favour shone faintly upon him once again, and the government of Pennsylvania was restored to his hands, he resolved to return to the province, which had been but little disturbed by the mighty changes at home. The flight of James and the accession of William had, in fact, made no particular impression upon the colonists, who paid scant heed to the startling news, but waited without impatience for further developments. James, they considered, might come

back, and the Prince of Orange might fly in his turn.
Neither possibility interested them very profoundly.
Those were happy days, when the serenity of one hemi-
sphere was not at the mercy of daily despatches from
the other. Nine months passed before the new reign
seemed so reasonably secure, that, in tardy little Philadelphia, William and Mary were proclaimed King and
Queen of England.

In matters nearer home, however, the colony was as
actively contentious as its neighbours, and even across
the ocean there had reached Penn's ears the echoes of
constant strife. "For the love of God, of me, and of
the poor country," we find him writing to Lloyd, "be
not so governmentish, so noisy and open in your dissatisfaction." He had failed to realize, amid the cares and
dangers that beset his path in England, how in far-away
Pennsylvania there was growing with every year a
spirit of strong and bitter opposition to his proprietary
powers. He thought that all would be well when he
was with his own people once again; but scarcely had
the words of welcome which greeted his return to
Philadelphia died away, when the struggle began which
in two years left little of his cherished laws, or of his
old authority. The Assembly was ready enough to
assist him in the suppression of smuggling and piracy,
which lawless but profitable professions had grown to
scandalous magnitude. On other points they met his
wishes with steady resistance, and the Christ Church

party, under the leadership of Robert Quarry, Judge of
the Admiralty, grew more hostile every month.   Penn
took up his quarters for the winter in the Slate Roof
House; but at the earliest approach of spring he went
gladly to Pennsbury, which had been furnished with a
degree of elegance hitherto unknown to the colony.

" THE SLATE ROOF HOUSE "

Turkish tapestry and satin hangings covered the bare
white walls, the first carpet carried over the ocean
adorned the drawing-room floor, silver and glass
sparkled on the massive sideboard.   Outside there were
lawns and terraces, made with infinite pains, to give
the house some sweet resemblance to an English
country home, and endear it in the sight of wife and
child; for Penn had married a second time, and his

family accompanied him now to the strange New
World, and liked it very little when they got there.

The successor of poor Gulielma Maria, who had escaped forever from careless servants and encroaching
friendships, was a "devout and comely maiden," Hannah Callowhill, the daughter of a Bristol merchant.
Her letters, which have been ardently recommended as
profitable reading for the young, show her to have been
a woman of force and character, well fitted for the
serious cares of life, and for the important part she was
destined to play in the history of the province. She
had three sons, one of whom, John Penn, was born in
Philadelphia, and was commonly called " the American,"
though he did as little as possible to merit the title,
or to make it an honourable distinction. "A lovely
babe," writes Isaac Norris, with breathless enthusiasm.
in 1701, "and has much of his father's grace and air.
and hope he will not want a good portion of his
mother's sweetness. who is a woman extremely well-
beloved here, exemplary in her station, and of an excellent spirit, which adds lustre to her character, and has
a great place in the hearts of good people."

Penn's only daughter, Letitia, and his scapegrace son.
William, the children of his first wife, had accompanied
him to the colony, and Letitia's discontent and home-
sickness fully equalled her stepmother's. The "fair
mansion house" seemed but a desolate dwelling-place
to these sedate Englishwomen, who never learned to

love such unaccustomed freedom, and never ceased to fear the silent forest that surrounded them, nor the "insolent bears and painted savages" that roamed — most uncongenial neighbours — through its sombre depths. Yet Penn maintained the dignity of his position in a manner that might well have satisfied, and even dazzled, the Bristol merchant's daughter. Four horses drew his state coach bumping and jolting over the rough, ill-made road from Penns-bury to Philadelphia; eight oarsmen rowed his barge when he took the smoother waterway. The colonists were impressed, amused, or exasperated, according to their dispo-sitions, by all this for-mality and display; but

PENN'S DESK

even those who least loved the Proprietor were com-pelled to admit that his was a nature broad enough to understand the needs of a community, and generous enough to begrudge neither labour nor wealth when the happiness of the people was at stake. Penn, like Washington, was a slaveholder, and, like Washington,

he treated his slaves with uniform kindness and humanity. He even urged upon the Assembly a bill obliging
all colonists to instruct their negroes in Christian
truths; and while the Quakers, as a rule, made but
little effort to convert the Indians about them, they
gave to the savages a rare example of that seldom
seen Christianity which consistently practised what it
preached.

Meanwhile the town grew and prospered. Active
measures were taken against the pirates who swarmed
along the coast,—unmitigated ruffians for the most
part, who had no wrongs to avenge like Kingsley's
warm-hearted and sentimental "Buccaneer"; but who
robbed honest men, and assaulted honest women, and
dishonoured the very seas over which their black
crafts sailed. The commerce they had blocked was once
again resumed. Emigration increased almost too rapidly, people thought, for the welfare of the colony.
It is curious to hear, echoed from the very beginning of the eighteenth century, the same apprehensive whispers that now disturb our peace. James
Logan, who came to the province as Penn's secretary
in 1699, and who was for many years the best, the
most loyal, and the most capable public servant that
Pennsylvania possessed, wrote doubtfully, after thirty
years of experience: "It looks as if Ireland is to
send all its inhabitants hither. The common fear is
that if they continue to come, they will make them-

selves masters of the place. It is strange that they
thus crowd where they are not wanted."

Not very strange, for the land was fertile and the
country was at peace, a peace to be broken and lost
before many years had passed through the harshness
and arrogance of these same Scotch-Irish emigrants,
who tilled the soil with splendid industry, and an
undeviating indifference as to its rightful ownership.
In 1701 Penn was recalled to England by a fresh
danger. Parliament was considering a bill for the
purchase by the crown of all proprietary rights; and
to defend both the independence of the province
and his own peculiar claims became the immediate
duty of the governor. Before he left Philadelphia,
the Assembly, ever prompt to secure an advantage,
obtained the Charter of Privileges, which gave it the
power to originate its own measures, and left to
Penn, of all his old authority, little but empty honours, and the quit-rents, which were destined in the
coming years to enrich his children and his children's children "beyond the dreams of avarice," as
the story books phrase it, though never beyond their
own avaricious desires.

Hannah Penn and Letitia rejoiced openly at this
chance of returning to England; but Gulielma Maria's
son was left in the colony, where it was hoped he
would gain steadfastness of purpose, and propriety of
behaviour. " Weigh down his levities, temper his re-

sentiments, and inform his understanding," wrote Penn
to Logan who remained as Hamilton's provincial secretary, and upon whose capable shoulders fell a
heavy burden of cares. The young man's resent-
ments and levities, however, so far outweighed his
understanding that no balance of sanity could be
struck, and his riotous conduct sorely scandalized the
quiet Quaker community. His father meanwhile settled once more into his old familiar life, became
rather a favourite of good Queen Anne's, succeeded in
checking the bill for the purchase of proprietary
rights, and spent much time at court, very pleasantly
and profitably, until overtaken by the serious financial trouble which shadowed and saddened his old
age. Many causes contributed to this disaster. The
difficulty of collecting quit-rents, the extravagance of
his dissolute son, and the greed of his parsimonious
son-in-law, William Aubrey, — " a scraping man,"
says Penn with his usual felicity of phrase, who
compelled the prompt payment of Letitia's portion
when so large a sum could hardly be raised without
ruin. Above all, an unjust steward — that character
as well known in the eighteenth Christian century
as in the first — completed the work of destruction,
and forced Penn to live for many months within
the confines of the Fleet prison.

It is not pleasant for us to contemplate the founder
of our Keystone State, the founder of our Quaker

City, pent up in a London jail. It is not pleasant
for us to remember that Robert Morris, who poured
out his wealth like water for the support of our en-
dangered commonwealth, was left to lie unhelped and
unheeded in a debtor's prison. It is never pleasant
to realize that every page of history is but a monotonous illustration of Tourgueneff's savage satire, a
monotonous repetition of that pitiless scene, where,
the virtues being gathered together in the azure
halls, it is discovered that Benevolence and Gratitude have never met before. Even in England and
in France, the spectacle of Penn's misfortunes could
not long be endured with equanimity, and his own
unbroken courage heightened the feeling of sympathy
and of resentment. A compromise was finally effected, money was raised by the English Quakers
for his release, and the man to whom had been
granted absolute rights over vast and unknown terri-
tories, was permitted to enjoy once more the fields
and the skies of his native land. He rented a modest country house in Buckinghamshire, and the remainder of his life — until paralysis clouded his
understanding — was spent quietly, though with little
joy, for ever and again some fresh contention with
the province disturbed his peace of mind. His last
sad, serious letter to the colonists shamed them into
an outburst of love and loyalty which came too late
for comfort. He died in 1718, being seventy-four

years old ; and his most sincere mourners were
found, neither in London nor in Philadelphia, but in
those trackless forests where the Indians — whose
friends had been but few — still cherished and honoured the memory of the "white truth-teller." They
sent gifts of skins over the sea to his widow, and
bewailed in savage fashion around their camp-fires
" the man of treaties unbroken, and friendships
inviolate."

Calumny, which loves a shining mark, has never
been sparing of her favours to William Penn. Many
are the arrows she has winged ; many are the accusations she has reiterated. In his own day he was
denounced by sturdy Protestants as a concealed
Papist, by angry Whigs as a rebel at heart, and by
clamorous preachers as a Jesuit in disguise, which
last accusation might have been spared a man who
had two wives and five children. He offended worldlings by his Quaker creed, which to them was mere
hypocrisy, and he scandalized the righteous by his
association with courts and courtiers. His personal
charm is vouched for by no less censorious a critic
than Swift, who says that he spoke "very agreeably,
and with much spirit." In 1710, Swift writes to
Stella that he met at Mr. Harley's, "Will Penn the
Quaker," and that they passed a lively evening,
being exceedingly well entertained by one another.
" We sat two hours, drinking as good wine as you

do," adds the great churchman with unwonted amiability; and it is perhaps the strongest proof of Penn's
lovableness that, after drinking good wine with him
for two hours at night, Swift has the next morning
no word of dispraise for his companion.

LOGAN ARMS

CHAPTER V

THE death of William Penn closes one period of Philadelphia's history. His proprietary rights passed to his widow, for the worthless son did not long survive his father, and Hannah Penn's children were still minors, under her exclusive guardianship. She remained in England, and was ably assisted in her cares by Sir William Keith, the governor of the province, a man who behaved with great discretion for years, and then, losing his mental balance under pressure of a too sustained success, quarrelled with Logan, defied the Assembly, and, returning to London, perished miserably in the Old Bailey. He it was who first suggested paper currency to supply the needs of the colony, continually drained of gold by the excess of its imports over its exports, — a dangerous measure, but one which, in prudent Quaker hands, succeeded beyond all anticipation. For fifty years the notes never depreciated, and only with the darkening of the revolutionary cloud came their melancholy and disgraceful downfall. In 1726, Franklin, then a sanguine young man of twenty, who, like other sanguine young men, believed in cheap money and plenty of it, rushed into the field with a pamphlet on "The Nature and Necessity of a Paper Currency," which, in the general absence of sounder arguments, created a wide impression, and brought its author into enviable notice. It was, nevertheless, a crude and shallow piece of reasoning, and Franklin in later years clearly recognized its folly. Older and wiser eyes saw, even amid the present prosperity, ominous shadows of trouble to come; and only three years after the publication of Franklin's glittering generalities, James Logan confessed that his heart was heavy with apprehension. "I dare not say one word against the paper money," he wrote sadly in 1729. "The popular phrensy will never stop till our credit be as bad as in New England, where an ounce of silver is worth twenty shillings of paper. They already talk of making more, and no man dares to stem the fury of the rage. The notion is that while any man will borrow on good security of land, more money should be made for him, without thinking of what value it will be when made. They affirm that, while the security is good, the money cannot fall. The King's own hand should forbid this folly."

For a while, however, and a long while too, all went merrily as wedding bells. The province grew stronger and more populous, the city increased yearly in size and wealth. Luxury and gayety began to manifest themselves, and we hear the echo of many an unheeded protest against the insidious encroachments of the world; against the use of snuff-boxes, for example, and of fans, which were carried even to the meeting-house, where they diverted women's minds from "inward and spiritual exercise." As early as 1726 devout female Friends were publicly cautioned against "the immodest fashion of hooped·Petticoats," and even against "imitations of them by stiffened or full Skirts, which we take" (very rightly) "to be but a Branch springing from the same corrupt root of Pride." They were also forbidden to wear striped shoes, to lay pleats in their caps, "to cut or draw down their hair on their Foreheads and Temples," or to put aside that badge of demure and domestic womanhood — the apron. Much scandal was given, moreover, by the readiness with which the merry wives of Philadelphia joined in their husbands' comfortable potations. The eighteenth century was the great drinking era, and our colony followed in no halting measure the jovial fashions of the day. In 1733 the *Pennsylvania Gazette* laments that Philadelphia women, "otherwise discreet," instead of contenting themselves with one good draught of beer in the morning, take "two or three drams, by which their appetite for wholesome food is destroyed."

Much might be written about the taverns which, from the very beginning, played an important part in this dull, cheerful, prosperous, unplagued colonial life.

Their faded sign-boards swung in every street, and curious old verses, copied by loving antiquarians, still remain to show us what our wise forefathers liked to read. One little pot-house had painted on its board, a tree, a bird, a ship, and a mug of beer, while beneath were these encouraging lines : —

"This is the tree that never grew,
This is the bird that never flew,
This is the ship that never sailed,
This is the mug that never failed."

When the increasing hostility to Great Britain disturbed more and more the peacefulness of province and of town, the sign-boards caught the restless tone of discontent, and became belligerent rather than festive and hospitable. A diminutive, one-storied tavern with high pitched roof, near the old Swedes' church, displayed a hen, a brood of young chickens, and an eagle hovering over them with a crown in its beak. Below, in large letters, was this patriotic sentiment: "May the wings of Liberty cover the chickens of Freedom, and pluck the crown from the enemy's head!"— a valiant display of metaphors irresistibly suggestive of Elijah Pogram, the immortal, and his eloquent words anent the impetuous Mr. Chollop: "He is a child of Natur' and a child of Freedom ; and his boastful answer to the Despot and the Tyrant is that his bright home is in the Settin' Sun."

When the colonists began to have sufficient leisure for ennui, the question arose in Philadelphia, as in every other community, "What shall we do to be amused?" and the answer was difficult to find. Amusements were held in no great esteem by decorous citizens, and for a while it seemed as if the primitive pastimes of cock-fighting and bull-baiting were the only admissible diversions. Cock-fighting, indeed, was

OLD HOUSE ON RACE STREET WHARF

so universally popular, that even in later days when Mr. Whitefield's eloquent preaching had persuaded good Philadelphians to deny themselves the sinful joys of dancing and of music, the personal friends and warm supporters of the uncompromising divine were still as careful as ever in the rearing of their young game-cocks. As for bull-baiting, it held its own until 1820, when Mayor Wharton put an abrupt and final end to the sport by confiscating the last bull ever seen in a Philadelphia ring.

Occasionally, across the arid waste of dulness, came jugglers and tight-rope dancers, lending to the virtuous little town a transient air of excess. In the winter of 1724, a band of these roving acrobats was kindly received by all but the Quaker colonists, and especial favour was shown to a child of seven, "who danced and capered upon the strait roap, to the wonder of all spectators." A few years later, an eight-legged cat was exhibited to the delighted public; also a moose, (spelled in the old notice, mouse, which is misleading) and "a beautiful creature, but surprising fierce, called a leopard." By the end of the century, our forefathers were still so easily entertained that they manifested wild enthusiasm for the skeleton of a mammoth, which had been found in a marl pit in New York, and which was brought to Philadelphia by the enterprising Mr. Peale, who generously restored all the missing bones; and it was not until a comparatively recent date that the first waxworks made their appearance, and were greeted with universal enthusiasm.

None of the gracious tolerance manifested for the cock-pit and other virile amusements was shown to the poor actors, who from time to time ventured to try their fortunes in the Quaker City. When, in 1749, a little troop of shabby players presented themselves forlornly in an improvised theatre, and gave to Phila-

delphia the unsolicited honour of seeing the first Shake-
sperian representation in the United States, they were
promptly suppressed by active magistrates, as "encouraging idleness, and drawing great sums of money [?]
from weak and inconsiderate persons." The stage,
however, in every land and in every century, has been
wily enough to present herself at first as a religious
and moral teacher, and to gain her first hearing on the
score of the good she hopes to do. She is like that
adroit demon of Benozzo Gozzoli in the Campo Santo
at Pisa, who enters the hermitage disguised as a pil-
grim, and, notwithstanding the palpable evidence of
horn and hoof, is welcomed joyously by the devout and
unsuspicious hermit. In 1754, Hallam's Company from
London established themselves modestly in a shop on
South Street, obtained with difficulty a license to act
for a few months, provided they offered "nothing indecent or immoral," and proceeded at once to stem the
stream of popular disapprobation by distributing on
the streets a slender pamphlet, setting forth the harmless nature of their occupation. The imposing title of
this pamphlet ran as follows : —

"Extracts of Several Treatises,
Wrote by the Prince of Conti;
With the Sentiments of the Fathers,
And some of the Decrees of the Councils,
Concerning Stage Plays.
Recommended to the Perusal, and Serious Consideration of the
Professors of Christianity, in the City of Philadelphia."

A curious pleading this, to urge against the ill-will of Quakers and Presbyterians who did not, as a rule, concern themselves deeply with the sentiments of the Fathers, or the decrees of the Councils, and for whom the opinions of the Prince of Conti must have carried marvellously little weight. A better argument in behalf of the players was the alacrity with which they gave the proceeds of one night's entertainment to the Charity School that had been established in connection with the newly founded Academy. But even this heavy bribe, which they could so ill afford, failed to soften the spirit of opposition, or to awaken general interest. Few people knew or cared anything about the actor's art; fewer still could be persuaded that it was a justifiable vocation. Science was much in fashion, thanks to Franklin and his discoveries, and young men of education and leisure preferred, or said they preferred, the lectures of Professor Kinnersly on electricity to the purposeless soliloquies of Hamlet, or the wild ravings of King Richard III. It is to be feared that little, learned Philadelphia was something of a prig, until those gay and graceless days when an English army held her in thraldom, and English offi-cers taught her seductive lessons, in which science and lectures played but scanty parts.

After an absence of five years, the indomitable Hal-lams returned to the city which had welcomed them so coldly, established themselves prudently outside the

town limits, and printed their play-bills in a wary
fashion ; promising as a rule " A Concert of Music," —
which sounded harmless — " to be followed by a moral
Dialogue on the Vice of Gaming," — or any other vice
suitable for the occasion. The word "play" was
always religiously omitted from these early notices.
We see "Hamlet" and "Jane Shore" described as
"moral and instructive Tales"; and sometimes the
whole entertainment, "The Fair Penitent," perhaps,
and "Miss in her Teens," is mendaciously advertised
as a lecture.

Of little avail, however, was all this strategy and
subterfuge. Quakers, Presbyterians, Baptists, and
Lutherans united their forces to rout from their virtuous town these brazen representatives of evil. The
urgent petition they addressed to the Assembly set
forth in no measured terms the mischief wrought in a
peaceful community by "idle persons and strollers, who
have come into this province from foreign parts, in the
character of players, erected stages and theatres, and
thereon acted divers plays, by which the weak, poor,
and necessitous have been prevailed on to neglect their
industry and labour, and to give extravagant prices for
their tickets ; and great numbers of disorderly persons
have been drawn together in the night, to the distress
of many poor families, manifest injury to this young
colony, and grievous scandal of religion, and the laws
of the government."

A heavy arraignment against a dozen poor mummers, who could plead nothing in their own behalf, save that they were striving to give pleasure and amuse, and whose flimsy pretence of moral instruction was swept away like a cobweb by these vigorous home truths. Philadelphia had all the moral instruction of which she stood in need, without any assistance from the stage; and so her citizens probably felt, for, after a struggle of some months, hostile virtue triumphed signally,—the little playhouse was closed, the plays forbidden, and the dejected actors set forth once more in search of colonies less stanchly wedded to electricity and rectitude.

But not for long. There is a power of resistance in the world, the flesh, and the devil, which the upholders of morality do not always take sufficiently into account. For seven years the Quaker City waxed fat in uncontaminated goodness, and then the fight with Apollyon was again renewed, and renewed under ominous disadvantages. Apollyon had built himself a home, a real playhouse this time, albeit a poor, shabby little structure, miserably inadequate to the cause of vice. In this playhouse, long known as the Old Southwark Theatre, actors strutted through their nightly parts, while the storm of righteousness rolled unheeded around them; and to this playhouse was accorded the honour of producing the first

American play ever publicly acted in the colonies.
A strictly moral drama it was, entitled "The Prince
of Parthia," written in deplorable blank verse, and
of a dulness so uniform and sustained that even a
lecture on electricity must have seemed sprightly by
its side. Its author, Thomas Godfrey, was an aspiring young watchmaker of Philadelphia, a protégé of
Franklin ; and he acquired an enviable reputation as
a poet in those halcyon days when literary criticism
had not yet crossed the Atlantic, and when a book
was necessarily a good book, a poem was necessarily a
good poem, and a play was necessarily a good play,
unless they offended public taste and decency.

Vehement were the remonstrances urged by the
elect against the Southwark Theatre, and the sinful
diversions it afforded. Play-acting, it was affirmed,
was "akin to image-worship," though the connection
between the two was not very clearly defined ; and
the Assembly was entreated to put an end to this
open scandal and iniquity. The Assembly, however,
had grown less hostile to the stage, and Governor
Penn stoutly refused to interfere with the actors.
They were tolerated from year to year, though never
assured of protection, and never released from assault.
In the *Pennsylvania Gazette*, Dec. 19, 1768, we find
a long communication from a sanctimonious gentleman, who laments the hold which the theatre has
gained upon the public mind. Young people, it

seems, were even guilty of going to the play on nights when they might have gone to church. He himself, so great was the general laxity, had been presented with a box ticket the day before; but "having no taste for theatrical performances," he had attended religious service instead, and had handed over the ticket to a black servant, whose soul, he plainly considered, could not be easily injured. The negro apparently thought otherwise. "The virtuous slave immediately sold the ticket for half price, and purchased a prayer book with the money. An example of virtue and religion in a slave, worthy the imitation of the greatest ruler upon earth."

It was not until after the Revolution that Philadelphia — no longer, alas! the Quaker City — ceased to look askance upon the stage. During those brief months in which the English army occupied the town, theatrical representations of every kind became a recognized source of amusement in a community which suddenly, amid dangers, battles, and bankruptcy, found out how delightful it was to be amused. The officers of General Howe's staff acted a number of plays in the Southwark Theatre, giving the proceeds always to the soldiers' widows and orphans. Major André and Captain De Lancey achieved especial distinction, not only as comedians, but as scene-painters, costumers, and property men. The famous drop curtain painted by Major André, and representing a waterfall in a forest glade, was held to be a triumph of art. It is described over and over again in contemporary letters as exceedingly

AN ALLEY

beautiful, and was used with much pride for years, until lost in the burning of the theatre.

Nor were the American officers averse, as a rule, to the seductions of the stage. Washington honestly loved a good comedy or a rattling farce, and was seen more than once in the east proscenium box of the Southwark Theatre, to the disedification of many good citizens. There must have been a sharp struggle now and then with deep-rooted prejudice on the one hand, and the respect it was impossible to withhold from the President, on the other. This conflict of feeling is amusingly apparent in a letter written by Senator Maclay, who, being honoured by a seat in Washington's box, is divided between gratification at the privilege and a strong distaste for the entertainment. "The play," he writes, "was the 'School for Scandal.' I never liked it. Indeed, I think it an indecent representation before ladies of character and virtue. The farce that followed was 'The Old Soldier.' The house was greatly crowded, and I thought the players acted well ; but I wish we had seen the 'Conscious Lovers,' or some play that inculcated more prudential manners."

It must be admitted that Philadelphia had wandered far from her early decorum, and the estimable "Prince of Parthia," when she sat, smiling and unconcerned, to see the "School for Scandal." The day was fast approaching when the stage, freed from the yoke of the pious oppressor, was to flaunt, a licensed libertine, unmindful of old promises, moral instruction, the decrees of the Councils, and the admirable opinions of the Prince of Conti. For many months the Dramatic Association had striven unceas-

ingly for the repeal of the Act of Prohibition, which
hung like the sword of Damocles over each actor's
head, blighting his peace of mind, and keeping him
up to an uncomfortably rigid standard of ethics.
At last, on the second of March, 1789, the efforts of
the Association triumphed over all opposition. The
obnoxious act was repealed, and the Southwark Theatre was opened "by authority" for the first time
since it was built. Polite deceptions were henceforth
at an end; moral dialogues and fictitious lectures
ceased to figure on the bills; a play was a play, and
a spade was a spade, for all the emancipated years
to come.

CHAPTER VI

THE BIRTH OF LEARNING IN THE QUAKER CITY

THERE is an especial charm to the modest student
of history in contemplating the little beginnings of
big things; and most big things, whose bigness is of a
lasting and satisfying nature, have started on so small
a scale that we can afford to feel familiar with them
from their birth. It is only in the present day, and
only in this impatient western world, that institutions
are expected to spring into existence, as Pallas Athene
sprang from the brain of Zeus, vigorous, mature, and

fully equipped for achievement. An impression prevails now among energetic people that a university can
be finished off-hand, and set running like a locomotive.
All we need are the stone walls, the apparatus, and
money to pay the professors. It is a mere question of
steam. But the wise old monk who said to the magnificent Medici, "Ah! Lorenzo, money does not make
masters; masters make money," knew whereof he
spoke. Our great, great grandfathers had but little
money when they planted the seeds of learning in the
infant colonies; but they gave unstintedly from their
narrow resources, and were content that future generations should finish their work, and reap the fulness of
their harvest. Two young men, one of them a chemist
and one a dentist, called together a few friends in their
own walk of life, rented a little room over a milliner's
shop, placed in it, with infinite pride, a dozen stuffed
birds and a jar or two of reptiles, and met there at
night to discuss "the operations of nature," pledging
themselves wisely to leave politics and religion entirely
out of their debates. From this modest beginning, this
insignificant society, sprang the Philadelphia Academy
of Natural Sciences, the oldest institution of its kind
in America, which has borne a part in Arctic expeditions, diffused knowledge over the eastern States, and
counted among its members the scholars and scientists
of the land.

In another small room in Jone's Alley, a few books,

G

loaned by a club of gentlemen, were kept in three little
bookcases for the benefit of members who might wish
to consult them, and these three little bookcases cradled
the infancy of the Philadelphia Library. The volumes
grew so shabby under constant handling that their
owners became dissatisfied; and into the fertile brain
of Franklin crept the project of a public library which
should differ from all other public libraries, inasmuch
as its books should be lent to subscribers, and carried
home " into the bosom of private families." Much was
hoped for the future, but little was exacted from the
present, Franklin being wise enough to recognize the
principle of growth. Fifty gentlemen willing to pay
forty shillings each were sought for anxiously, but, as
they were hard to find, half that number were held to
be sufficient for a foundation, and when the Library
Company saw itself in possession of forty-five pounds,
it determined to send to England for books. With a
modesty beyond all praise, the members of the Company acknowledged their unfitness to select these
precious volumes, and requested James Logan, "a
gentleman of universal learning, and the best judge of
books in these parts," to make out the necessary list.
When the infant library arrived in Philadelphia, — a
pedantic and somewhat ponderous infant it proved to
be, — the room in Jone's Alley was prepared for its reception; and from there it migrated to an apartment
in the State House, and afterwards to Carpenter's Hall.

The elate directors met at the house of Nicholas Scull, "who loved books, and sometimes made a few verses," elected a librarian, who only attended twice a week, designed a seal, and passed a resolution, placing their volumes at the disposal of any "civil gentleman" who wished to read them, though only subscribers were permitted to carry them away. A public library, it may be observed, was not then intended to provide young women with an inexhaustible supply of novels.

In 1733, Thomas Penn, second son of William Penn and Hannah Callowhill, visited the colony, and the adroit directors presented him with an address, asking his patronage for an institution which was to make Philadelphia "the future Athens of America." His Excellency was not averse to a little well-timed flattery, and was ready to assist inexpensively in moulding an American Athens. He presented to the Library an air-pump, a microscope, and the promise of a lot of land, which was not definitely secured until twenty-four years later. Other gentlemen imitated his generosity, and donated a cabinet of medals, a collection of Indian fish-hooks, some Chinese slippers, the hand of an Egyptian mummy, and various articles of the kind that museums are now expected to accept from anybody who wishes to be rid of them, but which were particularly undesirable in a library which lacked sufficient space for its books. The volumes remained in Carpenter's Hall until after the Revolution, and were an occasional solace to both the English and American officers, especially when the library-room was used as a hospital. Not a single book, it is said, was lost or mutilated during this period of usurpation, and the soldiers with scrupulous integrity or courtesy paid the customary fee for every work they read.

In 1789 the directors laid the corner-stone of the old library building in Fifth Street, with its curious homely inscription : —

> "Be it remembered
> In honour of the Philadelphia youth,
> (Then chiefly artificers)
> That in MDCCXXXI
> They cheerfully,
> At the instance of Benjamin Franklin,
> One of their number,
> Instituted the Philadelphia Library;
> Which though small at first,
> Is become highly valuable and extensively useful;
> And which the walls of this edifice
> Are now destined to contain and preserve."

In December, 1790, the books were triumphantly carried to this their first real home. A statue of Franklin, executed in Italy, was presented to the Company by Mr. William Bingham, and placed in a niche over the doorway. Tradition says that this statue cost five hundred guineas, and history records that, before it was ordered, a committee of the directors waited upon the illustrious scholar to learn his wishes in the matter, and reported to Mr. Bingham that Dr. Franklin desired "a gown for his dress, and a Roman head." The figure was accordingly draped in a toga, after the approved fashion of the eighteenth century, of which St. Paul's in London affords us so many delightful examples, and it looks like a benign old gentleman preparing decorously for his morning bath. It still stands over the portal of the new library building erected in Locust Street, in 1880, when the vast accumulation of books demanded a more spacious habitation.

For the few insignificant volumes in the little room in Jone's Alley have increased and multiplied exceedingly. In 1792 the Loganian Library, so called from its founder, James Logan, was added to the collection. In 1869 the bequest of Dr. James Rush placed at the disposal of the Company the beautiful building known as the Ridgway Branch of the Philadelphia Library. In this spacious mansion, stately, remote, and inaccessible, a hundred thousand volumes repose in dignified seclusion. It is a granite mausoleum where knowledge sleeps serenely, unvexed by would-be readers, and the noisy tumult of the world. Far different is the fate of the remaining books which number nearly a hundred thousand more, and which, in the less imposing edifice in Locust Street, are comparatively at the mercy of the crowd. Here, too, may be found a number of interesting historical relics

William Penn's desk, comfortable, commodious, and full of delightful little drawers; his clock, still bravely keeping time; Franklin's clock, which is far more

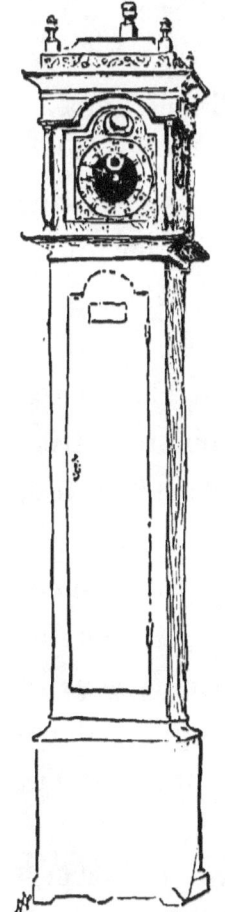

ornate and elegant; and the old inscribed corner-stone of the Fifth Street Library, which has been carefully transferred to the new walls. Here, in the words of the devout ornithologist, Alexander Wilson, we may

"Feast with sages, and give thanks to God;"

not altogether ignoring our debt of gratitude to the "artificers" of Philadelphia, who, nearly two centuries ago, planned and plotted, worked and saved, to leave to future generations the little library which, grown into such fair proportions, is an inheritance carrying down to us in every volume the wisdom and the good-will of our ancestors.

It is to Franklin that the Quaker City owes her college as well as her

FRANKLIN'S CLOCK

books. Indeed, we can no more escape from Franklin when studying the history of Philadelphia, than we can escape from Michelangelo when studying the treasures of Rome or Florence; and Mark Twain's ribald witticism is as applicable to the one case as to the other. Turn where we will, from the homeliest detail of practical life to the sharp strife of politics, the wild flights of philosophy, the freshly opened field of scientific research ; seek where we may for the beginning of everything that is most useful and most highly valued in the Philadelphia of to-day, and we are always confronted by the same ubiquitous figure. It was Franklin who invented the stove which warmed nearly every parlour in the town ; Franklin who invented the lightning-rod which protected nearly every farmhouse in the State ; Franklin who organized the fire companies ; Franklin who started the Philosophical Society ; Franklin who obtained from England a fair taxation of the proprietary estates ; Franklin who pranked it gayly at the French court, flattered by fair women, and cheered by the sapient mob ; and Franklin who, alarmed at the ignorance he saw on every side of him, resolved that the sons of Philadelphia citizens should have some higher education than that afforded them by the admirable but limited training of the Quaker schools.

In 1749, having thought the matter over for several years, he made known his views in a pamphlet entitled " Proposals Relating to the Education of Youth in Pennsylvania." Many of these " proposals," it must be admitted, are of a serenely chimerical order, and suggest the Utopian dreams of Milton, who held that schoolboys should never be permitted to eat their

dinners, uncheered by the ravishment of music.   For
music, indeed, Franklin cared but little ; and as for
dinners, they were to be of Spartan simplicity in the
new establishment.   " Poor Richard" was not likely

to see the college funds wasted in riotous living.   But
the school should be surrounded by an orchard and
many green meadows ; the students were to learn how
to write "a fair hand swiftly"; to acquire a moderate

knowledge of arithmetic, geometry, astronomy, and kindred subjects; and to read Pope, Addison, Tillotson, Algernon Sidney, and a translation of Cato's Letters, by way of acquiring good style and good principles. On Greek and Latin, alas! no time was to be wasted, — it is easier for a camel to pass through the eye of a needle than for a self-taught man to recognize the value of the classics, — but the grand underlying principle of the institution was that the students were to study nothing, unless they felt impatient to do so. Even a simple matter like geography was not to be essayed, until a familiarity with past events — how acquired we are not told — had awakened in them a desire to know the position and extent of countries where such events had taken place. Education, which hitherto had meant the goading on of reluctant youth, was now at last to assume its true character, — a free and joyous pursuit of knowledge, of such knowledge, at least, as the Philadelphia lads deemed it incumbent to acquire.

The breadth and depth of Franklin's theories did not for one moment interfere with his severely practical plans for the establishment and support of the Academy. The subscription he set on foot for this purpose met with extraordinary success, the number of students increased rapidly, and the trustees acquired for very little money the great barn-like building on Fourth Street that had been erected for the benefit of the Rev. Mr. Whitefield, after he had alienated the affections of his brother clergymen by passing "unwarrantable sentences on men, as if he were the supreme Judge,"—a habit ill calculated to promote charity and good-will. The selection of the Rev. William Smith for provost was due largely to another pamphlet— pamphlets carried wondrous weight in those colonial days—which that ardent young Scotchman had published a year or two before, and in which he gave *his* views upon the training and education of youth. Dr. Smith's literary methods were not wholly unlike those of our modern social reformers. Instead of dry, logical arguments, he contented himself with a lively description of an imaginary and ideal institution, the "College of Mirania," in which lads were taught, somewhat after the "Harry and Lucy" fashion, everything that mortal man could learn. Physics and fencing, mechanics and agriculture, the philosophy of politics and practical farming,—nothing came amiss to the Miranian youths, and nothing sated their inexhaustible thirst for information. Franklin, who knew most things himself, and saw no reason why other men should not know them too, was enchanted with the pamphlet, and eager to secure the services of its author. The trustees shared his enthusiasm, without his knowledge to excuse it; Smith was summoned from New York to Philadelphia; and—if we may trust the curriculum of the infant college which embraces every art and every science — the theories of Mirania were put as far as possible into practice.

The wisdom of Providence, however, has placed an insurmountable barrier between such theories and their accomplishment, in the steady, wholesome resistance of the average boy, who can be trusted impli-

" WOODLANDS "

After an old painting

citly to protect himself from the perils of over-instruction. Girl students are led with dangerous ease over the thorny paths where knowledge stalks unchecked; but the stolid sanity of the boy stays his footsteps in good time, and frequently a little earlier than need be. The lads who thronged with cheerful tumult and confusion into the old collegiate rooms on Fourth Street resembled but indifferently their Miranian models, and learned only as much of the abundance that was offered as it was wise and well for them to know.

It seemed inevitable that the college, though priding itself originally on its purely liberal basis, should gravitate towards the Episcopal and proprietary party. Where should it have turned, if not to its friends and supporters? The Penns, recognizing it as an able ally, gave liberally out of their abundance to its needs; and when Dr. Smith went to England to collect funds, he naturally addressed himself to dignitaries of his own church. The long list of clergymen, bishops, archbishops, and peers who swiftly responded to his appeal, proves the generous interest taken by the English establishment in the little colonial college; and the great universities of England held out helping hands to their small sister over the seas, who was battling against heavy odds for life.

For the Quakers were disposed to look askance upon Mirania, and the learned Dr. Smith, being the most belligerent of men, took infinite pains to arouse their resentment and animosity. After Braddock's defeat had awakened Pennsylvania to a sense of mingled shame and apprehension, he published two pamphlets, charging the Assembly with supine cowardice and neglect of its duties. The Indian massacres, in his opinion, were due wholly to the Quakers and their abominable religion, which left the province at the mercy of savages. It would be well, he gently asserted, to stamp this religion from the face of the earth, and to drive the Quakers from their places of authority, — or, if necessary, cut their throats. These Rienzi-like sentiments from a young man of twenty-nine were hardly calculated to soften the hearts of his opponents; and when he followed them up by enthusiastically supporting the seditious utterances of William Moore, the Assembly exerted its " tyrannous power," and clapped him into jail for libel.

This was a serious drawback to the prosperity of the college, but a magnificent opportunity for the warlike and oratorical provost. He made the most of it! The day of his trial was one of profound and delightful excitement. Dr. Smith in heroic periods defied the Assembly, refused to retract his statements, demanded a writ of *habeas corpus*, and swore that he would appeal to the crown. Storms of applause greeted him from his friends; but the unmoved Assembly remanded him to prison, where he remained, at some inconvenience to himself and others, for eleven weeks. The trustees of the college ordered that his classes should attend him there at their usual hours, and the enthusiastic students had the supreme felicity of swarming into the jail, and manifesting the exuberance of their zeal. It was a trifle demoralizing perhaps, and hardly conducive to the calm acquisition of knowledge; nothing of the kind had ever happened in Mirania; but for pure enjoyment it surpassed any diversion offered to the Miranian youths.

The provost wrote joyously to the Bishop of London that his cell was crowded with visitors from morning to night, and that he transacted there all the important business of the college. In fact, those who suffer persecution for justice' sake do not always have to wait for another world in which to meet with their reward. They are apt to get a large instalment of it here. Love and fame stand at the martyr's door. An interesting young woman gave her heart to the captive scholar, and promptly married him. When released from prison for the second time, for he had been rearrested after his first discharge, he sailed for England, and was received with that sympathy and admiration which every nation is so swift to manifest for another nation's ill-used patriots. The Church recognized in him a champion of the faith whom the tyrannous Quakers had signally failed to subdue. Oxford and Aberdeen granted him degrees. London gave him dinners and applause. His appeal to the Privy Council met with supreme success. The Assembly was censured for its unconstitutional disregard of a subject's rights and privileges, and, when Dr. Smith returned to Philadelphia, it was as a justified and triumphant man. The episode had sadly disturbed the serenity and the utility of the college ; but it brought unqualified satisfaction to the provost, and heartened him for fresh crusades.

It was a period of strange hostilities. The vain attempt to abolish the proprietorship left the province sullen and disturbed. The coming of the Revolution threw its mighty shadow over the hearts of men, and they wrangled bitterly, filled with mistrust and anger. In the first meetings held by prominent citizens of Philadelphia to express sympathy for poor locked-up Boston, we find the college provost emphatically asserting the indefeasible right of the colonies to vote their own supplies, — a right which they would never abandon. His seemed a voice destined to uphold the cause of freedom, and help an injured people to rebel; but the overwhelming speed with which rebellion, once set going, advanced, disconcerted him, as it did many older and wiser men. The college, moreover, was closely bound to England by ties of creed, by gratitude for favours given, and by that reverent admiration which every little, but right-thinking, school feels for the great universities, which stand crowned by the scholarship of the past, rich with the inheritance of the centuries. It was a loyal college ever; loyal to its own traditions, but more loyal still to the claims of the commonwealth which were stronger than any tradition. The stormy years of revolutionary war were ill adapted for the advancement of education; but the triumph of the Constitutionalists should have meant protection and safety for Philadelphia's scholars. This was what Franklin strove in vain to insure by a clause in the new Constitution, providing that all schools and all churches should be left in undisturbed possession of their privileges. What really happened is almost too scandalous to be told. The Assembly, composed now of extremists under the leadership of Reed, professed to doubt the patriotism of an institution which had never failed in respect and obedience to the national government, and which had for its trustees men like Robert Morris and James Wilson, who had signed the Declaration of Independence, and striven unceasingly for the freedom and the honour of their land. In 1779 the college charter was declared void, the Faculty was dissolved after the parliamentary fashion of Cromwell, and the property was handed over to new trustees, with directions to found a brand-new *alma mater*, which was to be modestly entitled, "The University of the State of Pennsylvania."

It was an act of spoliation, without excuse and without redress. Its immediate result was the collapse of education in Philadelphia. The old college, deprived of charter, roof-tree, and funds, refused to die peaceably when requested, but struggled on, crippled and wellnigh useless. Its provost, whose heroic pluck would never allow him to know when he was beaten, retired to Maryland, only to plan fresh campaigns for the future. The new "University" found its honours heavy to bear, and its task impossible of performance. The magnificent title mocked the feebleness of its intellect, the inadequacy of its work. Poor minion of fortune, it could not even rely upon its own friends. After nine years, the Assembly which had bidden it live, took from it all means of livelihood. The act of 1779 was pronounced "repugnant to justice, and a violation of the Constitution of the Commonwealth." The property was handed ruthlessly back to its rightful owner, the old College of Philadelphia, and Provost Smith, victorious and elate, took his place at the head of the institution.

But not for long. There could be no stability anywhere amid such hopeless elements of disorder. As the strife of factions ran higher and higher, scholarship sank lower and lower. The college and the university stood side by side, weakened and well-nigh weaponless. They could do nothing worth the doing apart, and it was hoped they might accomplish something together. With the consent of the Legislature, a union was effected in 1791; the simple old name was abandoned in favour of the more aspiring designation; and the trustees were impartially selected from every contesting clique and party the city could afford, in the hope, as Mr. Sydney Fisher aptly expresses it, "that

the more dissimilar and disunited they were, the more
they would work in harmony." Dr. Smith disappeared
forever from the collegiate halls, and education departed with him. Mirania was no more, and, in her
place, an enfeebled school, calling itself a university,
struggled for existence, and graduated a pitiful handful of students every year. Only the medical department, established in 1765, was strong enough to resist
the dismal influence of the times; and through the
unceasing efforts of Dr. Shippen, Dr. Rush, Dr.
Wistar, and other physicians of distinction, advanced
steadily step by step to the splendid future that
awaited it. In medicine and surgery Philadelphia
always claimed preëminence, and her doctors to-day
need look back upon no period of their history with
shame in their hearts for its dishonourable inactivity.
But it was not until after the Civil War that the University began slowly to raise its downcast head, that
head now held aloft in conscious and justifiable elation. In 1871, one of Franklin's early "Proposals"
was realized in part by the erection of the new college
buildings in West Philadelphia; where, if no green
meadows and fruitful orchards win the students from
their books, and no river rolls invitingly under collegiate windows, there is at least a campus and a little
breathing space, turf under foot, and blue sky over-
head. In these buildings, which from year to year have
received important additions, the college which has

LIBRARY OF UNIVERSITY OF PENNSYLVANIA

passed through so many vicissitudes, so many changes of scene and fortune, has at last fulfilled the proudest hopes of those who first sped her on her way for the help and enlightenment of posterity.

Six years before the ever famous " Proposals " saw the light of day, another and very different scheme of education was being slowly shaped into action by the resistless energy of Franklin. In 1743 he conceived the admirable idea of forming a society " for promoting useful knowledge among the British plantations in America," or, in other words, for connecting the aspiring science of the New World with the supercilious science of the Old. The members of this society were naturally chosen from the " Junto," a club organized by Franklin " for mutual improvement," when he was but twenty-one years old. The Junto was a serious club, not given to youthful frivolities, still less to youthful indiscretions. It met, indeed, in a tavern ; but the members asked each other difficult questions, such as " Is there any essential difference between the electric fluid and elementary fire ? " or " What becomes of the water constantly flowing into the Mediterranean?" and took a sincere pleasure in endeavouring to answer them. In fact, they solemnly promised, on admission, not only to love truth for truth's sake, but to receive it impartially themselves, and to communicate it industriously to others.

Here was exactly the material needed by Franklin

for the formation of a Philosophical Society. Young
men who diverted themselves in this exemplary manner
were surely born to be philosophers. Nevertheless,
the old Junto did not, as is commonly supposed, melt

DOORWAYS IN PINE STREET

at once into the new organization. It held together
as a club until 1766, when it became the formidable
"American Society for promoting and propagating
Useful Knowledge;" and it was not until three years
later that the Philosophical Society and the American
Society united their forces, and became one. Franklin

was elected the first president of the combined fraternities, and held that position until his death. Richard Penn, the most affable of the proprietors, consented to act as patron. The Quaker Assembly looked with favour upon philosophers who proposed to push their investigations into practical matters, and who, in the intervals of discussing the best form of government, or the secret of happiness, were not above a care for smoky chimneys, and a farmer-like regard for manures. In fact, "the useful science of agriculture" occupied a great deal of their leisure and attention. Franklin's enthusiasm for rice equalled Napoleon's for beets, or Edmund Burke's for carrots. Thomas Jefferson, who was at one time president of the philosophers as well as of the United States, designed a model plough, almost as good in its way as Franklin's model stove. The Assembly generously voted a thousand pounds to assist the Society in planting mulberry trees for the benefit of silkworms, which were to be invited to emigrate to the New World and feed on them.

"Botany, medicine, mineralogy, chemistry, mining, mechanics, arts, trades, manufactures, geography, and topography," also appear on the list of subjects to be studied and discussed; yet, even under this severe pressure of erudition, the genial philosophers found time to give themselves, and occasionally their neighbours, very good dinners, and to turn their minds to the consideration of those practical details which philosophy is wont

to ignore, but upon which the comfort of colonial life
was largely dependent. This was in keeping with
Franklin's character, and avowed inclinations. "No
other writer," says Mr. MacMaster, "has pointed out so
clearly the way to obtain the greatest amount of comfort out of life;" and the old panegyrist who penned
this glowing tribute, —

> " Immortal Franklin, whose unwearied mind
>   Still sought out every good for all mankind ;
>   Searched every science, studious still to know,
>   To make men virtuous, and to keep them so,"

would have been nearer the mark if he had written
the last line, —

> " To make men prosperous, and to keep them so."

To increase the comfort and prosperity, as well
as the scholarship of the province, was the laudable
ambition of the Philosophical Society. Its members,
drawn from every creed and every rank of life, present
a curious medley of colonial pundits. David Rittenhouse, the astronomer, who succeeded Franklin as
president ; ex-governor Hamilton, the distinguished
leader of the proprietary party ; and Brother Jabetz,
Prior of the Ephrata cloister, who was wont to walk
eighty miles, it is said, to attend the meetings, and
whose tall spare figure in flowing robe, girt by a
hempen cord, added a charming element of picturesqueness, as well as a flavour of asceticism which

seemed just what the philosophers required. It was this unworldly monk who, after the Revolution, translated the Declaration of Independence into seven languages, and proved himself of great service to the State in reading diplomatic correspondence. Tradition says that for all this work he never demanded, and alas! never received a penny of pay from a too thrifty government. The Prior, however often he may have walked the eighty miles, had neglected to learn one important lesson from the lips of Franklin, who would have taught him plainly that the labourer is worthy of his hire.

The first momentous task undertaken by the Philosophical Society was the scientific observation of the transit of Venus, in 1769. This was an enterprise requiring a large expenditure of money, as well as the closest care and calculation; but it was the looked-for opportunity for the colonial scientists to associate themselves with the scientists of Europe, and to add their quota to the accurate information of the world. Observatories were erected in Philadelphia, in Norristown, and at Cape Henlopen. The Assembly voted one hundred pounds for the purchase of a telescope. Thomas Penn sent a second admirable telescope from England. The day of the transit, June third, was one of unbroken clearness and brilliancy, nature having abandoned her usual perversity for this ever memorable occasion; and the observations taken were so completely successful that Dr. Maskelyne, the astronomer royal, pronounced them enthusiastically to be an honour to Pennsylvania, and to all the learned gentlemen whose indefatigable exertions had accomplished this splendid result.

With the approach of war, the zeal of the philosophers for scientific research grew visibly less. It was not a time for study; and during three tumultuous years the Society never held a single meeting. Its members were mostly occupied in making history, and had scant leisure for the calm pursuit of agriculture or astronomy. On the fifth of March, 1779, they reassembled to gather up the broken threads of their past work; and a year later they were granted their first charter, and a lot of ground adjoining the State House on which to build a hall. In 1787 this hall was completed, and still stands undesecrated, save in a few details, by modern renovations. Here on their dusty shelves are the ancient volumes which Franklin and Rittenhouse handled; here are many curious relics of the Society's vigorous youth, and of days so long past we have well-nigh forgotten the lessons that they taught us. In one of these beautiful rooms Washington was painted by the three Peales, and the historic mantel-shelf which forms the background of the portrait has now, alas! been dug from the wall, and banished as lumber to the cellar. When La Fayette returned to America, the Philosophical Society entertained him under its own roof-tree, and Mr.

Charles Ingersoll delivered an address of such flattering eloquence that it would have abashed Napoleon, and made Cæsar blush beneath his civic wreath, though, to the insatiable vanity of the genial Frenchman, it was probably no more than a bare recognition of his merits.

Among the philosophers may be found long lists of distinguished names, both European and American. Noah Webster, Washington Irving, George Bancroft, Dr. Holmes, James Russell Lowell, Louis Agassiz, and Joseph Leidy were members. Even women are not altogether lacking from the rolls. Mrs. Somerville, Mrs. Agassiz, and Mrs. Seiler were elected as valued members; and also that very different exponent of feminine scholarship, rich in knowledge and in many experiences, the Princess Daschkof. The Empress was not pleased at her favourite's acceptance of the proffered honour. Catherine the Second never liked Benjamin Franklin, and had scant tolerance for his philosophy. She refused coldly to receive him, and refused to give any reason for her denial. It was not for the ruler of all the Russias to cheapen her deeds with reasons. "I do not care for him," was the only opinion she ever vouchsafed. The same imperial and comprehensive criticism was passed by Elizabeth of England upon John Knox, when she forbade him English soil.

CHAPTER VII

THE STATE HOUSE AND ITS MESSAGE

THE birth of law in Philadelphia was as modest as the birth of learning, at least so far as outward circumstances were concerned. When Penn returned for the first time to England in 1684, he left the little Letitia House to his secretary, Markham, and directed that it should be at the service of the Provincial Council. The wine and beer stored in the cellar were placed at the disposal of the deputy governor, Thomas Lloyd, "for the use of strangers," a kindly and hospitable thought. Penn's periwigs, which were of the finest order, were also consigned to the care of Lloyd, who was permitted to wear them during their owner's absence, and had, as it chanced, an admirable opportunity to wear them out in the fifteen years that followed. The Letitia House was, accordingly, for some time the State House of the province; and in its small, low-ceilinged rooms the men who carried their country's cares upon their shoulders met in anxious deliberation. Four years later, we find Penn writing that he fears the cottage is too contracted for such a purpose, and that the Council should have a building fitted to its needs. The Council thought otherwise. Debt was a thing its members abhorred as only Quakers can, and money was hard to find in the prosperous little colony, already drained of gold by the number and variety of its imports. So for twenty-five years the lawmakers of the province met wherever they could find accommodation,— under the roofs of private citizens, in schoolrooms, and in the Quaker meeting-house. Those were primitive, almost Arcadian days, when the character of public men, and the nature of the laws they enacted, were deemed of greater importance than stone walls, marble floors, and upholstery. The country court-house, the "Towne House" as it was called, was finished in 1709, and in this unpretentious little

building the Colonial Assembly and the Supreme
Court of the province held their sessions. It was
not until the issue of paper currency made money

THE "TOWNE HOUSE"

seem more abundant, and relaxed the vigilant economy of our forefathers, that Philadelphia aspired to
a State House of her own; and even after two
thousand pounds had been appropriated to this purpose in 1729, the work proceeded very slowly, and

with a due regard to the reluctance of tax-payers, — a class of people who, however contumeliously they may be treated now, were then held in the greatest consideration and esteem.

In 1735 the Assembly met for the first time in the new State House, which was still far from finished. The great chamber now known as Independence Hall was not completed until seven years later; the modest wooden steeple was not added until 1751. A bell was felt to be an imperative necessity, and was ordered forthwith from England, its cost not to exceed two hundred pounds. It was cast in White-chapel, and around its sides ran the prophetic words, "Proclaim Liberty throughout all the Land, to all the Inhabitants thereof." This English bell, to the bitter disappointment of the colonists, was cracked at its first trial by a stroke of its own clapper, and had to be recast in Philadelphia before it was hung honourably in the little steeple which had been built for its accommodation. The graceful outlines of the State House, an admirable example of colonial architecture, full of dignity, and with an exquisite sense of fitness and proportion, were rendered still more charming to the eye by the deep green of the magnificent trees that surrounded it. These veterans of the primeval forest, the last survivors in Philadelphia of the mighty woods which had gained for Pennsylvania its sylvan name, were sacrificed, one by one, to the indifference or the dislike of the colonists. Penn had dearly loved the deep shadows of their spreading branches. He had hoped and desired that his settlers would spare the trees when possible, and would build their homes at reasonable distances, "so that there may be ground on each side for gardens or orchards, and that the town may be a green country town, which will never be burned, and always be wholesome."

But the early Philadelphians pressed their houses closer and closer together, and they cut down their beautiful trees to economize space, or under the strange pretext of guarding "against fire and stagnant air." The State House was gradually denuded of its green girdle, and stood bare and desolate until after the Revolution; when more room was added to its shabby enclosure, new trees were planted, new walks laid out, a new brick wall built to protect it from vulgar intrusion, and, under the new and dignified name of Independence Square, the old State House yard became for a few years a fashionable loitering-place, upon whose genteel and urban charms Philadelphia poets wrote stilted verses in the columns of the local press.

There were other and far different scenes, however, to be enacted on this hallowed ground before the citizens of the young Republic had leisure for sylvan strolls and verse-making. No building in the United States has an historic interest comparable to that of

the Philadelphia State House, the birthplace of our
national life. Its venerable walls heard the vehement
denunciations hurled against the Stamp Act, and the
still more vehement resolutions which sent Captain
Ayres and his ship-load of tea back to the port of

OLD STATE HOUSE

London. Here, after the battle of Lexington, assembled that eager, angry crowd who expressed the
sentiments of the whole people in a single curt resolution, "to defend with arms their property, liberty, and
lives." Here Washington was appointed, by the second
Continental Congress, commander-in-chief of the army ;

and here Richard Henry Lee of Virginia moved on the seventh of June, 1776, that "these United Colonies are, and of right ought to be, free and independent States; that they are absolved from all allegiance to the British Crown, and that all political connection between them and the state of Great Britain is, and ought to be, totally dissolved."

From the little observatory, the "awful platform," as John Adams calls it, that had been erected in the State House yard for the peaceful study of Venus, the Declaration of Independence was read aloud to the people of Philadelphia, — to the few at least who gathered to hear it, and by whom it was received in serious and puzzled silence. The dramatic side of this great historic event was not, as has been often observed, apparent to men who thought less of the document itself, than of how it was to be supported and enforced. They had thrilled with anger and pity when Boston called to them for help. They had exulted jubilantly over the repeal of the Stamp Act, and had watched with proud hearts the last white sail of Captain Ayres' tea ship, *Polly*, as she turned seaward with her hated cargo. But it was no longer a time for passing resolutions, and rejecting tea. Grim war was at their doors, and the horror of it sobered their enthusiasm, and chilled the first wild rapture of defiance. The men who signed their names to the Declaration of Independence realized to the utmost all

THE STATE HOUSE

the consequences it involved, and the terrible responsibility they had placed upon their own shoulders. The State House bell rang out its message, proclaiming for the first time "liberty throughout all the land, to all the inhabitants thereof"; but the people listened gravely, and with no apparent response. Those who knew what it meant, knew also that liberty is not to be won by proclamation, but bought with the life-blood of brave men who die that their brothers may be free.

CASE CONTAINING ORIGINAL OF DECLARATION OF INDEPENDENCE

CHAPTER VIII

FOR nearly a century the history of Philadelphia is a placid record of unbroken good fortune. The tireless wrangling of two great conflicting interests injured the province very little, and gave her that most precious boon, — a standing quarrel which could be taken up by the combatants whenever they had leisure to engage in it. Had the Assembly and the proprietary party worked together in accord, the colonists would have suffered grievously from the benumbing of those angry passions which childhood is bidden to restrain, but which make life a thing of abounding interest to healthily contentious men. The Indian wars, though they cost Pennsylvania both troops and money, left the city undevastated by the horrors which dyed deep with blood the annals of less fortunate communities. The stubborn and conservative Quakers guarded their town — Penn's precious legacy — with a wise watchfulness, and she waxed fairer and stronger every year. Her prosperity was not, indeed, a matter of sudden acquisition, like the affluence of New Zealand, where, Mr. Froude assures us, the labourers eat hot-house grapes. It was built up on solid foundations of industry and thrift, having Franklin's maxims for its week-day sermons, and Franklin's shining example to illustrate the text. The man who amassed his fortune penny by penny, and retired from business at the early age of forty-two, with a modest income of three thousand dollars, taught his neighbours a triple lesson of assiduity, economy, and moderation. It is only to be regretted that the edifying spectacle of colonial honour and enterprise should be marred by the dark shadow of privateering. In the Spanish war, and in King George's war, the virtuous Quaker City sent forth these armed marauders to snatch what prey they could; and that she was proud of their success, and pointed them out with elation to strangers visiting her busy docks, proves the exactness of Sydney Smith's cynical observation anent the stanch moral support to be derived from the most dubious of theories.

The increasing wealth of the province manifested itself in farmhouses so strongly and admirably built that time leaves no impression on their massive walls; in country-seats more spacious and beautiful than could be found in any other State save Virginia; in the fast-growing luxury of town life; and in a sane philanthropy, devoid of whims and sentiment. The charity of the Quakers has always extended to the bodies as well as to the souls of men. In 1713, when the city was still in its infancy, they built "for

the habitation and succour of the poor and unfortunate," the pretty rural cottages long known as the

QUAKER ALMSHOUSE

Quaker almshouses. Each cottage had its patch of
ground, where the aged inmates — unshamed by the

stigma of pauperism — cultivated bright flowers and healing herbs. It was a peaceful haven, affording, not only shelter, but, as an old historian earnestly assures us, "opportunities for study and meditation." We smile when we read the words, but we sigh, too, recalling the bleak desolation, the abiding horror of a modern almshouse, and comparing it with the decent privacy of the happier poor nearly two hundred years ago, when the wisdom of our forefathers drew a deep line of distinction between the old and helpless, "the afflicted of God," and the sturdy beggar or shameless wench, for whom was made sharper and sterner provision. It is to the Quaker almshouse,

> "Home of the homeless,
> Then in the suburbs it stood, in the midst of meadows and
> woodlands,"

that tradition points as the final meeting-place of Gabriel and Evangeline; and antiquarians who disprove the story with aggressive and importunate details might find a better use for their time and knowledge. In the graveyard of old St. Joseph's — hidden away in Willing's Alley from the wrath of hostile creeds — the lovers slept side by side; and the clamour of a great city echoed but faintly through the narrow, walled-in strip of consecrated ground, where, after so many years of sorrowful wandering, their faithful hearts found rest.

What the college was to the Episcopal and pro. prietary party in Philadelphia, the Pennsylvania Hospital was to the Quakers, — a party stronghold, as well as a cherished and admirably administered institution. On its ancient corner-stone was cut deep this cheerful and devout inscription : —

> "In the year of Christ MDCCLV,
> George the second happily reigning,
> (For he sought the happiness of his people)
> Philadelphia flourishing,
> (For its inhabitants were public-spirited)
> This Building
> By the bounty of the government,
> And of many private persons,
> Was piously founded
> For the relief of the sick and the miserable.
>
> May the God of Mercies bless the undertaking."

Of the public spirit here gratefully commemorated, the erection of this hospital gives abiding proof. When, in 1750, Dr. Thomas Bond and a few charitable citizens realized the necessity of providing shelter for "sick and distempered strangers," their appeal for funds met with an immediate response. The Assembly voted at different times five thousand pounds to help them with the work. All classes endeavoured honestly to assist. An especial subscription was asked from "rich widows and other single women," and they answered nobly by raising a fund sufficient for the purchase of drugs. Although most of the money came from the Quakers, who kept the hospital always under their control, yet other churches contributed with amazing generosity. The pious free-lance, Whitefield, collected, after an ardent and persuasive sermon, one hundred and seventy pounds. England, ever liberal to colonial charities, lent such material aid that the directors found their burden almost easy to bear. An Act of Parliament gave to the hospital all the unclaimed funds remaining in the hands of the trustees of the Pennsylvania Land Company in London, and this extraordinary windfall amounted to thirteen thousand pounds. The Proprietors, Thomas and Richard Penn, gave a portion of the land on which the building was erected, and an annuity of forty pounds a year. Finally, Dr. John Fothergill of London sent a beautifully articulated human skeleton, and so admirable a collection of anatomical models and drawings that the thrifty Friends refused to exhibit them gratuitously to the public. They were placed in a room apart, and Dr. Shippen explained them learnedly every other Saturday afternoon to such seekers after knowledge as were willing to pay a dollar for its acquisition.

It does not surprise us to find the name of Benjamin Franklin on the first board of managers. In point of fact, a Philadelphia board of managers which did not include Franklin would have been as great an anomaly as a Roman or a Florentine church without a trace of Michelangelo. It was Franklin who drew up the very sensible rules for the direction of the hospital, Franklin who was elected president of the board in 1756, and Franklin who characteristically proposed the distribution of tin boxes, lettered in gold, " Charity for the Hospital," and destined to receive the chance donations of benevolent friends and visitors. A penny given was a penny made, and the yearly reports of the institution show how much of its income was derived from the small contributions of well-wishers whose narrow means forbade a larger dole. Gifts of various kinds were proffered by prominent citizens; among them a second skeleton (skeletons were rare enough to be held in high esteem) which, being presented by Miss Deborah Morris, after the death of her brother, Dr. Benjamin Morris, was, we are assured, "gratefully received, and honourably deposited in the apothecary's shop."

The site on which the hospital was erected—not without long contention, for the Proprietors had wished to donate a less available piece of ground—was admirably chosen, and the building itself, like all other important buildings of the time, is a model of dignified simplicity, finely proportioned, and free from meretricious decoration. It is well for us who live in an age of over-ornamentation that we can rest our weary

PENNSYLVANIA HOSPITAL

eyes upon the graceful severity of colonial architecture where nothing needless can be found. The ample lawn was shaded by two rows of beautiful trees planted by Hugh Roberts, one of the first managers, in 1756, and among them grew and flourished a scion of the famous Treaty Elm, pleasantly refuting the slanderous tongues which mocked that historic monument, that mute witness of a nation's peace.

The prosperity of the hospital was unbroken, its efficiency unimpaired, until the dark days which followed the Revolution, when the terrible depreciation of the currency, the chaotic confusion of the public service, and the determination of the legislature to tax charitable institutions, crippled and well-nigh ruined it. Resolute labour and resolute resistance on the part of the managers averted the impending shipwreck, but years dragged by before the old sphere of quiet usefulness was even partially regained. It is pleasant to record that at this juncture the First Troop of Philadelphia City Cavalry gave to the Pennsylvania Hospital the entire sum received by it for services during the Revolutionary war; and the maternity ward for poor married women was built and endowed with this money. A very different, but equally welcome donation was the picture of "Christ Healing the Sick," which Benjamin West generously presented to the institution in 1817, and which awakened such enthusiasm in the hearts of our uncritical grandfathers that the adroit managers of the hospital — mindful still of Dr. Franklin's maxims — placed it on exhibition, and realized nearly twenty thousand dollars from the eager crowds

A BIT OF PENNSYLVANIA HOSPITAL

who thronged to see it. The big canvas is a replica of the painting originally intended by West for Philadelphia; but which, when it was seen in London,

excited, we are told, "such a glow of admiration that
nobles and commons, rich and poor, united in the determination to retain it in the country." Verily, an
artist so blessed by the patronage, so burdened by the
praises of his own generation, might well afford indifference to the acrimonious verdicts of posterity.

It was not in philanthropy alone, in the building of
almshouses, libraries and hospitals, that the rich colonists of the Quaker City found a use for their ample
incomes. They spent their money, after a reasonable
fashion, upon creature comforts, and in moderate display. Within their red brick houses, "stately and three
stories high, in the mode of London," writes Gabriel
Thomas as early as 1696, reigned security and modest
affluence. Balconies and sun-dials lent to these demure
homes an occasional air of gayety and picturesqueness.
"Every necessary for the Support of Life throughout
the whole Year," might be found in the far-famed
Philadelphia markets; and, if we may trust the evidence of colonial letters and diaries, more ingenuous
and less jubilant as a rule than colonial chroniclers,
our forefathers heartily enjoyed the good things which
Providence had kindly placed at their disposal. In
the published journal of Jacob Hiltzheimer, who lived
to see the Revolution, and was apparently but little
interested in that great crisis, we find such scandalous
entries as this: "Feb. 14th, 1766. At noon went to
William Jones's, to drink punch; met several of my

friends, and got decently drunk. The groom could not be accused of the same fault." Whether this means that the groom drank not at all, or that his libations went beyond the limits of decency, does not very clearly appear; but noon seems an early hour to settle down seriously to punch, even on Saint Valentine's day. On other occasions we read that Mr. Hiltzheimer went with his two sons and Daniel Wister to Joseph Galloway's place, "to eat turtle,"—a more innocent indulgence; that on the tenth of May he saw a "ten-pound race between Joseph Hogg's and John Buckingham's horses"; and that—being well disposed to divers sorts of entertainment—he found equal pleasure in bull-baiting, and in witnessing the performance of "Romeo and Juliet," at the Old Southwark Theatre. An opportunity for especial festivity was the King's birthday, June 4th, when he dined on the green banks of the Schuylkill, in company with three hundred and eighty loyal citizens, all in most jovial humour. Any number of healths were drunk at this gay repast, "among them Dr. Franklin's, which gave great satisfaction to everybody." A long boat was then dragged to the water's edge and launched, while the firing of "many great guns" announced King George's birthday to the town.

No one was better disposed towards a moderate conviviality than Franklin himself, for all his maxims and apothegms. In that old house on High Street where he lived and died, where, in the garden, he flew his immortal kite, and where he attached his own lightning-rod to his own wall, thereby greatly entertaining his curious neighbours, there reigned always hospitality and good cheer. True, he sent his sister Jane a spinning-wheel instead of the coveted tea-table, desiring her to be a "notable housewife." True, he recommended the "Whole Duty of Man," and the "Young Lady's Library," as proper reading for his daughter Sally, in place of the novels for which her spirit yearned. But, nevertheless, there remains now in the possession of the Pennsylvania Historical Society that delightful punch-keg which could be rolled so easily from guest to guest, and which carried the generous liquor circling around Franklin's board. A curious little keg this, pretty, portly, and altogether unlike other punch-bowls left us from colonial days. And what of that often quoted letter written by Franklin in England to his wife, and promising her, not spinning-wheels and decorous dull books, but the foreign crockery dear to the hearts of all colonial dames. Yet not every spouse would have felt pleased by this dubious compliment from an absent husband.

"I also forgot to mention among the china a large fine jug for beer, to stand in the cooler. I fell in love with it at first sight; for I thought it looked like a fat jolly dame, clean and tidy, with a neat

blue and white calico gown on, good-natured and
lovely, and put me in mind of — somebody."

Praise is not always charming. Had Mrs. Franklin loved poetry as well as she loved her husband,
which happily does not seem to have been the case,
she would have felt more pain than pleasure at hearing her merits extolled by him in such halting verses
as these : —

"Not a word of her face, of her shape, or her air,
  Or of flames, or of darts, you shall hear ;
  I beauty admire, but virtue I prize,
  That fades not in seventy year.

     *   *   *   *

"In peace and good order my household she guides,
  Right careful to save what I gain ;
  Yet cheerfully spends, and smiles on the friends
  I've the pleasure to entertain."

Well, the lines show at least that Franklin did
like to entertain his friends, and that it gladdened
him to see his wife lay aside her customary frugality
on those blithesome occasions, when the punch-keg
went rolling round. Mrs. Franklin — being but a
woman, albeit a great man's helpmate — found per-
chance a keener joy in furnishing her house than in
feeding her husband's guests. There is a delightful
blending of conscious thrift and timorous extravagance in the account she writes him of her modestly
garnished chambers.

"The chairs downstairs are plain horsehair, and look as well as Paduasoy, and are admired by all. In the little south room is a carpet I bought cheap for its goodness, and nearly new. In the parlour is a Scotch carpet which has much fault found with it. In the north room, where we sit, we have a small Scotch carpet, the small bookcase, brother John's picture, and one of the King and Queen. In the room for our friends we have the Earl of Bute hung up, and a glass."

The simplicity of the philosopher's surroundings contrasted sharply with the beauty and elegance of more pretentious dwellings; with Edward Shippen's house, for example, which is described by a contemporary chronicler as a veritable palace of delights, girt by an ample park, "and having a very famous and pleasant summer-house erected in the middle of his garden, abounding with tulips, pinks, carnations, roses, and lilies, not to mention those that grew wild in the fields ; and also a fine lawn upon which reposed his herd of tranquil deer."

A herd of deer reposing on South Second Street seems as strange an anomaly as the concealed staircase, the "priest's escape," in James Logan's country-seat, "Stenton." Who in that dignified and law-abiding household could ever have needed to escape, save from importunate visitors, or from the friendly Indians who came again and again to Logan, as to their truest ally, seeking counsel and aid in their difficulties. It was not unusual for several hundred Indians to stay a week encamped in the Stenton woods, and treated always with the greatest kindness and hospitality by the master of the house, whose public duties left him scant leisure for rest. Small wonder that Cannassetego, chief of the Onondagas,

STENTON

bewailed the approaching end of their most trusted friend, and touchingly entreated the Council that when Logan's soul went to God, another might be chosen in his place, "of the same prudence and ability in counselling, and of the same tender disposition and affection for the Indians."

The beauty of Stenton lay in its broad lands. its superb avenue of hemlocks, which tradition pleasantly

K

but mendaciously asserted to have been planted by William Penn, its lofty wainscoted rooms, its generous fireplaces, ornamented with blue and white tiles, its graceful staircase, - that test of colonial architecture,— its air of dignified and scholarly repose. Here, in the well-lit library, were ranged those noble old books which subsequently became the city's legacy; and looking at them with love and pride, their owner felt a not unreasonable regret that no one in the future was likely to cherish them as he did. " I have four children now with me," he writes to Thomas Story in 1734, " who I think take more after their mother than me, which I am sure thou wilt not dislike in them ; yet if they had more of a mixture, it might be of some use to bring them through the world ; and it sometimes gives me an anxious thought that my considerable collections of Greek and Roman authors, with others in various languages, will not find an heir in my family to use them as I have done, but after my decease may be sold or squandered away."

If ghosts can reasonably rejoice as well as groan and rattle chains, then must the spirit of James Logan, scholar and statesman, have exulted over the patient toil of his grandson's wife, heir of his name though not of his blood, as she faithfully and intelligently sorted, copied and annotated the important letters stored in the Stenton library, and wrought from them a lasting record of his life and work. The "Penn and Logan Papers," with their wealth of historic and colonial interest, might never have seen the light, had not Deborah Logan worked year after year with unwearied and unrewarded fidelity in those too scant hours of leisure which the mistress of a large and busy household could dare to call her own.

We think of Quakers now as clad perpetually in sober drab, with close bonnets or broad-brimmed hats ; but for many years after the founding of Philadelphia they wore no exclusive costumes, contenting themselves with avoiding in a general way the allurements of fashion and finery. Hence the stern warnings, the sharp reproofs directed from time to time against those daughters of Eve who yearned after fancy fig-leaves, who let their hair stray wantonly over their brows, or sought to widen their modest petticoats with the seductive crinoline. As Thomas Chalkley vigorously but vainly remarked, "If Almighty God should make a woman in the same Shape her hoop makes her, Everybody would say truly it was monstrous ; so according to this real truth they make themselves Monsters by art."

Nor were the female Friends averse to glowing colours, remembering perhaps Penn's sky-blue sash which gave them warrant for their weakness. Their silk aprons rivalled the rainbow, and not infrequently their gowns were of red or green, instead of that dove-

like hue which Whittier loved and praised. Sir Godfrey Kneller's portrait of Sarah, elder daughter of
James Logan of Stenton, and wife of Isaac Norris of
Fairhill, shows us a stately young woman dressed in
deep blue, and with the air of an English court
beauty rather than a colonial Quaker matron. Thomas
Lloyd's daughter, Mary, who married Isaac Norris the
elder, is also painted in a blue gown relieved with
crimson; and her granddaughter, Mary Dickinson,
appears all in red, that deep seducing red which the
Paris artists of to-day love better than any other
shade. These women, despite their partiality for vivid
tints, were strict Quakers, but Quakers upon whom
the rigid rules of an exclusive costume had yet to be
imposed. Perhaps Mrs. Dickinson was one of the
last to rejoice in the glory of colour, for we find *her*
daughter, Maria Logan, painted in the orthodox dress
of the Friends, and presenting a curious contrast to
her resplendent kinsfolk. There is ample evidence
to show that the scarlet cloaks so popular in provincial
England (who does not remember poor ill-fated Syl-
via's?) found their way over the ocean, and created
much disturbance among the sober-minded and austere.
That one of these gay garments, "almost new, with a
double cape," was stolen from Franklin's house in 1750,
proves that the philosopher did not seek to restrain
the natural longing of wife and daughter for the
shining, dress-laden booths of Vanity Fair.

Gayer and gayer grew the Quaker City that had been so demure in childhood. Coaches emblazoned with heraldic devices rolled through the ill-paved streets. In the bitter cold of winter days the frozen Delaware was covered with merry throngs; and there is a pleasant flavour of colonial simplicity in the interesting information, wafted along a century and more, that the best skaters of their day were General Cadwalader and Massey the biscuit-maker. In the bitter cold of winter nights, wax candles shone softly down on Philadelphia's sons and daughters, as they met for the famous Dancing Assemblies that date from 1749, and lend an air of prim worldliness to the uneventful annals of the town. Dancing seems never to have been regarded with the same stern disapprobation that made the theatre a forbidden joy. Whitefield, indeed, who was impartially opposed to cakes and ale in any shape, waged an earnest crusade against this, as against all other diversions, and set himself the serious task of remodelling the nature of youth. But before he came to make a dull world duller, the colonists who were not Quakers had smiled indulgently upon such harmless mirth; and the Quakers, though not dancing themselves, had been serenely content that others should. Mr. Richard Castelman, writing in 1710, records with a grateful heart the kindness and courtesy of " the facetious Mr. Staples, the dancing-master, who was the first stranger of Philadelphia that did me the

honour of a visit. To his merry company I owe the
passing of many a sad hour, that might have hung
heavy upon the hands of a man deprived of friends and
fortune in an alien land."

Thirty years later, we find several dancing-masters
prepared to teach "fashionable English and French
dances,after the newest and politest manner practised
in London, Dublin, and Paris"; and, with the perfection of such accomplishments, there came naturally
in time subscription balls, in which the graces thus
acquired could be properly shown to the world. These
balls, if they somewhat scandalized the elect, were
favoured with the approbation and patronage of the
Episcopal clergy, who were well disposed towards any
form of entertainment which the Quakers rejected, and
of which the Presbyterians disapproved. The Assemblies were not scenes of wild dissipation, nor was there
any excessive extravagance to provoke the direful eloquence of the pulpit. They began at precisely six
o'clock in the evening, and by midnight the dancers
were all wending their ways homeward. The old
subscription ticket cost forty shillings; and for this
moderate outlay a gentleman could take the lady of his
choice to sixteen or eighteen entertainments, the dances
being given every Thursday night in the winter and
early spring. The supper was of the very lightest
order, consisting, it was said, "chiefly of something
to drink"; a not inadequate description of a repast

where five gallons of rum and two hundred limes were consumed in punch, and nine shillings' worth of "milk bisket" represented the solid food,—a half-pennyworth of bread to this intolerable deal of sack. Card-tables were prepared for the amusement of those who did not dance, and who appear to have been less patient then than now, and less disposed to play a purely passive part.

The invitations were often printed on the undecorated backs of common playing-cards, blank cards of any kind being exceedingly scarce, and spades and hearts being only too abundant in an age which had not yet learned to repudiate gambling as a sadly unprofitable vice. No wife nor daughter of mechanic or tradesman was suffered to enter the Assemblies which were rigidly aristocratic, and no flippant coquetry was permitted to interfere with the decorous order of procedure. The ladies who arrived earliest had places duly assigned them in the first set, and those who followed were distributed throughout other sets, either at the discretion of the directors, or according to the numbers they drew,—a melancholy arrangement, fraught, like the modern dinner, with many painful possibilities. It was Miss Polly Riché who in 1782 first revolted against this stringent rule, and insisted on standing up in any set she fancied, thus precipitating a quarrel between the gentlemen who supported her recusancy and the managers of the

Assembly. But what other conduct could have been expected in 1782? Cornwallis had surrendered; the war of the Revolution was practically at an end; independence had been won, and Philadelphia was slowly struggling to emerge from chaos into a new law and order. An evil time this for conservatives, as Miss Polly Riché doubtless understood; so she struck her little blow for liberty, and struck it not in vain. The exaltation of freedom manifested itself on all sides in a general disposition to obey nobody, and the hour was ripe for revolt.

FRANKLIN'S PUNCH KEG

CHAPTER IX

WHILE the province was growing rich in long years of peaceful industry, the Proprietors were amassing noble fortunes from the increased value of their quit-rents. John Penn, "the American," visited Philadelphia in 1732, and was received with clamorous delight : flags flying, cannon thundering, addresses without stint, and a grand banquet which cost the town exactly forty pounds, twelve shillings, and twopence. It is pleasant to find the little twopence so faithfully and accurately recorded. Thomas Penn, John's younger and cleverer brother, lived for nine years in the colony, and showed equal ability in the management of public affairs and of his own interests. He had more than his father's shrewdness, but lacked the distinction of character which made Pennsylvania's Founder a marked man, whether he lived in the two-storied Letitia House, or in the courts of kings. Thomas had no mind for two-story cottages. He purchased in 1760 Stoke Park, which had been the home of Sir Christopher Hatton in the days of Queen Elizabeth ; and his son John made of

137

this noble old place, and of Pennsylvania Castle, his other country-seat on the Isle of Portland, two great estates, famous during half a century for their elegance and beauty.

There is no denying that it was the persistent peace policy of the Quakers which secured for Pennsylvania its unmarred prosperity, and that this policy received the support of the people, notwithstanding the clamour raised by angry and belligerent agitators. What did the Quaker Assembly care if Spanish privateers flaunted their hostile colours in Delaware Bay? They knew enough about privateering themselves to be well aware that no serious injury was to be feared from these rovers of the sea, who preferred robbing to fighting any day, and who sought easier prey than a town protected by the dangerous shoals in its river bed. The war with Spain seemed no concern of Philadelphia's, and for a long time the wars between France and England fretted her but faintly. She protected her merchant ships with convoys, and she listened calmly to glowing harangues, mostly preached from Episcopal pulpits, which described the horrors to come: the city wrapped in flames, fathers slain, children homeless and weeping, desolation and ruin everywhere, —all because the Quakers would neither fight themselves, nor vote money to pay for fighting men. Pamphlets circulated at this time resemble in tone the appeals made to rural and provincial England, when every week brought a fresh rumour that Napoleon and his troops had landed upon English soil.

Occasionally, but not often, the Quakers put forth a defensive pamphlet of their own. They were never much addicted to talking nor to printing; and the wealth of argument, animadversion, and personal application of strong passages from Holy Writ, launched at their devoted heads, won little response, save that of quiet and obstinate resistance. Abusing them was like hurling a missile against a padded wall; there was not even a rebound. The Assembly was as willing that Franklin should organize the first militia company as that he should organize the first fire brigade. It even permitted him to buy gunpowder with some of the money voted for "wheat and other grains," and serene Friends frankly acknowledged that they did not condemn the use of arms in those who thought it right to bear them. But they were determined that the peace of the province should not be lightly broken, and they were disposed to temporize as far as possible when the growing hostility of the Indians brought real danger close to their city's doors.

The cause of this hostility is not hard to find. Every year, as the colony increased, it became more difficult to control the frontiersmen, who had no scruples in occupying the Indians' land, and no hesi-

tation in shooting the Indians, if they presumed to
interfere. Sturdy farmers, Scotch-Irish and Germans principally, deemed it as preposterous to talk
about the rights of savages as the rights of wolves
and foxes. God never intended the fertile soil to be
wasted on wandering heathens. Even Franklin philosophically remarked that rum, which had already
wrought dreadful havoc among the tribes of the sea-
coast, was perhaps the means appointed by Providence to destroy a race that blocked the way of
advancing civilization. The shameful " Walking Purchase " was another wrong that sank deeply in the
Indians' hearts. They knew they had been outwitted
by the Proprietors, and they felt themselves at the
mercy of the Six Nations, whom the white men had
summoned as allies. The Albany Treaty of 1754, by
which the colonists gained the fertile land lying west
of the Susquehanna, destroyed the last sentiments of
good-will that lingered in the red men's souls.
Driven practically out of Pennsylvania, and forced
to seek shelter amid alien tribes, their anger and
deep humiliation made them only too ready to listen
to the wily advances of the French, who were then
planning a chain of forts to stretch from the Great
Lakes to New Orleans. That tenacious memory of
the Indian, which never permitted him to forget
either benefit or injury, had its serious inconveniences. He was still well disposed towards the

Quakers, still loved and honoured the name of William Penn, "the white truth-teller," who had so consistently practised what he preached. But new wrongs could no more be forgotten than old friendships. The long peace of seventy years which Penn had bequeathed to his colony was drawing to a close; and the savages, once helpless as well as harmless, but now made sullen by ill-usage, and dangerous by the French alliance, had become a menace to the safety of the province, pacified and bribed into inaction by generous presents from the Assembly.

This was a state of things which could not long endure. The treaty between England and France was broken in 1755, and Major-General Braddock was sent to stop the advance of the French troops and their Indian allies. The Assembly, though occupied at this time in a particularly lively quarrel with Governor Morris, recognized the greatness of the emergency, laid aside its scruples anent war, and borrowed twenty thousand pounds on its own credit to supply Braddock with horses and provisions. The result of the campaign is too well known to need another telling. Not only Macaulay's omniscient schoolboy, but less admirably instructed people remember well what happened. Seven miles from Fort Du Quesne the English forces were surrounded by the French and Indians, and killed, easily and ruthlessly, like wild beasts in a trap. Of thirteen hundred men, only four hundred and sixty escaped that dreadful slaughter; sixty-three out of eighty-six officers were slain or wounded. The French loss was slight, and the fifty or sixty Indians whom the hemmed-in English succeeded in shooting could easily be replaced. It was a massacre rather than a battle, and it left Pennsylvania at the mercy of her foes.

The time for temporizing was past. The Indians, savagely elate that their day of reckoning had come, ravaged the province, and their stealthy attacks filled all the land with terror and despairing rage. It was absolutely necessary to send troops to the frontier, and the Assembly was ready and eager to vote the necessary funds, either by a new issue of paper currency, or by direct taxation, from which it justly insisted the estates of the Proprietors should no longer be exempt. To these measures, however, Governor Morris refused his consent, and for a while it seemed as if all the farmers of Pennsylvania might be scalped, because the Proprietors would not relinquish their privileges, nor the Assembly its constitutional rights. Happily, before the country was rendered wholly desolate, a compromise was reached. Thomas Penn offered in his own name, and in the names of his brothers, to contribute five thousand pounds towards the expenses of the war; the Assembly responded with equal generosity by raising the really noble sum of sixty thousand pounds, independent of the proprietary estates, and by promptly passing Franklin's militia bill, which sent a thousand sturdy men at once to the frontier.

It is a little surprising, accustomed as we are to the inevitable appearance of Franklin in all emergencies, to find him, not only organizing the militia, — there was nothing on earth he could not organize, — but actually marching at its head into the Lehigh Valley, prepared to defend his country with his sword or his rifle, whichever he carried, and surpassing in this one respect, at least, the labours of Michelangelo for Italy. He built some little forts in the valley, and succeeded in partially checking the Indian raids. Only ten farmers, we are told, were massacred in that district during his two months' occupancy; and while this does not sound to us now like satisfactory protection, it seems to have been considered at the time a very creditable piece of work. Franklin returned to Philadelphia to be made a colonel, and receive the ovations of the populace; and his fort at Gnadenhutten, being surprised by the savages while its garrison were skating one fine afternoon, the village it defended was burned to the ground, and nearly all the inhabitants slain.

Mr. Sydney Fisher has pointed out with admirable accuracy and good temper that Pennsylvania, so far from being the languid, supine province which Mr.

Parkman is never weary of contrasting with vigorous and altogether inimitable New England, was in reality playing an active and prominent part in these years of hand-to-hand struggle with the Indians. She gave men, and she gave money with unstinted liberality, but she asked in return the preservation of her own rights; and the governors who fancied that the exigencies of war could be used as a weapon to wrest from the Assembly an authority cemented by seventy years of masterdom, found themselves signally mistaken in their calculations. The violence of party spirit was now so thoroughly aroused that even a common danger was powerless to allay it. The Quakers clung stubbornly to their prerogatives, and their opponents appealed to England for protection, asserting that the safety of the colony was at stake. It was at this juncture that Provost Smith made his furious attack upon the Assembly, and the exuberant impetuosity of his sentiments reflected fairly the hostile attitude of the Episcopal and proprietary party. It was but natural that the Privy Council should lend an attentive ear to complaints urged against men who had ever opposed the voice of home authority. The Penns were assured that unless the Friends acted "a more rational and dutiful part," they should not be permitted "to continue in stations to perplex the government"; and an imperious message was sent over the seas, condemning in no stinted

ST. PETER'S CHURCH

L

terms the tardiness of the provincial rulers in prose-
cuting the war, and defending their own frontiers.

Historic fiction is deathless. It can never be silenced nor discredited. The Quakers have always
borne the blame for Pennsylvania's failure to beat
back her savage foes. It is true that, when the message of the Privy Council was received, the Assembly
at once passed a compulsory militia bill, and that the
governor promptly vetoed it; true that the Assembly
voted a second grant of one hundred thousand pounds
—an enormous sum in those days—for the expenses
of the war, and that the Proprietors still refused to
bear their share of the taxation. But these details
are wisely ignored by historians, as both annoying
and unmanageable. Once weakly admit such in-
trusive facts into history, and the smoothness and
brilliancy of the narrative is forever destroyed.

What does seem tolerably sure, is that while Quakers
and Episcopalians contended for mastery, the Indians
had things pretty much their own way, and came
within thirty miles of Philadelphia. Penn's city of
peace bid fair to become — as in later years — the
headquarters of war, when the wise and energetic
measures of the elder Pitt restored some semblance
of harmony to the combative colonists, and infused
fresh vigour into the provincial government. The
Prime Minister's clear eyes saw the absurdity of the
situation, his impregnable common-sense mastered its

difficulties. Born ruler of men, he knew when to abandon the policy of coercion for one of conciliation and kindness. His counsel and generous assistance put the wearisome struggle with the Indians on a wholly fresh basis. Arms, ammunition, and other necessities for the troops were despatched at once from England; three thousand recruits, raised in Pennsylvania, promptly joined the expedition against Fort Du Quesne; and the Quaker Assembly voted another hundred thousand pounds to meet the emergencies of this final struggle. A bounty of five pounds was also offered for every volunteer, thus putting a positive premium upon war; while at the same time, to leave no stone unturned, the Moravian missionary, Frederick Post, was sent on an embassy of peace to the Shawanese and Delaware Indians, who, though alienated from the English, were not closely allied with the French. Post was as successful in his negotiations as were General Forbes and Colonel Bouquet in their military manœuvres. A convention was held at Easton, three hundred chiefs of various tribes being present. The Proprietors, through their agents, restored to the savages a large portion of the land taken from them by the Albany Treaty; and the chiefs solemnly declared themselves satisfied with the restitution, and despatched at once to their young braves the white wampum belt, emblem of peace and good-will. No words can adequately praise the heroism, the quiet unflinching courage which carried an unarmed Moravian with two or three devoted followers into the very heart of the hostile country, where death lurked day and night amid the sombre woods.

In the meantime, arguments of a different order had been brought to bear upon the allied French and Indians at Fort Du Quesne, and they were found to be so convincing that, after two assaults and one long bloody battle, the French troops withdrew from the fort, setting fire to it before their departure, and carrying safely away their guns and ammunition, though beset by an invading army outnumbering them ten to one. Their departure restored safety and tranquillity to Pennsylvania. Thousands of farmers returned to their abandoned homes. Fort Pitt was built for their protection on the site of Fort Du Quesne, and where the city of Pittsburg now stands, commemorating the name of the great statesman to whom was mainly due the renewed prosperity of the province. Forbes, shattered in health, was carried back to Philadelphia, where he died the following spring, and was buried in Christ Church. For a few years peace reigned in the city of peace, and the Assembly gained a real and lasting victory when Franklin, who had exchanged military glory for the more congenial field of diplomacy, obtained the consent of the Privy Council to a bill authorizing the taxation of the proprietary estates.

This was the most important service he had rendered yet to the commonwealth. It had cost him two long years of hard work and weary waiting in England; it had taxed his ingenuity, his resources, his patience to the utmost; but it established his fame as a diplomatist, and was the beginning of his successful public career.

In 1763 the treaty of Paris ended the war with France. There was a reasonable hope in every heart that the evil times were over, and that the old days of peace and comfort had returned to the province, now more thickly settled, more assiduously cultivated than before. But although the French had been driven westward, the Indians remained, and the settlers, having learned nothing from experience, treated them more cruelly and contemptuously than before, believing that, unaided by European allies, they were no longer to be feared, and that they should be punished for all the trouble they had dared to give. Perhaps it is never wise to provoke a savage foe beyond his rather limited powers of endurance. When the game seems easiest, then is danger near at hand. The story of Pontiac is no part of Philadelphia's history, save that his ruthless and terrible wars brought devastation to the fertile farms and smiling hamlets of Pennsylvania; for this Indian Attila, who combined the fierceness of the barbarian with the genius of a great commander, had organized the scattered tribes into a destroying army, infinitely more dangerous because ruled by a single mind, bent on the extermination of the white man. Fort Pitt, the one defence and stronghold of the province, was surrounded and patiently besieged by the savages; but the splendid courage of its Swiss commander, Captain Écuyer, nerved his soldiers to resolute resistance, and they held out bravely until relieved by Colonel Bouquet who, with a mere handful of veterans, went gallantly to the rescue of his countryman. He asked help in this desperate enterprise from Pennsylvania's frontiersmen, from those Scotch-Irish farmers to whose hostile attitude was due much of the present trouble; but not one of them consented to accompany him. The glorious battle of August 5th, which saved Fort Pitt, checked the triumphant advance of the Indians, and warded off from many a hearth the torch and the scalping knife, was fought by two regiments of English soldiers, so enfeebled by service in the West Indies that many of them died in the long, cruel marches before their goal was reached.

The danger once lifted, however, the hearts of the settlers grew hot with rage, and they formed themselves into companies for the easy extermination of scattered and often harmless bands of Indians, whose depredations had never gone further than a gypsy-like pilfering of hen-roosts. The history of the so-called Paxton Boys is one of the dark stains on Pennsylvania's record. It has been told many times already, and each new telling makes it seem more thoroughly disgraceful than before. A little band of friendly Indians, direct descendants of the savages with whom William Penn had made his first successful treaty, was settled at Conestoga, near Lancaster. All its members had long since been converted to Christianity by the kind Moravians, and supported themselves by basket-weaving, that time-honoured industry of their race. The wrathful colonists of Paxton, inflamed by the preaching of the church militant, as embodied in the fierce harangues of John Elder, determined to pluck out, root and branch, these abominations, hated of the Lord. With this pious purpose, fifty-seven of them went at daybreak on the fourteenth of December, 1763, to the Indian village, and found there only three men, two women, and a young boy. One hundred and forty of the tribe had been carried off to Philadelphia the day before, and fourteen of them were wandering about the country, selling their baskets and brooms. Though sorely disappointed by the smallness of the catch, the Paxton rangers promptly killed the men, the women, and the boy, set fire to the village, and retired jubilantly, trusting that Providence would soon deliver a more satisfactory prey into their hands.

They had not long to wait. The Lancaster sheriff, hearing what had been done, and eager to avert further bloodshed, collected together the fourteen Indians who had escaped the massacre, and lodged them for protection in the jail. His action was kindly meant, but the jail was old and weak. The Paxton Boys knew now where to find their victims. They rode in a body to Lancaster, thrust aside their pastor, John Elder, who vainly strove to turn them from the meditated murder, beat down the jail doors, and cut the fourteen Indians, men, women, and children, into pieces with their hatchets. And these were the settlers who had refused their aid to Bouquet's fever-stricken troops, when they were asked to defend their own province in open and honourable warfare.

The deed awoke shame and anger in every honest breast. Brave men loathed its cowardice, good men its sickening brutality. Franklin laid aside his philosophic theories concerning savages and the march of civilization, and wrote his famous "Narrative," telling in simple, straightforward phrases the whole horrible story, and sternly reminding the colonists that, even in the improbable event of the butchered Indians having been on friendly terms with hostile tribes, the lawless murder was no less a crime against God, against the commonwealth, and against the very essence of civilization, which such acts of violence inevitably and hopelessly blighted. As for the Quakers, who felt themselves in an especial manner outraged by the cruel slaughter of their helpless dependents, they were aroused to a state of un-Quakerlike wrath, which it is both pleasant and wholesome to contemplate. Governor Penn issued two proclamations, denouncing the murders, and instructing the magistrates to arrest the murderers, which, of course, they never did. On the contrary, the Paxtons found themselves so agreeably free from molestation that they grew valorous, and set out for Philadelphia, with the openly avowed intention of killing the one hundred and forty Moravian Indians who had been taken there for safety.

The Friends prepared to give the invaders a hot welcome. They even took up arms with an alacrity foreign to their principles, and which left no shadow of doubt as to the course they intended to pursue. English regulars were summoned to their aid, and the city swarmed with defenders. It had been deemed prudent to place the frightened Indians out of harm's way by sending them to a distance, but neither New Jersey nor New York would consent to receive them. Apparently there was no such thing as a colonial government which did not fear a mob.

Philadelphia honourably resolved that no power on earth should wrest from her these poor hostages to fortune. They were lodged in the soldiers' barracks, freshly fortified with trenches and cannon, and we see the ubiquitous Franklin assuming the personal charge of their defence. When the Paxton

rangers, now numbering a thousand or twelve hundred
men, reached Germantown, they found matters not
at all to their liking. Here was no question of easy
butchery, but of stout fighting, if they were to attempt carrying out their purpose. The prospect
cooled their ardour, and they announced themselves
ready to negotiate. Franklin was thereupon sent
to meet them, and to him they forthwith presented
a memorial of their grievances, as if they had been
sinned against, and were innocent of crime. Their
complaints were many, but first and foremost on the
list was the discontinuance of the "scalp bounty," by
which a useful industry had been weakened and well-
nigh destroyed. It did not profit settlers, they said,
to kill stray Indians, unless the government would
encourage them by paying for the scalps. Time was
when an adroit backwoodsman could make a comfortable living by tracking down savages and their
squaws; but the withdrawal of the bounty at the
close of the French and Indian wars had made this
species of hunting unsatisfactory and unremunerative.
They prayed that the matter might be reconsidered,
and honest labour meet its just reward.

Having presented their petitions, and having assured
themselves that martial measures would be ill-advised,
the rangers disbanded and went home. They had
offered no injury to Philadelphia, nor to the poor
fugitives they had sought to slay; but, on the other

hand, they had been received with a good deal more civility than rioters and law-breakers had any reason to expect, and they felt tolerably sure that the Conestoga murders would never be avenged. Nor were they. Party feeling ran so high, the hostility between rival churches grew so bitter, that from more than one pulpit were heard in time condoning words anent that cruel slaughter. The Germans, always on friendly terms with the Quakers, condemned it strenuously; and the ever-widening breach determined the Assembly to make the strongest effort in its power to bring about the final overthrow of its enemies. The King was petitioned to abolish the Proprietorship, and to govern Pennsylvania as a royal province.

It is easy to trace the troubles and provocations which led to this extraordinary step. The Quakers had always been deeply antagonized by the Scotch-Irish settlers, at whose doors they laid the blame of most of the Indian disturbances. They abhorred the Presbyterian creed, with its marked preference for the Old Testament, and its vigorous, unmerciful interpretation of Hebrew sentiments and standards. They resented the position of the Church party, which, for purely political reasons, lent its moral support to the Presbyterians; and they were reduced to a state of chronic irritation by the perpetual encroachments of the English governors upon their ancient privileges. Above and beyond all, they were discouraged by the impossi-

bility of keeping faith with the savages, whose scanty
rights — even the one poor primitive right of living —
were   now openly ignored. For the Proprietors,
with a callousness that seems in-
credible in any of their name
and lineage, had gratified
the active frontiers-
men by renew-
ing the scalp

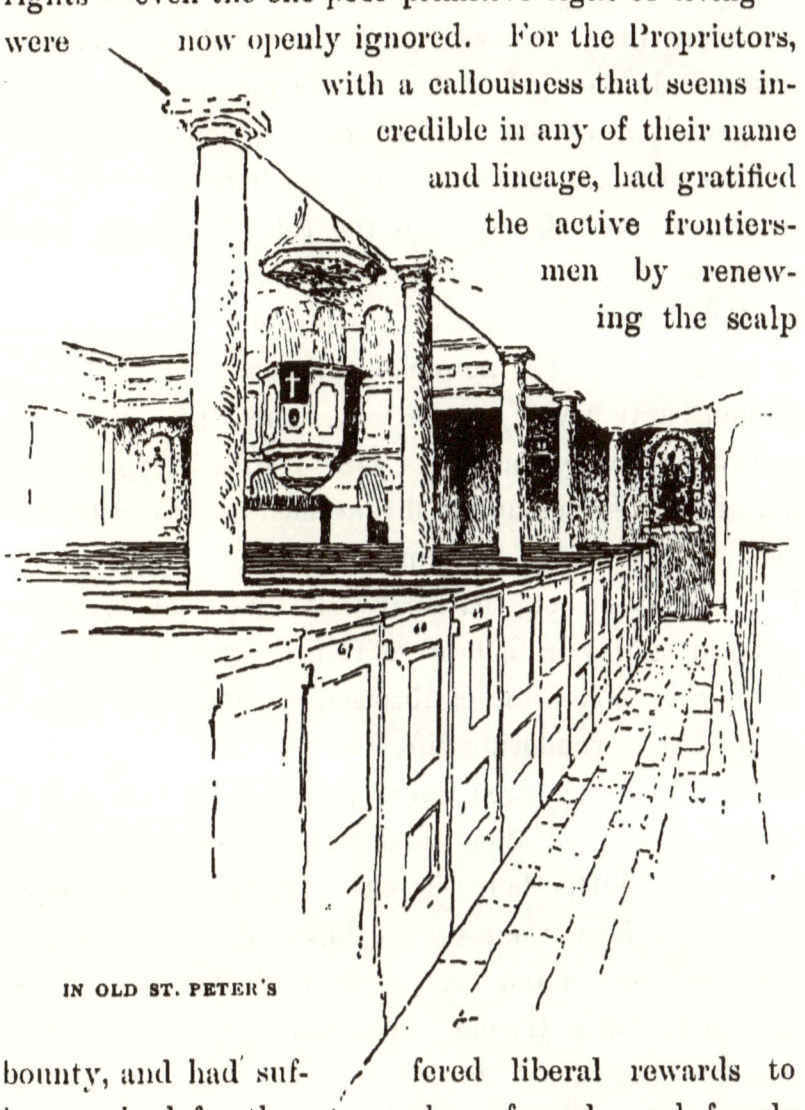

IN OLD ST. PETER'S

bounty, and had suf-   fered liberal rewards to
be promised for the   scalps of male and female
Indians. "Such," says Mr. Sydney Fisher sadly, "was
the melancholy end of Penn's Indian policy; a policy

which for its justice and humanity had at one time
aroused the admiration of all the philosophers of Europe.
But now the tribe with which he made the famous
treaty had dwindled to a miserable remnant, . . . and
his grandson was offering bounties for women's scalps."

There was the less excuse for this barbarous iniquity
in which white men played the rôle of savages, inasmuch as Pontiac's wars had been brought to a close
in 1764 by the successful expeditions of Bradstreet
and Bouquet. The power of the organized tribes was
broken, a treaty of peace was signed, and Bouquet,
returning triumphantly to Pennsylvania, brought back
with him over two hundred ransomed captives who had
been carried away from time to time by the Indians.
It is worthy of note that many of these poor prisoners
were strangely reluctant to return, and to take up
anew the bonds of civilization. Men had grown
wedded to a wandering life, and to the wild pleasures
of the chase; children clung piteously to the squaws
who had adopted them, and were dragged away by
force amid bitter lamentations; white women parted
with tears from their savage husbands, and often, on
the homeward march, escaped by night from the tents,
and stole back through the forest paths to their
deserted wigwams. It was truly discouraging to the
soldiers who played the gallant part of liberators to
find their efforts so often baffled by the mysterious
intricacies of the human heart.

Bouquet was received with wild enthusiasm in Philadelphia, and the Assembly willingly voted fifty thousand pounds to pay the expenses of his campaign. It was the refusal of the Proprietors to give their share of this money which precipitated the final quarrel between them and the Friends, and which brought about the memorable petition for the abolishment of the proprietary government.

The converting of Pennsylvania into a royal province had always been looked upon as a remedy — though a somewhat dangerous one — for the many ills that from time to time had beset colonial life. William Penn had himself resolved upon the step in the profound discouragement of his later years, and only the swift failing of his mental powers prevented him from carrying it into execution. The Christ Church party had in its day presented a similar petition, believing that the crown would readily grant it privileges denied by the obstinate Quakers; and now the Quakers were playing in their turn the part of the clamorous frogs, and begging for a king to eat them up.

The measure, however, was not one to be lightly carried. If it had sanguine friends, it had also mortal foes; and the fury of the combat may be gauged by the number of pamphlets, all couched in the most intemperate language, that have come fluttering down to us from these stormy days. "In the whole history of the province," says Mr. MacMaster, "there had never been in so short a time such a number of pamphlets issued"; and we know what that must have meant. Franklin took an active share in this paper war, and stoutly advocated the petition. Joseph Galloway, a brilliant lawyer and an accomplished gentleman, was its most ardent upholder. John Dickinson, afterwards made famous by the "Farmer's Letters," fought bravely on the other side, defending the ancient charter with rugged eloquence, and pointing out to the colonists that it was at all times better to endure the ills they had, than to fly to others that they knew not of. Though the Quakers triumphed, and the popular discontent carried the petition through the Assembly, yet the feeling against it was so strong that neither Franklin nor Galloway was returned at the next election. Galloway retired for a time to private life, but Franklin was naturally appointed to carry the petition to the King. This appointment was hotly opposed by Dickinson, who detested the philosopher with all his heart, and who brought forward a heavy array of arguments against the perpetual employment of his services. Philadelphia, however, was too well accustomed to these services to dream of setting them aside. A public mission, great or small, conducted by anybody but Franklin, would have been so serious an innovation that the Assembly could hardly have been expected to countenance it.

So the triumphant diplomat sailed over the sea with his precious paper, leaving behind him a final pamphlet, by way of Parthian dart; and on the tenth of December, 1764, he reached the city of London. Here in due time he presented the petition,—and nothing came of it. The English Ministry, then meditating the famous Stamp Act, had apparently no desire to dispossess the Proprietors. King George III, who was determined a few years later to coerce the colonists at any cost into obedience, seemed quite indifferent to this opportunity of extending his royal power. The situation was unusual, and a little absurd. On the one hand, a province, upon the very eve of rebellion, asserting its absolute confidence in the justice of a king, and offering its constitutional rights as pledges of its credulity. On the other hand, a monarch and a ministry prepared to force their unwelcome measures at the point of the bayonet, but ignoring this easy means of strengthening their hands. Franklin himself seems to have wellnigh forgotten the petition, in the new excitement of opposing the threatened Stamp Act. His prophetic eyes saw clearly the manifold evils that would result from any form of taxation to which the colonists had not yielded their consent. He was a man of peace, for all his little toyings with Indian warfare, and he struggled honestly and impotently to avert the coming strife. As well have tried to beat back from the shore the broad, resistless roll of the encroaching wave.

CHAPTER X

THE EVE OF THE REVOLUTION

IT is hardly a matter for surprise that Pennsylvania should have been more languid than Massachusetts or Virginia in asserting her independence; that Philadelphia, destined to be the birthplace of the nation, should have been slower than restless Boston to defy authority, and take up arms against her King. To the sane and somewhat sluggish minds of wealthy merchants and well-paid mechanics, a principle is not always worth fighting for, unless its sacrifice involves a serious loss of personal comfort or well-being. And for nearly a century the Quaker City, though sometimes weary of wrangling, had been exceedingly comfortable, and had lacked nothing that the colonial heart could reasonably ask or desire. The gentlemen who drove every evening, after the easy cares of the days, to their beautiful country-seats, — to Stenton, to Mount Pleasant, to Cliveden, or to Bush Hill, — must have found life very well worth living. It was the custom of all wealthy citizens to build these country-seats, and their tranquil beauty did much to foster the spirit of conservative content. Belmont Mansion stood looking over

woods and water, boasting the finest avenue of hemlocks in the country, a stately, strong old house, full
of traditions and memories. William Peters, who
purchased the estate and lived there many years, was
a strict churchman and an unflinching Tory, detesting
Quakers and patriots with the impartial sincerity of

BELMONT MANSION

Praed's delightful "Quince." Not so his son Richard,
afterwards Judge Peters, who threw in his lot with
the revolutionists, and kept for us some lively records
of that stirring time. His unconquerable vivacity left
him light of heart when others chilled with despair,
and never for one moment does he appear to have
doubted the ultimate success of his cause. A genial

and hospitable host, he made Belmont the gayest house
of its day. There Washington sought respite from
anxiety and care ; there La Fayette planted a walnut
tree, and John Quincy Adams ate one of the best and
merriest dinners of his life, — a life in which good and
merry dinners seem to have played a somewhat con-
spicuous part. Judge Peters enjoyed an enviable
reputation as a wit, and some of his pleasantries have
come floating down to us in cold unsympathetic print,
illustrating, as a captious biographer expresses it, "the
great difference between hearing a joke and reading
one." The Indians, whose councils he occasionally
attended, and who are not a humorous race, christened
him the Talking Bird. It is a pity ever to waste wit
upon Indians.

There is hardly one of the noble old country-houses
that girdle Philadelphia which has not its historic
interest, its close association with names and incidents
inseparably interwoven with the annals of the province,
and sometimes with the broader annals of the land.
To Mount Pleasant, embedded in trees, and famous
alike for the breadth of its stairs and the depth of its
capacious fireplaces, Benedict Arnold brought home
his bride; the pretty, vivacious, self-willed Peggy
Shippen, daughter of Edward Shippen, afterwards
judge of the Supreme Court, and chief justice of
Pennsylvania. The estate was Arnold's marriage
settlement upon his wife, and beneath this roof their

first child was born to them, in the innocent, happy years, undimmed by trouble, untainted by the shadow of approaching shame.

Cliveden, the home of Chief Justice Chew, and better known to Philadelphians as Chew House, has a different history, for here occurred that memorable struggle by which victory was snatched from the very arms of defeat. The barricading of Chew House by Colonel Musgrave with six companies of the Fortieth Regiment, the fruitless assault by the American forces, the delay and danger thus occasioned, and the final routing of our soldiers from the hotly contested field, are well-known details of the battle of Germantown ; as familiar to readers of American history as is the death of that gallant English officer, Brigadier-General Agnew, in the old Wister homestead, where the blood from his many wounds stained deeply red the smooth and polished floor. Agnew had fought bravely for the colonies in the French and Indian wars, and the inexorable voice of duty had sent him back to fight against them, when they threw off their allegiance to the King. His last act was an effort to save a German servant-maid from danger. Two hours later he was carried back to her master's roof, a dying man, yet so tranquil and content that, in the simple words of his aide-de-camp, it was "with seeming satisfaction" he passed quietly away from strife. He was buried in the Germantown graveyard, finding rest in the alien

land to which he had been both friend and foe; and
years afterwards his grandchildren came over the sea
to visit the place where he lay.

More peaceful associations cling around other historic
homes: Bush Hill, the country-seat of the Hamiltons

WISTER HOUSE

before Woodlands was built; Walnut Grove, the most
demure of houses, erected by Joseph Wharton, the most
sedate of Quakers, yet destined to be the scene of the
gayest, maddest, richest, courtliest frolic that Philadelphia has ever witnessed; and Fairhill, the home of Isaac
Norris, and afterwards of that contentious, letter-writing
patriot, John Dickinson. The gardens of Fairhill,

grave English gardens with gravelled walks and well-clipped hedges, were esteemed the fairest in the province; and Francis Pastorius, who dearly loved their orderly charms, was wont to pronounce them the fairest in the world. Here grew strange exotics brought from distant lands, and here were found the first willow trees that ever drooped over Pennsylvania's soil. Isaac Norris owed these trees to the keen observation of Franklin, who noticed the sprouting of a willow wand, woven into a rough basket which lay on the deck of a boat moored in the Delaware. He carried the brave little sprout to Debby Norris, who planted it with care, and it became in time the parent of a numerous progeny, much admired because so little known.

Fairhill was destroyed during the Revolution. Its beauties are now only a tradition of the past, as are also the beauties of another famous country-seat, Lansdowne Mansion, built by John Penn, grandson of the Founder, in the romantic glen which bears its name. After Penn returned to England, Lansdowne was purchased by William Bingham who had amassed what, for those primitive days, seemed a colossal fortune, in the West Indies, and who made this lovely spot for many years his summer home. He married Ann Willing, the sixteen-year-old daughter of that able judge and very moderate Whig, Thomas Willing; and the letters and diaries of the day teem with descriptions of the young bride's beauty, her distinction of manner, her luxurious surroundings and wonderful gowns. Even in Paris these gowns won ample recognition, and so deeply impressed Miss Adams, daughter of John Adams, then busy with negotiations in France, that she filled up her journal with ardent accounts of their splendour.

We know from other equally enthusiastic contemporaries how handsomely Lansdowne and Mr. Bingham's town house were furnished, how the sofas were covered with Gobelin tapestry, and the folding-doors were inlaid with mirrors, into which awkward or absent-minded guests walked blunderingly. We are even familiar with the chairs, upholstered in crimson and yellow brocade, their rosewood backs shaped like lyres; and we are informed by Mr. Wansey, an English traveller who enjoyed much Philadelphia hospitality, that the drawing-room " was papered in the French taste, after the style of the Vatican at Rome," a suggestive but enigmatic statement which leaves us sunk in the depths of speculation. From all this magnificence the gay and graceful hostess was summoned too soon by the unkindly fates, and her husband, detesting the empty splendour of his home, abandoned it forever, and lived in Europe until his death. Joseph Bonaparte occupied Lansdowne House for several years, adding to the interest with which the fine old place was always regarded, until it was burned to the ground on the fourth of July, 1854, sacrificed, like so many other homes, and like so many lives, to our peculiar methods of celebrating our great national anniversary.

In sharp contrast to the stately country-seats which were the especial delight of wealthy and aristocratic Philadelphians, stood and still stands the old stone house, simple and beautiful, of John Bartram the botanist, whose famous gardens sloped down to the river's brink, and were the wonder and admiration of his day. Bartram's history is as interesting as that of Gilbert White of Selborne. Where the Englishman turned his keen and thoughtful eyes upon bird and beast, the American fixed his upon every green leaf that sprang from the fertile soil. Both men laboured quietly within their narrow bounds, both thought much of their work and little of the public, and both added generous shares to the useful knowledge of the world.

It was while ploughing his field that a little white daisy forced the current of Bartram's thoughts into a studious channel. The flower made its innocent appeal to him as to the pitying, passionate eyes of Burns, but the Quaker ploughman was no poet. He could only regret that his rude labour destroyed so many nurslings of the earth, and resolve to foster them in the future as far as lay in his power, and to learn what he could of their structure and existence. This was a harder matter than the Scotchman's inspired song. Bartram bought a Latin grammar, and to the profound annoyance of his wife, who, like all good helpmates, was steadfastly opposed to her husband's inexplicable crotchets, he studied earnestly until, with the help of a neighbouring school-master, he had acquired a sufficient knowledge of the language to enable him to read and understand several works of Linnæus. From that time forward, the joy of a beloved pursuit filled his life with sober happi-ness, and he illustrated, as did Gilbert White, how much can be accomplished by the close observation of a single student, working year after year within a limited com-pass. Watson, a very doubtful authority, asserts that, prior to the Revolution, Bartram enjoyed a small pension as botanist to the royal family. This, if true, was a pleasing token of appreciation on the royal family's part; but it does not appear that the Quaker farmer ever lacked sufficient means for his modest wants. He built in 1731 his quaint stone house, with his name and his wife's name cut into the wall; and forty years later he chiselled this couplet over the window of his study where all who passed might see it: —

> " 'Tis God alone, almighty Lord,
> The holy One by me adored."
>
> John Bartram, 1770.

In this house, "small but decent," as St. John de-scribes it, he lived a life of almost patriarchal simplicity. His family, his visitors, his hired servants and negro slaves all sat at the same board, his slaves below the salt, as the Saxon thralls of old. Yet his armorial bear-ings hung blazoned on the wall, for this Pennsylvania

Quaker boasted a descent from one of the Norman knights who had stormed England under the Conqueror's banner, and he was most inconsistently proud of his strain of noble blood, which perhaps, indeed, furnished the keynote of his character, and accounted for the very simplicity of a household resembling in some respects the ancient château in Languedoc, where Eugénie de Guérin toiled in the great kitchen, directing and assisting the peasant servants in their homely work. Perhaps, too, this Norman lineage rendered John Bartram, gentle and peace-loving though he seemed, a little impatient of spiritual control; for we find him accused of Unitarianism by the Society of Friends, and exceedingly indifferent to its strictures. In 1741 a subscription was raised to enable him to travel through the neighbouring colonies in search of flowers and plants; and, as his knowledge widened, he wandered still further afield, — to Virginia, to Carolina, to Canada, and even, when nearly seventy years of age, to Florida, where he navigated the St. Juan in a clumsy boat with three oars and a sail, exploring those marshy and unfrequented shores, upon which, as his old chronicler delightfully expresses it, " the wild birds are held in awe by the thunder of the devouring alligator."

Of John Bartram's twelve children, only one, William Bartram, inherited his father's tastes and studious habits, with an additional aptitude for writing verses, which local critics, after the time-honoured custom of their race, compared favourably to the poetry of Burns. William died childless, and the property passed into the hands of his grand-niece, Ann, whose husband sold it after her death to Andrew Eastwick. Mr. Eastwick erected a more commodious residence on the estate; but the old Bartram homestead has been pre-

OLD BARTRAM HOUSE

served with great care, as well for its beauty as for its interesting associations. Strength, simplicity, an instinctive and unfailing sense of appropriateness, — these are the characteristics which, when seen in a house, indicate some corresponding qualities on the part of the man who built it, and these are precisely the characteristics that took flight for many a year from the fantastic and paltry architecture of the land.

Into this peaceful province, so rich, so comfortable, so thoroughly satisfied, came rolling in 1765 the apple of discord in the shape of an obnoxious, unconstitutional Stamp Act, and the voice of the coming Revolution bade men arise from their pleasant hearths, and do battle for their civic rights. They were not quick to obey, though the call sank deeply into their hearts. Principle, not prosperity, was at stake, and the shadow of strife cast a disagreeable and ominous chill over the first buoyant enthusiasm for resistance. Moreover, there were many reasons moving many minds through different channels into the same sluggish course. The Episcopalians entertained honest sentiments of loyalty, as well they might, towards the crown, and towards the English establishment which had so often befriended them in their need; and they knew that only by help of the mother country, and the mother church, could they maintain their political importance. The Germans were just as honest in their way, being absolutely indifferent to the situation, and absolutely untouched by the restless and fast-growing spirit of discontent. The Quakers, though their entire history had been one of determined opposition to attempted encroachments upon the constitutional privileges of the colony, were far from desiring any radical change of government; and they mistrusted profoundly the movement for independence which threatened the complete overthrow of their present power and of their past work, of

that fair structure upon which they had toiled patiently
and lovingly for nearly a century of progress.

It would be difficult to overrate the influence of the
Quakers in Philadelphia immediately before the Revolution, an influence which melted wholly away during
those years of warfare, carrying with it much sanity
and moderation that could ill be spared. They held a
large part of the city's commerce in their capable hands,
and the fortunes they acquired were spent with liberality and discretion. If they did not give their wives
and daughters Paris gowns, nor cover their sofas with
Gobelin tapestry, nor scandalize the town by aspiring,
like Mrs. Bingham and her friends, to private boxes at
the theatre, yet life held for them many demure and
sober gayeties. John Adams, who has left us such
epicurean descriptions of Philadelphia dinners and
suppers that a feeble digestion is wrecked by even
reading a list of the things he ate, or tried to eat,
acknowledges that it was often under Quaker roofs he
encountered these "sinful feasts." It was a Quaker
hostess who pressed upon him at a single meal, "ducks,
ham, chickens, beef, pig, tarts, creams, custards, jellies,
fools, trifles, floating islands, beer, porter, punch, and
wine." It was, he confesses. at the solicitation of a
Quaker host that he "drank Madeira at a great rate,
and found no inconvenience,"— for which the incredu-
lous reader can only take his word.

In the interesting journal of Elizabeth Drinker,

begun in 1759, and continued with occasional inter-
ruptions for nearly fifty years, we find, before the
peaceful days are over, a perpetual record of tea-
drinking and other gentle dissipations. Such items as
" Drank tea at Joseph Trotter's," or " Peggy Parr with
her sister-in-law, Nancy, and Polly drank tea with us,"
appear on every page ; and it is plain this sedate young
Quakeress has a lingering love for diversion. She
flatly declines hearing an instructive lecture on electricity, which is greatly to her credit ; but she pays
two shillings to see a lioness which a wandering show-
man is carrying through the town. She " spends the
day " — that old-time entertainment — at the houses
of youthful friends ; and she writes with inexpressible
demureness that Henry Drinker, her future husband,
has stayed until eleven o'clock at night, — " unseasonable hours," as she admits, adding softly, " My judgment doesn't coincide with my actions ; 'tis a pity, but
I hope to mend." Strictly conservative, and innocently
loyal, she records with sadness, December 26, 1760,
" the Death of our good old King, George the Second,"
— the news being then two months old ; and this
contentment with the ruling powers, and with the
placid tranquillity of the province, illustrates very accurately the attitude of the Quakers before the great
division in their ranks. They, at least, had few complaints to offer. A wealthy and prominent Friend,
meeting one of the " Apostates " or Free Quakers,

bravely girt with a sword, said to him, " Why, what is
this with which thou hast bedecked thyself? Surely
not a rapier!" "Yes," was the staunch reply, "for
liberty or death is now the watchword of every one
who means to defend himself and his property."
"Ah!" sighed the serene old Friend, "I had not
expected such high feelings in thee. Thy mind has
become as fierce as thy sword. As to property, I
thought thee had none, and as to thy liberty, I thought
thee already enjoyed it through the kindness of thy
creditors." A purely commercial view, one may ob-
serve, to take of the situation.

It is well for us that the leisure of those days gave
people time to keep journals, for it is to such records
we must turn if we wish to understand the ordinary
life and common sentiments of men and women who
do not appear on the canvas of history, but who reflect
with unconscious sincerity the public temper which
made public action possible. The diaries of Elizabeth
Drinker and Christopher Marshall, the memoirs of
Dr. Graydon and Thomas Twining, give us, not only
a number of interesting facts, but also the atmosphere
of the last century which eludes all modern histories,
and leaves them unsympathetic and judicial. We
learn from Dr. Graydon that the letters of Junius
awakened such a thrill of excitement in quiet Philadelphia that it became "highly fashionable" — delightful phrase — to discuss them on all occasions; and

that the Rev. Mr. Duché published a series of papers
on the subject, signing himself "Tamoc Caspipina,"
an acrostic — wholly impenetrable — upon his rightful
title, "The Assistant Minister of Christ's Church and
Saint Peter's, in Philadelphia, in North America."

As for Tom Paine and his seething sentences, we
know from many sources what influence he acquired;
how "Common Sense" was eagerly read by the colonists, and how the "Rights of Man" was quoted on
every side during those unsettled, turbulent years
which followed the Revolution. Dr. Graydon tells us
that ardent patriots were wont to denounce Burke's
"Reflections on the French Revolution" as "heavy
and tedious," fit only to serve as a foil for the shining
qualities of Paine. He himself, however, though sincerely patriotic and an officer of the Revolutionary
army, was disinclined to accept this verdict. Having
nourished his youth upon English classics, Fielding,
Smollett and Richardson, he naturally found the "Revolution" less tedious than the "Rights"; and our
sudden fierce enthusiasm for France, the tri-colour,
and the guillotine, struck him as a little absurd and
very dangerous. We had travelled far afield by 1791;
but in 1765 even "Common Sense" had not yet
dawned luridly upon our peaceful path. The province, though sufficiently ill-disposed towards unconstitutional taxation, was at heart loyal to the English
crown; and Franklin, even while upholding his coun-

try's cause, could find no words too forcible in which to give this loyalty expression. He was wont to say that the colonists loved England better than they loved each other. The time was fast approaching when the first of these laudable affections died a natural death, and the second ceased to be so apparent as to justify its use when a strong comparison or illustration was desired.

N

CHAPTER XI

THE DAWN OF THE REVOLUTION

THE Stamp Act was passed in March, 1765, notwithstanding the strenuous opposition of Franklin and the American agents in London, who, however, were not authorized by the colonies to give their consent to any other proposed measure for the raising of money. Its immediate result in Philadelphia was a sudden decrease of extravagance, a sudden passion for frugality, which would have delighted "Poor Richard's" heart, had he been there to witness it. The merchants and traders bound themselves to import no goods from England until the Act had been repealed; they would not even suffer the "pestilential cargoes," as John

Dickinson called them, to be unloaded at the docks. and self-denying citizens resolved to wear no English cloths, to eat no English mutton, to drink no English beer, while the law remained in force. They stinted themselves even in the matter of funerals, and one patriotic alderman who died in these troubled days left directions that he should be buried without a pall, and that his family should wear no crape nor other mourning for him. To John Hughes, a member of the Assembly and a keen partisan of Franklin's, was given the sale of the hated stamps; not a pleasant duty, as it chanced, for the mob, having hanged him in effigy, gathered around his house with muffled drums, and tried vainly to force him into yielding up the appointment. He was even expelled from his fire company — a sad affront, and equivalent to being expelled from a club — on account of his contumacy and lack of public spirit.

The repeal of the Stamp Act, in March, 1766, changed all this bitter discontent into general gladness. The colonists believed that they had won their battle, and the brig, *Minerva*, which brought the happy news to Philadelphia, was welcomed with universal rejoicings. Bonfires blazed all night long, bowls of punch were emptied under opulent roofs, kegs of beer were rolled into the streets to intoxicate the poor. Every sailor in the crew received a handsome cadeau, and to the captain was presented a fine gold-laced cocked hat. The mayor and aldermen celebrated the occasion with a great civic banquet, at which the King's health was drunk with extravagant demonstrations of loyalty; and we know that these sentiments had by no means abated when June brought round the royal birthday, and Jacob Hiltzheimer went forth with nearly four hundred citizens to dine on the banks of the Schuylkill, and empty a score of glasses in honour of good King George.

It is a pity that this general satisfaction should have been so exceedingly short-lived. In the following year another colonial tax-bill, placing duties on paper, glass, paints, lead and tea, renewed the consternation of the province; and John Dickinson fanned the flame of popular resentment into an angry blaze with his timely " Letters of a Farmer of Pennsylvania to the Inhabitants of the British Colonies." Once more Philadelphia prepared to offer a passive resistance to the obnoxious law by steeling her heart against imported luxuries, taxed or untaxed, with the result that patriotism on the one hand, and self-indulgence on the other, waged a steady conflict for mastery. A weak-minded citizen, overcome by the pleadings of his appetite, ventured to surreptitiously purchase some English cheese from the mate of the *Speedwell;* but his dastardly deed was discovered before he had time to eat the coveted delicacy, and he was compelled to give it, untasted, to the poor debtors in prison. There was more difficulty experienced in persuading women to do without their tea. Notwithstanding its ruinous cost and painful unpopularity, it was never wholly banished. Shopmen escaped detection by selling it in sealed packages, under the name of tobacco, snuff, or any other innocuous merchandise, — just as whiskey is sold in prohibition towns; and fair recalcitrants kept it discreetly hidden in hot water pots, while the empty coffee urns were placed conspicuously in posts of honour, to give their lying evidence to visitors who were not in the secret.

Smuggling grew so common in these days that it wore an air of persecuted honesty; smugglers were as highly esteemed in virtuous Pennsylvania as in lawless Spain; and prying citizens who gave evidence against this illicit trade were promptly tarred and feathered by the mob, to teach them the inadvisability of interference. There was a confused impression in the minds of the angry, illogical colonists that smugglers were patriots; and abstract patriotism had gained so much favour under the stress of general discontent, that sober Philadelphians celebrated with a grand banquet the birthday of the Corsican, Pascal Paoli, and uttered fervid sentiments that would not have shamed a Jacobin club in Paris.

The autumn of 1773 brought a new complication into this uneasy turmoil. An Act of Parliament permitted the East India Company to carry its tea to

America free of all duty, save the trifling three-penny colonial tax. This gave the colonists cheaper tea than England had ever enjoyed, and the temptation was well-nigh irresistible after long months of enforced abstemiousness. It was all very well for ardent and acrimonious Whigs, like Christopher Marshall, to compel their families to drink that vile domestic beverage known as "balm tea"; but the hearts of women had grown rebellious as the weary weeks went on, and there was every danger that this wily measure on the part of England would break down at last the stubborn opposition of the colonies. The committee of merchants determined that no choice between principle and comfort should be permitted; that the weaker portion of the community should have no chance given them to succumb. When the tea ship, *Polly*, reached Gloucester Point, her captain was invited, or rather bidden to come ashore, and told as briefly as possible that he would not be allowed to land his cargo, and that any attempt to do so would place him in great personal danger. He acquiesced philosophically in a situation which could not be remedied, tarried but a few hours to lay in fresh supplies, and set sail with the outgoing tide for his long homeward voyage. The whole important matter, notwithstanding the usual array of half-mad pamphlets, and the riotous demonstrations of the mob, had been conducted with moderation and dignity. It was not nearly such

good fun as pitching the tea-chests into Boston harbour, and it does not make a lively historic anecdote
for schoolboys to read; but it has the advantage
of greater honesty, of self-respecting decorum, and
of being a daylight performance, in which all the
actors gave their names to the public before they
played their parts.

In May, 1774, Boston port was closed, and Paul
Revere brought the news to Philadelphia, where
it was received with astonishment and indignation.
Christopher Marshall tells us that nearly every shop
was shut on the first of June, when Revere's message
was given to the people, that the flags were lowered
to half-mast, and the churches being opened as though
it were Sunday, huge congregations attended, and
listened grimly to appropriate sermons. There was
no service, indeed, at Christ Church, but her bells rang
a muffled peal all day long, as was their wont in time
of public calamity. "Sorrow and anger," says the
sympathetic Marshall, "seemed pictured in the coun-
tenances of the inhabitants, and the whole city wore
the aspect of deep distress, it being a most melancholy
occasion."

Revere's letters were addressed to Joseph Reed, and
to that fighting Quaker, Thomas Mifflin. Through
the influence of these citizens, a meeting was called in
the City Tavern, at which Dickinson and Charles
Thomson spoke with great eloquence and fervour;

and Boston was assured of sympathy and support in
a letter written by Provost Smith, but which the
friends of Dickinson always stoutly declared to have
been his composition. A more important gathering
met in the State House on June 28th. Thomas
Willing and Dickinson presided, much oratory was
let loose, and some definite measures decided upon.
The governor was asked to call together the Assembly,
a committee of correspondence was appointed, and —
most momentous step of all — a resolution was passed,
recommending a congress of all the colonies, which
should assist the Assembly — and override it — in deal-
ing with the grave emergencies of the time.

The Continental Congress assembled in Philadelphia
in the autumn of 1774, and held its sessions in Carpenters' Hall, a fine, simple old building which had
been erected a few years before by the guild of carpenters and house masons. Eleven only of the thirteen provinces sent delegates, but these were men
capable of overriding any Assembly, and of forcing
their own measures upon a hesitating country. Among
them were John and Samuel Adams, Richard Henry
Lee, George Washington, and Patrick Henry, whose
glowing periods won him scant favour in a town
which had not yet wholly relinquished its ancient
gift of silence. Peyton Randolph of Virginia was
elected president, and Charles Thomson — he who
knew so much and divulged so little of his country's

history — was chosen to be the secretary. The Rev.
Jacob Duché — "Tamoc Caspipina" — was invited to
act as chaplain, to his unquali- | fied delight. "He
appeared," says John Adams, | "with his clerk, and
in his pontificals," and offered | eloquent prayers,

CARPENTERS' HALL

which were much admired and quoted until such time
as he abandoned the cause of liberty and became a
devout Tory, when the angry Whigs ceased praising
his orisons, and promptly confiscated his estate.

For six weeks the Congress deliberated on the
manifold difficulties of the situation, cheered mean-

while by much Philadelphia hospitality. Adams
was not the only delegate who ate and drank himself
into permanent indigestion amid the seductions of
a society, "happy, elegant, tranquil, and polite." A
grand banquet was given by prominent citizens to the
city's guests, when their first work was done. Five
hundred covers were laid in the great State House
chamber, and innumerable healths were drunk, the
first and foremost toast being still King George III.,
for the colonists had by no means given up hoping
for a peaceful adjustment of their troubles. The
resolutions adopted by the Congress were moderate
in tone, but expressed steadfast resistance to any form
of taxation imposed by the English government while
the provinces remained unrepresented in Parliament,
and a steadfast rejection of all imports upon which
such unconstitutional taxes were levied. The Assembly professed great satisfaction with most of the
measures proposed, especially with those which sought
to encourage domestic manufactures; and Franklin,
returning to Philadelphia in May, 1775, was immediately appointed a delegate, that he might add his
share of sagacity and experience to the counsels of
men so heavily burdened with responsibility, so new
to the perils of their parts.

And, indeed, the country had sore need of all the
wisdom she could muster, in a situation of which no
man could reasonably foresee the end. It was a time

pregnant with hopes unspoken, and with fears unchecked ; a time of deep disquiet, with darkening skies, and universal discontent. Strange omens — like to those which presaged the coming of the great Plague — were witnessed by the apprehensive ; and Marshall notes in his diary, without a tremour of disbelief, that a headless snake was seen by many, writhing in the heavens. When this snake shook its tail, there came a trembling vibration like an earthquake shock, and balls of fire descended from the skies upon the doomed houses of men. Past were the old easy days when life held few perplexities, and when the standing quarrel between Quaker and churchman, Assembly and governor, carried with it no deadly frustration of power or purpose. Now any division in the ranks meant certain peril, and possible ruin. How far could the Quakers be cajoled or bullied into open rebellion against England? How far could they be persuaded to advance in a movement which threatened destruction to the laws they had made, and which had been their pride and glory for a hundred years? A most inconvenient people to deal with, these Quakers, for all their mildness and general sanity ; a people whose religious scruples were as binding as moral laws, and in whom "the noble firmness of the mule" was backed by a reasonably clear conception of their own interests, and of the material interests of the commonwealth. Equally averse to barracks and

to law-courts, they refused to support the one by
paying military taxes, or to assist the other by acting
as jurors, witnesses, or clients; and it must be confessed that, left to themselves, they had apparently
no need for either of these ornaments of civilization.
They kept their peace with the Indians, unaided by
the convincing voice of firearms, and they settled
their own disputes, without assistance from advocate
or judge. The "Committee of Monthly Meetings,"
aided and abetted by the still more awe-inspiring
Quarterly and Yearly Meetings, held them in thrall,
and gave them all they wanted in the way of laws
and penalties.

It was natural that a people so wedded to peace,
so content with their own rules of life, and so mistrustful of change, should have been hard to influence
in a great public crisis, of which nothing but the insecurity could be wholly understood. "The leading
members of the Society," says Mr. Charles Wetherill
in his history of the Free Quakers, "were men who
had grown old in the habit of loyalty to the crown,
and had been rewarded by dignities and wealth."
The somewhat clamorous eloquence of the patriots
moved them less than the rippling of the wind; the
fast-growing authority of the mob filled them with
serious apprehensions. At the Yearly Meeting held
in Philadelphia, 1774, a solemn letter of warning
was prepared and sent to all the Friends in the colonies,

bidding them to beware of sedition and strife, and
to assume no part in the defiant rebellion against
their King. This letter was generally respected and
obeyed, for it needed a moment of supreme urgency
to awaken in the hearts of all men the common instinct of self-protection, and to startle even the young
Quakers into war.

Yet the determination of the Society to hold itself
aloof from any hostile demonstrations veiled an equally
obstinate determination to yield no civic rights, no
long-contested privileges. The delegates to the Continental Congress knew little of the Quaker temperament, or of the Quaker history, else they would have
been aware that what was needed to push these strong
conservatives into opposition was, not enthusiastic
speech-making on their part, but continued injustice
on the part of England. It was hard, however, to
wait for such slow conversion in a time of profound
impatience and restless fear. It was hard to refrain
from attacking and alienating a people whose attitude
of reserve was more trying than open disaffection.
Men had grown suspicious of one another in these
weeks of anxious waiting for — they knew not what.
At last, on the twenty-fourth of April, 1775, there
came an answer to many an unspoken question. It
was brought by a weary and travel-stained rider who
alighted at the City Tavern, and asked to see some
members of the Committee of Correspondence. The

news he carried was strange indeed, yet no man was surprised by it. Rather it seemed as though all had been waiting for this hour, and for the word it bore. The English soldiers and the New England militia had fired on one another at Lexington. The first blood had been shed in the great struggle for independence. The Revolution had begun.

INKSTAND IN INDEPENDENCE HALL

CHAPTER XII

WAR

THE history of Philadelphia for the next six years is, in reality, the history of the country. It is impossible to divorce her records from the broader annals of the united colonies, who looked to her as to the central stage on which was played the great drama of rebellion. If she still hesitated, it was, not at action, but at calling that action by its proper name. She flew to arms, but seldom spoke of battle; she prepared decisively for war, but hardly confessed that England was her antagonist. When the encounter at Lexington was made known to the public, an angry and excited crowd of eight thousand men assembled before the State House, declared their intention of defending their rights and liberties, and advocated the immediate enrolling of new bodies of militia. We learn from many sources with what ardour young and old offered their services in the first flush of enthusiasm, and how they drilled day and night to be prepared for an imperative emergency. Dr. Graydon who belonged to the third battalion, commanded by John Cadwalader, and sarcastically called the "Silk Stocking Company," in reference to supposed fine feathers and good birth, tells us that he and his companions practised shooting at a target on Race Street, and that one of the party shot a child, which was discouraging, but hardly a matter for surprise.

Congress reassembled on the eleventh of May, and a Committee of Safety was appointed, with Franklin at its head, to look after the needs and the defences of the city. This committee determined to be healthy, wealthy, and wise, by following one of its great leader's maxims, and met every morning at the bracing hour of six. The members found plenty to do in preparing for war, and in trying to preserve order, for already the disturbed condition of the public mind had broken the barriers of security. The mob grew bolder and bolder, until at last, in playful mood, it openly set fire to the jail, as the easiest way of liberating two counterfeiters who were confined within its walls. What wonder that a sober citizen like James Allen, son of Chief Justice Allen, should, even while ready to shoulder a musket in the "great and glorious cause," have confided most despondent sentiments to the secrecy of his diary. "The madness of the multitude," he writes, "is but one degree better than submission to the Tea Act. . . . Many thinking people believe America has seen its best days, and even if we be victorious, peace and order will with difficulty be restored. The inconveniences are already sensibly felt. Debts as yet are paid, but this cannot last long, for people begin to plead their inability."

The manufacture of gunpowder, and the building of gunboats to defend the river's front, occupied much of the committee's attention; but it found leisure to inquire very curiously into the goings and comings of men who were suspected of Tory proclivities. It was a time of active interference with other people's affairs, and Joseph Galloway protested that he could not retire for a night to his country-house without explaining publicly why he did not sleep in town. A favourite diversion of the mob was the dragging of Tory citizens in carts through the streets, to the spirited music of the "Rogue's March," until they "politely acknowledged" the erroneous nature of their convictions, and uttered more patriotic sentiments, to the huge delight of their captors. Occasionally the crowds which assembled for this sport were cheated out of their triumph. Dr. John Kearsley, though so roughly handled that the blood

o

streamed from his hurts, merely swore with ever-increasing vehemence at his tormentors, who were about to offer the final argument of tar and feathers when their victim — still swearing — was snatched away from them by the militia, and carried back to his house, where the lively populace had broken all the windows. A yet more defiant combatant was Major Skene, who, after his third bottle of port, flung open the shutters, and roared out with drunken loyalty over the heads of the angry rabble, "God save great George, our King."

The Continental Congress, having recommended the people to "abstain from vain amusements," was not disposed to tolerate anything in the nature of gayety, and this resolution checked Philadelphia's generous hospitality. With the approach of war, the Assemblies were given up ; but youth is always youth, and as eager to dance in dark days as in bright ones. The presence of Mrs. Washington and Mrs. Hancock in the city during the autumn of 1775 gave excellent excuse for a ball, at which these ladies readily promised to attend. But it was not to be. That portion of the community which never went to balls had for once the power to chill unseasonable mirth. A committee of citizens waited upon Mrs. Washington, and requested her not to grace the festivities, while her "worthy and brave husband was exposed in the field of battle, in defence of his country's liberties." The lady, with great good nature, acquiesced in her visitors' views, assured them that "their sentiments on this occasion were perfectly agreeable to her own," and promised to remain at home. As a consequence, the ball was abandoned, to the unfeigned regret of many young girls who, being under no anxiety on the score of worthy and brave husbands, would have welcomed a little cheerful variety.

There was some excuse for the arbitrary behaviour of the Whigs, inasmuch as they had to deal with so many disunited elements. Men who had nothing to lose were eager for radical measures. Men who, like Mr. Chew, Mr. Tilghman, and Mr. Shippen, enjoyed offices of trust and distinction, were more prone to consider consequences. Men with easy minds, like Mr. John Ross, declared in much the same words as the philosophical Vicar of Bray, "Let who will be king; I know that I shall still be subject." Men as wise and wary as Benjamin Franklin calculated every step they took in such parlous times, and permitted their final decisions to remain long a matter for conjecture. "Franklin's demeanour towards the conflicting parties," says Dr. Graydon, "was so truly accommodating, that it was doubtful where he really belonged. No man had scanned the world more critically than he, and few had profited more by a knowledge of it, or managed that knowledge more to their own advantage."

Meanwhile events were hastening forward with a ruthless speed that was sadly disconcerting to those who had not yet made up their minds what part to

play. Washington was appointed commander of the national forces, and joined the army before Boston, taking with him the first American flag, which then bore in the corner a red and blue cross in place of the thirteen stars. Paul Jones hoisted his rattlesnake flag — no pleasing emblem — over one of the new American cruisers.

HOUSE OF BETTY ROSS, WHERE THE FIRST FLAG WAS MADE

The troops drilling in Philadelphia demanded from the Assembly money for arms, accoutrements, and support. Lead was so scarce that all the fine old standing clocks were robbed of their weights, and stood mute and helpless in their corners. The battle of Bunker Hill added to the general agitation; the departure of the English army from Boston quickened the colonists' hopes. Tom Paine, that "disastrous meteor" as Adams calls him, published his "Common Sense," and at once became the most popular man in the country. Even Dickinson's fame paled before the new light, and the "Farmer's Letters" were well-nigh forgotten in the rabid enthusiasm which greeted Paine's bolder theories. Men were just in the humour to believe that governments were antiquated devices, and that the voice of the populace was the voice of God. Each reader felt his soul expand at this splendid recognition of his individual importance, and of his right to clamour with the loudest. In every Philadelphia shop was seen the familiar advertisement, "Common Sense for eighteen pence," and thousands of purchasers thought the article cheap at that very moderate price. Adams, James Allen, and others who disagreed violently with Paine's definition of sense were not slow in putting *their* opinions into print. Indeed, the approaching election brought down upon the anxious public a storm of pamphlets, in which political opponents under the names of Cato, Cassandra, Forrester, etc., enjoyed such a prolonged and lively combat that if the voters did not know what line of conduct to pursue, it was certainly not from lack of cheap and copious instruction.

For the last time the moderate party triumphed in the Assembly, a dearly bought victory destined to lead the way to the final overthrow of the constitution. Congress, on the tenth of May, 1776, passed a resolution recommending to all the colonies a radical change of government, that they might be better equipped to meet the serious emergencies of the war. The Committee of Safety, now grown imperious and despotic, held a week's conference in Carpenters' Hall, and determined that a convention should be called to frame a new constitution. At the inevitable dinner with which this conference terminated — dinners, unlike balls, were considered patriotic amusements — the King's health was not drunk, but, in his place, " The free and independent States of America " were toasted with loud acclamations. The petition sent to the crown met with no response, as the colonies were in open rebellion long before the " dutiful and humble " paper reached England; and it became more and more apparent on both sides that the war was, not for terms, but for freedom. The old Assembly, which had for almost a century watched faithfully over the interest of the province committed to its charge, was rapidly nearing its end, choked out of existence by the vehemence of reformers who scorned the wisdom of the past, and felt an easy confidence in their power to regulate the future. With its destruction, the political power of the Quakers came to an abrupt close. They had done their work for many years wisely

and well. The tasks which awaited their successors
were of a different order, and demanded different
hands. There was both rank ingratitude and rank
injustice in the treatment the Friends subsequently
received; but gratitude has never been a lively fac-
tor in politics, and men, when sick with apprehension or elate with victory, are hardly sane enough
to know what justice means.

The Convention of 1776 amply satisfied the public
appetite for novelties. It was generous and even pro-
fuse in the matter of new laws, both big and little.
Nothing was too important to be settled offhand, nothing too trivial to occupy its attention. Pennsylvania
was declared an independent state; delegates were
sent to Congress; heavy taxes were laid on Germans
and Quakers who refused to serve in the militia. A
new constitution was prepared which received Franklin's enthusiastic support. In place of the single governor with whom Pennsylvania had always quarrelled
lustily in the past, twelve governors, forming a council,
were given her as suitable antagonists for the future ;
and a "General Assembly" was furthermore provided
to fight fairly and squarely with the twelve. Then,
lest an ignoble tranquillity should still be possible,
a second council, called the Council of Censors, was
appointed, the members of which had the pleasant
duty of finding fault with both the executive and the
legislative bodies. Altogether there was abundant

opportunity for hostilities, and no sooner had the new laws gone into operation than hostilities began with fervour. The province was sharply divided into two irreconcilable parties: those who upheld this constitution, and those who saw in it certain and disastrous ruin. Philadelphia was the battlefield on which the opponents prepared for the coming combat.

But other and larger issues, weighted with the welfare of the whole nation, were pressing hard for recognition, and it was no longer possible to ignore or to stifle the agitation in favour of independence. The Pennsylvania delegates to Congress in the spring of 1776 were Franklin, Morris, Willing, Morton, Humphreys, Wilson and Dickinson; men of moderate views who were keenly anxious that the province should be won over wholly to the cause of freedom, before it was forced to yield its consent to a measure which could never be retracted. It was not in their power, however, to restrain the impetuosity of the Virginia and Massachusetts delegates, and, on the seventh of June, Richard Henry Lee offered his resolutions, absolving the colonies from their old allegiance, and proclaiming them free and independent States.

The following weeks were absorbed in strenuous debate. Seven of the thirteen colonies were in favour of the resolutions; six, with Pennsylvania at their head, held firmly back, believing that the time had not yet come for open and absolute rebellion. But

the fierce enthusiasm of the majority was well calculated to override the prudent hesitation of the
minority. Enthusiasm, moreover, is contagious, and
hesitation is ever an ungrateful part to play. Agents
were sent by Congress to quicken the spirit of revolt
in New York, New Jersey, Maryland and Delaware.
Every argument was used to persuade the colonists
that only by the closest union could they hope to
achieve their freedom, or even to preserve their safety;
they *must* hang together, as Richard Penn dryly observed, unless they wanted to be hanged separately.
The nine hours' debate of July 1st left four colonies
still unconvinced. Pennsylvania and South Carolina
voted against Lee's resolutions, Delaware was hopelessly divided, and New York refused to vote at all,
her delegates having received no authority from home
to support the popular measure.

The final decision was deferred until the next day,
and a last urgent appeal made to the conservatives
who still held back from action. It was not without
avail. By the evening of July 2d, South Carolina
and Delaware, either converted or overwearied, voted
for independence. Pennsylvania was still disunited.
Three of her delegates, Franklin, Wilson and Morton,
supported the resolutions; Willing and Humphreys,
consistent to the end, bravely and obstinately opposed
them; Morris and Dickinson evaded the necessity for
a decision by keeping out of the way. Their absence

enabled the advocates of liberty to carry the Pennsylvania vote by a handsome majority of one. New York, waiting like Casabianca for orders that never came, declined with an almost sublime apathy to take any part in the proceedings. Twelve of the thirteen colonies, however, had now been won over; and before sunset, July 2, 1776, Lee's resolutions were passed by an almost unanimous vote. The nation had determined to be free.

Two days later the Declaration of Independence was formally adopted, and on July 8th the document was read to the people — to the few at least who gathered to hear it — from the observatory in the State House yard. One unseen auditor there was who has left us an account of that day. Deborah Norris, then a girl of fifteen, had climbed her garden wall to catch a glimpse of what was going on. The reader was hidden from her by the side of the observatory, but she heard distinctly from her high perch every word he uttered, and was awed into a childish terror as the grave voice — Charles Thomson's voice, she fancied, but it was really that of Captain John Nixon — repeated slowly those memorable words, the full significance of which she was too young to understand. "It was," she wrote years afterwards, "a time of fearful doubt and great anxiety with the people, many of whom were appalled by the boldness of the measure; and the first audience of the Declaration was neither very numerous, nor composed of the most respectable class of citizens." The church bells, however, were rung assiduously, and a few bonfires were lit at night, that being a form of celebration as popular with the boys of 1776 as with their successors to-day.

The Declaration of Independence was not signed until August, and in the meantime the anger of the

ROOM IN STATE HOUSE WHERE DECLARA-
TION WAS SIGNED

community, now directed against the Pennsylvania delegates who had refused it their support, assumed more and more ominous proportions. Morris and Wilson were indeed reëlected to Congress on the twentieth of July, and subsequently became signers; but Wilson was not so easily pardoned, and Dickinson, once the idol of every heart, was loaded with recrimination and abuse. "Popular enthusiasm is a fire of straw," says

Mr. Froude; and the crowd who had hailed the "Farmer's Letters" as a veritable message from the gods, now found no words of contumely strong enough for its author. If he had been unduly elated by success, he was at least tolerably resigned to injustice. There was still work to do, and he marched with his battalion straight to the field of war. When the malice of his many enemies, striking hard at his honour, left him no battalion to lead, he simply shouldered a musket and served as a common soldier, determined to aid his country, notwithstanding the opposition of his countrymen. It may be observed that Dickinson and McKean were the only members of the Continental Congress who ever saw active service, a circumstance which posterity has thought it worth while to remember.

Philadelphia was a proud, but not altogether a comfortable city, after her ancient State House had witnessed the signing of the Declaration of Independence. In the first place the new Constitution was manifestly unpopular, which was hardly surprising; and in the second place the depreciation of the paper currency had begun, and the necessities of life were growing terribly dear. Above all, the scarcity of salt was working serious evil. In the autumn of 1776, fine salt was selling at twenty-five shillings a bushel. In December, the Rev. Henry Muhlenberg notes in his diary: "The people push and jostle each other wherever there is the smallest quantity of salt to be found about town. The country people complain bitterly because they suppose there are hidden stores in Philadelphia."

Meanwhile every effort was made to strengthen the defences of the city, and to increase the "flying camp" which grew but slowly, although a bounty of three pounds was offered for every volunteer, and a reward of three pounds for the arrest of every deserter. Graydon's account of the difficulties he experienced in raising recruits is pathetically droll. Men would utter sentiments of glowing patriotism, and would drink copiously to their country and their country's cause; but when pressed to enlist, they melted away like snowflakes, leaving him not a single soldier out of a most promisingly noisy crowd. It was a season of disasters. The colonists' high hopes grew fainter and fainter as the weary months brought nothing but tidings of defeat, and the lines of war drew ever closer to Philadelphia. Sick and wounded troops were brought in great numbers to the city, and the Pennsylvania hospital was set apart for their exclusive use. Camp-fever and small-pox raged among these unfortunates, destroying ten good men, says John Adams, where the enemy killed one. Shallow trenches were dug in Washington Square, and two thousand corpses were buried hastily in that field of death where, years before, the Guinea negroes had been wont to steal at dusk, or in the early dawn, with little offerings of food and rum for their departed kinsfolk.

On the nineteenth of November the news reached Philadelphia that General Howe had taken Fort Washington, and was marching on the city. Graydon, who was made a prisoner on this occasion, has left us a lively description of the fray, of his own capture, and of the kindness of the big Scotch sergeant who said to him, as to a froward child, " Young man, ye should never fight against your King." Some of the English officers, however, spoke to him so rudely, that he confesses he was unmanned. " I was obliged to apply my handkerchief to my eyes," — an avowal which sounds more like the sensitive Mr. Pecksniff than an American soldier. He was subsequently released on parole through the kindness of General Howe, and his fighting days were over.

By the second of December the British were at Brunswick, and a general panic ensued in Philadelphia. Christopher Marshall's diary describes the lamentable confusion : " Families loading wagons with their furniture, and all ranks sending their goods out of town into the country." Even the Congress departed with what speed it could to Baltimore, leaving a committee in charge of affairs, with the unterrified Morris — who had so much to lose — as chairman. Washington appointed General Putnam the military governor of the city, and this peremptory officer ordered all able-bodied men to muster at once for the militia, and all merchants to receive the Continental currency at its full value, neither of which mandates was obeyed. In fact, the

Committee of Safety was so determined that the people *should* accept the paper money for more than it was worth, that it was made a criminal offence to ask higher prices for merchandise when the depreciated notes were offered in payment. This is the kind of lawmaking which is happily always rendered inactive by its own viciousness, and by the plain common sense of the people. It was the last authoritative act of the Committee, before its power passed into the hands of the Supreme Executive Council, organized March 4, 1777.

When General Howe reached Trenton, he issued the proclamation which won over many wavering Tories, like Galloway and the Allens, who placed themselves under his protection. There is little doubt that the general insecurity of the country impelled them to take this step. James Allen's diary is half comical in its mournful, but not unreasonable lamentations over the marauding habits of the undisciplined militia, and the obstinacy of his tenants, who plainly intimated that a patriotic landlord would never expect them to pay their rents in such a troubled time. "The prevailing idea," he writes angrily, "is that no man has any right to property that the public has use for, and it is seldom they even ask the owner." On the other hand, Philadelphia was actively engaged in strewing the Tory path with thorns. In July, 1777, forty gentlemen were arrested on the charge of disloyalty to the Government. Among them were John Penn, Jared Ingersoll, Benjamin Chew, and the always unfortunate Provost Smith, who was the stanchest of patriots, — save that he would fain have delayed the Declaration, — and who had exhausted himself in fervid speech-making at every stage of the fight. A few of these prisoners were committed to jail; but the greater number were banished from the city, confined in their own homes, or released on parole, with the certainty of being suspected and closely watched in the future.

On the fourth of July, 1777, Philadelphia celebrated for the first time our great national holiday, and set the example which has been followed — with modifications — for more than a hundred years. There was much firing of guns all day, a civic banquet in the evening, notwithstanding the dearness of provisions, and a brisk smashing of Quaker windows at night, to keep up the spirits of the mob. Elizabeth Drinker, whose husband, Henry Drinker, was one of the banished Friends, writes tersely and without comment in her invaluable diary: —

"July 4th, 1777. The town illuminated, and a great number of windows broken on ye Anniversary of Independence and Freedom."

The new oath of allegiance to the State, which was exacted from all citizens under penalty of being deprived of every office and every civic right, caused

great division in the Quaker ranks. Hitherto the
Friends had played a purely passive part in the general excitement. They had issued their yearly warnings against deeds of violence, and open rebellion,
and they had stayed quietly at home when other
people fled from the city. It seemed as if, in their
aversion to war, they regarded even running away
— that very material part of contest — as opposed to
their principles. But all this time dissentient voices
had been heard uttering strange heresies, and insist-
ing that upon the shoulders of every man lay the
sacred duty of defending his country from oppres-
sion. These voices had grown stronger and more in-
sistent with the rush of events during the past twelve
months, and the leading spirit of revolt was Samuel
Wetherill, Junior, a great-grandson of one of the
first settlers of New Jersey. He had come to Philadelphia as a boy, had been apprenticed to Mordicai
Yarnall, a wealthy house carpenter, and had in the
course of time married his master's daughter, after
the good old fashion approved by Hogarth. He
helped to found the first factory for weaving cloths
in the colonies, and was an influential man, deeply
respected by the Quakers until he severed himself
abruptly from their ranks.

For it was not enough for this ardent combatant
to take the oath of allegiance publicly and gladly at
the head of a band of resolute young Friends. It

P

was not even enough to advocate the bearing of arms, or to give money generously for the defences of the town. He must needs, following the example of those about him, rush into print; and, as the "Meeting Record" attests, "violate the established order of our discipline, by being concerned in publishing and distributing a book tending to promote dissension and division among Friends." For these unpardonable offences he was formally but very gently cut off from the Society, with none of the "current compliments of theological parting"; but rather with regret at his obstinacy, and a pious hope that he would one day see his errors, and be restored to membership.

There was no room for repentance, however, in Samuel Wetherill's belligerent soul. He was a Quaker war-horse, scenting the battle from afar, and eager to rush into the thickest of the fray. Followers he had in plenty, men, who like himself, were disowned by the Friends because they advocated forcible resistance against foreign enemies and oppressive laws, and because they declared—of course in print —that no man nor woman could justly be excommunicated from any Christian church, provided he or she believed in the word of God. This was the substance of Wetherill's famous "Apology for the Religious Society, called Free Quakers, in the City of Philadelphia," which made him many converts and many

enemies, both of which acquisitions he thoroughly
enjoyed. " Free Quakers" was the name given to
themselves by these determined seceders; but the
people generally called them by the more stirring
title of " Fighting Quakers," which was well deserved,
and the Friends never mentioned them save briefly
as " Apostates." — " T. Matlock takes upon himself
to be speaker for ye Apostates," writes Elizabeth
Drinker, as usual without comment. She possessed
the unfeminine gift of expressing her sentiments fully
without help from explanations or expletives.

For several years after their expulsion from the
Society, the Free Quakers met for worship in private
houses, or in one of the college rooms. They considered, however, that they had a legal right to occupy
the old meeting-house, and applied for permission,
which was naturally but civilly refused. They also
boldly announced that they meant to use the Friends'
burial ground, without asking leave, whenever they
required it. " For however the living may contend, surely the dead may lie peaceably together."
This was not so easily accomplished as they fancied.
The dead, indeed, were peaceable enough, and cared
little who lay by their sides; but the burial ground
was under the control of the living, who would have
none but orthodox graves dug within its tranquil enclosure. The would-be intruders then took a step
alien to all Quaker principles, and to the whole his-

tory of their church: they appealed to the civil authorities to interfere in their behalf, setting forth their own claims as loyal citizens, and plainly intimating that their opponents were Tories, royalists, and traitors at heart to the Republic. This petition was promptly met by a memorial from the Friends, stoutly denying any treasonable intent, and asserting that they too were loyal and law-abiding men, who, in the matter of the meeting-house and burial ground, merely followed the rules of their community, and the dictates of their consciences. The lawmakers with unwonted sapiency decided that religious dissensions were no concern of theirs, and left to the pious disputants the privilege of settling the quarrel as best they could alone.

They did not settle it at all. They quarrelled bravely on, and the Free Quakers built a new meeting-house at Fifth and Arch Streets, a quaint little edifice of red brick, to which Washington, and Franklin and a great many distinguished people lent liberal aid. On a tablet inserted in the wall are cut these four lines: —

> "By General Subscription,
> For the Free Quakers.
> Erected A. D. 1783.
> Of the Empire 8."

The word "Empire" has puzzled good Republicans for more than a century. A prominent member of the first congregation being asked why it had been used, replied valiantly, "I tell thee, Friend, it is because our country is destined to be the great empire over all the world,"—a loyal sentiment, but one that affords no explanation.

During the Revolutionary war, and in the troubled years which immediately followed it, the Free or Fighting Quakers enjoyed great popularity, and were far better off than their persecuted brethren in the fold. They took an active part in politics, and even the women gave distinguished proof of their devotion to the cause of liberty. Lydia Darragh, who brought to Washington's camp at White Marsh news of the English army's intended attack, and Elizabeth Ross, who made the first flag carried by the American army, were both Free Quakers. But when the Federal government was firmly established, and the bitterness of dissension was at an end, the little congregation shared the fate of so many vigorous branches lopped from a parent stem. Some of its members returned to their old allegiance, and were received back into the Society of Friends; some died, and their families gradually ceased to attend the Sunday meetings. Elizabeth Ross, afterwards Elizabeth Claypoole, the last of the original seceders, lived until 1836, but was too old and infirm to leave her own roof. Finally, John Price Wetherill, son of Samuel Wetherill, who had inherited his father's undaunted spirit.

was reduced to the mournful necessity of worshipping alone, or nearly alone, for several years, a strain too great to be endured by any man. Accordingly, one Sunday morning he closed the meeting-house for the last time, and acknowledged the long, long struggle to be over. As a religious society, the Free Quakers had passed out of existence.

Yet a career of true usefulness remained to make the name honoured and beloved. Mr. Wetherill, clearly recognizing the needs of the community in which he lived, devoted himself to organizing a committee, the members of which should use the funds at their disposal for charitable and philanthropic purposes. If they could no longer minister to the souls of men, they could at least feed their bodies and their minds. So the red brick house at Fifth and Arch Streets was made over to the Apprentices' Library, then the only free library in Philadelphia; and for many years the nominal rent of fifty dollars was regularly given back, to be spent in "good and useful books." Other charities were added from time to time as the income of the society permitted; and even now this admirable organization continues to do its work, without parade, without salaried officials, without asking help from the public, and without any shadow of sectarianism. The Quakers, whether " Free " or in subjection, have never sympathized with the pious almsgiving peculiar to Christian churches, which follow the example of the careful Jacob, and bestow their mess of pottage, only at the price of a brother's birthright. The making, especially the buying of converts, finds no place in the annals of the Friends.

Nor did the spirit which impelled these obstinate schismatics to play their part in the Revolution die with the death of their schism, and the closing of their meeting-house. It survived to face another great emergency, and, with the breaking out of the Civil War, the old combative instinct flared into vehement life. Once more the Free Quakers became Fighting Quakers, and marched gayly to the front; while the treasurer of the Society, too old for active service, raised and equipped a company of soldiers at his sole expense, and presented them, ready for service, to the State. And still inherited characteristics survive, giving ample promise for the future. In the sudden mad revolts of organized labour, in the bloody scenes at the roundhouse of Pittsburg, and in the Homestead riots, the Philadelphia militia were never without some representatives of the Society, some descendants of the Fighting Quakers, ready and keen to preserve unbroken the ancient traditions of their name.

CHAPTER XIII

A GAY CAPTIVITY

THE defeat of Washington's forces on the Brandywine brought the victorious English army within twenty miles of Philadelphia. The successful night attack on Wayne's camp at Paoli disheartened still further the American soldiers, unused to the fearful vicissitudes of war. It only remained for General Howe to outmanœuvre Washington at the Swedes Ford by swift marches and counter-marches on the west bank of the Schuylkill, which tactics enabled him to elude his enemy, cross the river unopposed, and enter the city on the twenty-sixth of September, 1777. Word was sent to the townspeople, through Thomas Willing, that they should remain quietly in their homes, and a promise was given that no one should be molested in person or in property. This promise was kept, for although the soldiers could not always be restrained from committing depredations, they were punished with severity every time they offended, even when soft-hearted sufferers, like Mrs. Samuel Morton, tried hard to beg them off. Many prominent Whigs had already left Philadelphia. The citizens who remained regarded the advent of the English with conflicting emotions, in which the irrepressible spirit of commerce played a weighty part. Robert Morton, aged seventeen, wrote in his diary: "Sept. 26th. This day has put a period to the existence of Continental money in the city. 'Esto Perpetua!'"

It was no pleasant matter, however, for a town of thirty thousand inhabitants to be suddenly called upon to shelter an invading army nearly eighteen thousand strong. The soldiers found quarters wherever they could, the artillery and the Forty-Second Highlanders remaining near the State House, while the State House yard was filled with formidable cannon. The officers were billeted upon wealthier households, not always to the satisfaction of their hosts, though, on the whole, sufficiently amicable relations were maintained. Lord Cornwallis with a numerous suite established himself in the home of Isaac Norris; but when Mrs. Norris represented to him that it would be impossible for her to remain under her own roof with so large a company of soldiers and servants, he courteously expressed his unwillingness to cause her any annoyance, and betook himself that very afternoon to other lodgings. General Howe lived first in General Cadwalader's house on Second Street, and afterwards in the house of Richard Penn, which subsequently became the residence of Washington, when President. We have an

amusing account in Elizabeth Drinker's journal of
her reluctance to receive an English officer during
her husband's enforced absence, and of her relief
when she found the unwelcome guest to be "a
thoughtful, sober young man," with an equally
thoughtful, sober servant, neither of whom caused
any disturbance beneath her quiet roof. In fact,
" our Major," as she affectionately calls the intruder,
became after a month or two the object of her careful
solicitude. He developed, amid the fast growing gayeties of the town, a taste for late hours and supper
parties, and she gave him excellent advice, of the
" early to bed and early to rise " order, which he accepted with great good-humour, and ill-kept promises
of amendment.

Howe's first care was to strengthen the defences of
Philadelphia by placing batteries along the river front,
and building a line of redoubts from the Delaware to
the Schuylkill. Until these defences were completed,
a portion of his army was left to guard Germantown,
and the exposed position of this camp determined
Washington to risk an immediate battle. He divided
his forces into three columns, the first led by Arm-
strong, the second by Green, the third by Wayne and
Sullivan. The attack was made at early dawn on the
fourth of October. The English, taken by surprise, retreated in some disorder, closely pursued by Wayne,
until Colonel Musgrave with his six companies of the

Fortieth Regiment flung himself into the Chew Mansion, and effectually checked the progress of the triumphant Americans.   In vain they essayed to storm this strong old country house, thus suddenly turned into a fortress.   It was not built in this era of feeble, flimsy architecture, and Musgrave's men poured a

"THIS STRONG OLD COUNTRY HOUSE"

deadly and continuous fire upon the attacking column.   To complete the misfortunes of the day, a thick autumnal mist shrouded the combatants; and Green's division, pressing eagerly forward along Mill Street, was mistaken by Wayne's soldiers for the enemy.   The confusion that followed was irreparable; the battle which had promised a victory ended in defeat; and noon saw the American forces retreating northward to White Marsh, leaving the English in possession of the field.

To Philadelphia, the news of the struggle at her gates brought a fever of excitement. All morning she waited in suspense, and by afternoon the first wagon-loads of wounded soldiers were dragged through her thronged streets. The hospitals were filled to overflowing; and Robert Morton tells us that Dr. Foulke, demonstrator of anatomy at the Medical College, was held to be a far more skilful operator than any of the English surgeons: so that the wounded Americans had at least the sad comfort of having their arms and legs cut off in half the time, and with half the suffering endured by their unfortunate opponents. In those old terrible days, when the supreme mercy of anæsthetics had not yet been granted to the world, it made a vast difference to the poor shattered wretch to know that his agony would last twenty instead of forty minutes, and would be alleviated by the firm, sure touch of a practised and pitying hand.

The battle of Germantown left Howe free to complete his line of redoubts, and to turn his attention to the *chevaux de frise* — Franklin's invention — which still stretched across the channel, protecting the American ships, and separating the English effectually from their fleet, which lay outside under the command of Admiral

Howe. The invading army depended upon this fleet
for provisions, for the country about Philadelphia was
closely watched by detachments of soldiers under
Wayne's command; but the Admiral was unable to pass
the *chevaux de frise* while the three forts, Mifflin, Mercer
and Billingsport, were still in the hands of the Americans. The reduction of these forts became an absolute
necessity, if eighteen thousand men were not to starve
in the city they had taken; but though Billingsport
was surrendered early in October, Fort Mifflin and Fort
Mercer held out gallantly for more than a month; desperately attacked and desperately defended, costing
more lives than were wasted in many a great decisive
battle, and abandoned by their garrisons, only after they
had been battered into mere unrecognizable heaps of
tumbling stones and mortar. In the meantime, the
colonies had gained elsewhere their first decisive victory.
The battle of Saratoga had been fought, and Burgoyne
with six thousand men had surrendered to General Gates.
But Gates was far away from the poor little besieged
forts, and made no great speed to draw nearer. When
they fell, the *chevaux de frise* was removed, the American war vessels were captured by the superior English
fleet, and supplies of every kind were brought in great
abundance to the city. General Howe and his army,
free from all immediate apprehensions, settled down
comfortably for the winter; and Washington withdrew
to his dismal quarters at Valley Forge, with no prospect

of anything resembling comfort in the long, cruel months of inactivity.

If, at first, Philadelphia seemed a trifle dull to the English officers, they rapidly proceeded to remedy that evil. The water was pronounced at once too bad to drink, but wine could always be substituted, and the town had long been as famous for its fine Madeira as for its West India turtle. The damp, unwholesome climate was also roundly abused, and, unhappily, no substitute was in this case attainable. The women were declared with one accord to be both gay and charming, and they lent themselves with easy humour to strange surroundings, and to the unwonted quickening of social life. The deference shown them moderated in some degree the reckless dissipation of the younger men, cadets often of noble houses, to whom the snatching of every possible pleasure was as much a part of the soldier's life as hard fighting in the field, and grim endurance when there were no pleasures to be snatched. The weekly balls at the City Tavern had for these English lads a keener attraction than even the cock-pit in Moore's Alley, or the wild suppers at the "Bunch of Grapes," or the club dinners, "late and long," in the rooms of the "Indian Queen." The shabby little theatre on South Street no longer languished in disgrace, but afforded endless entertainment, notwithstanding its truly destitute condition. With military readiness of resource, the Englishmen were prepared to be actors,

actresses, scene-painters, supernumeraries, costumers and
audience. They were equally willing to try their hands
at tragedy, comedy, farce, or melodrama; and their
winter's repertoire included such fine contrasts as " The
Constant Couple," " Douglas," " The Deuce is in Him,"
and the first part of " King Henry IV."

The best actor in the troupe, the best scene-painter,
the best costumer, and the only man who could be
depended upon to write a really
witty prologue was Major André.
In all the frivolities of this frivo-
lous time, his was the central figure. His gay good humour, his
handsome face, his charm of voice
and manner, made the art of
pleasing a perilously easy art for
him to practise. Light of heart
and steadfast of purpose, he
shrank from no danger, and neglected no amusement. He was

MAJOR ANDRÉ

but twenty-seven years old, and his friend and fellow
actor, De Lancey, was younger still. Indeed, many
of the officers were mere boys, to whom a skirmish
or a cricket match were equally acceptable entertainments. That careless dare-devil, Tarleton, who divided
his time between riding races and making love, was
only twenty-one, and a match in precocity for the gallant young American, " Major Stodard," whom Miss

Sally Wister extols in her journal as "justly celebrated for his powers of mind," and who had gained this enviable distinction at nineteen.

We can best understand what sober Philadelphia was really like in this winter of mad and modish gayety when we read contemporary letters, especially the letters of women, who have ever been wont to think more of pastimes than of politics. Just as Miss Wister, in the retirement of country life at Gwynedd, fills up her diary with descriptions of the American officers whom the chances of war brought under her father's roof, with minute accounts of the bewitching costumes she wore for their subjection, and with accurate reports of all the flattering things they said to her, and of all the vivacious things she said to them; so the fair Tories in the Quaker City describe with equal ardour and fidelity the more varied dissipations which filled their nights, and filled their hearts, to the exclusion of graver issues. Miss Rebecca Franks, who played a prominent part in these few months of frolic, can find no words vehement enough to express her enjoyment of the situation.

"You have not the slightest idea," she writes to her friend, Mrs. Paca, "of the life of continued amusement I live in. I can scarce have a moment to myself. I have stole this while everybody is retired to dress for dinner. I am but just come from under Mr. J. Black's hands, and most elegantly am I dressed for a ball this evening at Smith's, where we have one every Thursday. ..

You would not know the room, 'tis so much improved. I wish to Heaven you were going with us this evening to judge for yourself."

No doubt poor Mrs. Paca, being still young and giddy, wished so too, especially when her correspondent goes 'on to assure her that there is never any loss for partners, and that she herself is engaged to seven different gentlemen for the evening, as no lady dances more than twice with the same cavalier. There is the ring of true girlish friendship in the closing lines of the letter, an impetuous, generous desire to share all this fun with a companion.

"Oh! how I wish Mr. P. would let you come in for a week or two. I know you are as fond of a gay life as myself. You'd have an opportunity of rakeing as much as you choose, either at Plays, Balls, Concerts, or Assemblies. I've been but three evenings alone since we moved to town. I begin now to be almost tired."

No wonder that downcast Whigs grew sore at heart when they contrasted all this jollity with the hardships endured by Washington's ragged army at Valley Forge, or with the still sadder lot of the American prisoners in Philadelphia, herded together in the old jail on Walnut Street under the charge of a brute named Cunningham, who proved his total unfitness for such an office by wanton cruelty and abuse, and who, it is a profound comfort to know, was finally hanged as he deserved after his return to England. No wonder that

Q

dull exiles from the city found it hard to listen with tranquillity to letters brimful of plays and dances. No wonder that James Allen growled deeply over Philadelphia's "rollicking winter," when he remembered his unpaid rents; or that Christopher Marshall, shut up in stupid Lancaster for safety, and well-nigh mad-dened by his isolation, — not from balls, but from the progress of events, — relieved his mind by storming alternately at General Howe, as a "savage monster," and at General Washington, as a supine sluggard, — equally unmerited reproaches. The situation was particularly trying to those Free Quakers who were rich, thrifty, disinclined for active service, and discontented with the behaviour of everybody about them. "This is a strange age in which I now dwell," writes Marshall angrily in his "Remembrancer," "because nothing can be had cheap but lies, falsehood, and slanderous accusations. Love and Charity, the badges of Christianity, are not so much as named amongst us."

It is a painful proof of the bitterness of spirit, which grew deeper with every year of warfare, that when Mr. William Atlee of Lancaster was moved by pity to take under his roof a young English officer, a fever-stricken prisoner who bore Mrs. Atlee's maiden name, though claiming no relationship, this act of "Love and Charity," so far from winning Marshall's approbation, rouses him to a whole page of wrathful anathemas upon the lukewarm patriotism which made friends of enemies, and weakened the cause of freedom by ill-timed lenity and vacillation.

Meanwhile Philadelphia, careless of the darkening future, grew gayer and gayer as the spring advanced. An occasional skirmish outside the lines hardly sufficed to remind the soldiers that there were still military duties and dangers to be encountered. Once, indeed, La Fayette with twenty-five hundred picked men advanced half-way from Valley Forge; and General Howe, eager to defeat this little force and to capture its gallant leader, marched hastily to meet them. But the Americans, eluding attack, retreated in safety, and nothing came of the manœuvres on either side, save some brisk and healthy exercise. England, however, was of the opinion that the war might be carried on with more fervour; Howe was recalled in May, to the unfeigned distress of both officers and soldiers with whom he was equally popular, and Sir Henry Clinton succeeded him in the command.

The famous fête called the Mischianza, of which so many accounts have been written, was designed as a farewell to Howe, and as a testimony of the affection felt for him. The open dissatisfaction expressed by the home government for the languor and negligence of his campaign merely stimulated his staff to more extravagant expressions of their love and loyalty. Twenty-two field-officers planned an entertainment which in beauty, novelty and costliness surpassed all

balls and banquets that Philadelphia had ever known
in her hundred years of existence.   It comprised a
regatta, a tournament, and a dance; and no pains were
spared to make it as splendid as colonial resources
would permit.   Walnut Grove, the country-seat of
Thomas Wharton, was selected as a desirable site; and
the gay company who met at Knight's Wharf between

WALNUT GROVE

three and four o'clock on the afternoon of the eighteenth
of May were carried in decorated barges to the land-
ing-place at Old Fort, whence they were escorted by
troops to the wide lawn on which the tournament was
held.   The English fleet lying at anchor with stream-
ing colours, and the thousands of spectators who
crowded the wharfs and transport ships, lent picturesqueness and brilliancy to the scene.   On the lawn,
suitable pavilions had been erected for the ladies,

twenty-one of whom were dressed in Turkish costumes, designed by the indefatigable André, and presenting a delightful mixture of the Oriental and the Parisian. André was wont to declare that the Mischianza had made of him a most capable milliner; and he wrote blithely to Miss Shippen, offering his valuable services, and confessing himself ready to enter "into the whole details of cap-wire, needles, and gauze."

The tournament was the remarkable feature of the entertainment. The Knights of the Blended Rose and the Knights of the Burning Mountain — it all sounds horribly Masonic to our dull nineteenth century ears — defied each other to mortal combat, shivered their lances in orthodox fashion, fired their pistols, — a sad anachronism, — and engaged valorously with their swords, until the Marshal of the Field ordered them, in the name of the ladies, to desist. The company then passed under triumphal arches, and between files of soldiers, into a spacious hall, where the Knights received their favours at the hands of the Turkish damsels, and refreshed themselves with lemonade and other cooling drinks. After this the doors of the ball-room were thrown open, revealing a charming apartment decorated in pale blue and gold, with hanging garlands of roses, painted by André and De Lancey, and with eighty-five mirrors on the wall, reflecting the beauty of the scene. The Knights and their Turkish ladies opened the ball, which began early, after the primi-

tive fashion of our ancestors, and was interrupted at ten
o'clock by a magnificent display of fireworks. At midnight, supper was served to the exhausted merrymakers,
who must by that time have been perilously nigh the
brink of starvation. A very fine supper it was, with
four hundred and thirty covers, and fully twelve
hundred dishes. Twenty-four black slaves in Oriental
costumes, with silver collars and bracelets, waited on
the guests. The walls of the banqueting room were
also gayly painted and hung with mirrors, while more
than a thousand wax tapers shed their soft brilliance
over scarlet uniforms and silken gowns. At the conclusion of the feast, a herald, gorgeously attired and preceded by trumpeters, proclaimed a number of toasts,
— the King, the Queen, the Army, the Navy, the
Commanders, the Knights and Ladies, — after which
ceremony all returned to the ball-room, and danced
indefatigably until four o'clock.

Thus the Mischianza lasted, from beginning to end,
fully twelve hours, and reflected credit on the magnificent endurance of the English army and of our American women. "It was the most splendid entertainment
ever given by soldiers to their General," writes André,
contentedly; and it was certainly one of the longest
entertainments ever given in modern times to anybody. Six days later, Howe sailed for England, amid
the lamentations of his officers, and to the unfeigned
regret of the rank and file who loved him better than

any other commander in the field. Even the phleg-
matic Hessians felt for him something akin to affection; and General Knyphausen broke down in the
middle of a farewell address, and forgot in his honest
dejection all the complimentary speeches he had meant
to utter.

With the Mischianza, Philadelphia's season of reckless levity came to an abrupt termination. Surely
the gay Tory dames, the fair Shippens and Chews, the
vivacious Miss Franks who, with the far handsomer
Miss Auchmuty, had been crowned Queen of Beauty
at the tournament, and many another pleasure-loving
maid must have felt the grey dawn strike chillingly to
their hearts, as they wended their way homeward, and
thought of the changes to 'come. For already there
was an ominous stir in the camp at Valley Forge,
where the sharp lessons of suffering and experience
had made of undisciplined and often cowardly militia,
soldiers worth leading to the field. That very night,
while Philadelphia's daughters were dancing in the
rose-garlanded ball-room, McLane with a few troopers
and four squads of infantry had sharply attacked the
redoubts, firing the abatis which adjoined them. But
while the English officers danced, or gambled at the
faro tables which the Mischianza had liberally provided, the English soldiers kept watchful guard. Surprise was impossible, and the bold assailants were so
swiftly repelled that the breathless girls, who paused

with startled eyes to listen to the thunder of the guns, were not even permitted to hear the disquieting news. It was a salute, their partners said, a salute to honour them; and with light laughter at their easily awakened fears, they turned joyously back to the dance.

It is a painful truth that not Tory ladies alone graced the Mischianza by their presence. The wives and daughters of many incorruptible Whigs found the temptation too great to be resisted, and their offence was hardly of so heinous a nature as to merit the severe strictures passed upon it. A ball is always a ball, no matter by whom it may be given; but when to a ball is added the startling novelty of a tournament, with Knights of the Blended Rose, and Turkish maidens carrying favours in their turbans, what wonder that curiosity and desire grew too strong to be controlled by the abstract spirit of patriotism! General Wayne, who could never bring himself to forgive the light-heartedness of women, wrote crossly and sarcastically anent their misbehaviour in coquetting with "the heavenly, sweet, pretty redcoats," adding, in the true tone of "Parent's Assistant": —

"The Knights of the Blended Roses and of the Burning Mount have resigned their laurels to Rebel officers, who will lay them at the feet of *those* virtuous daughters of America who cheerfully gave up ease and affluence in a city for liberty and peace of mind in a cottage."

Alas! and alas! outside the covers of Miss Edge-

worth's admirable tales, rewards and punishments are
not meted out with this scrupulous fidelity to deserts.
When the Americans regained possession of the Quaker City, and began to give balls in their turn, they laid
their laurels — not yet imposing wreaths — somewhat in-
discriminately at the feet of pretty Whigs and Tories;
and the fair Vicaresses of Bray, who had danced all
night at the Mischianza, showed the same irresistible
vivacity when Arnold opened his doors for an entertainment which rivalled in beauty and extravagance
the gay routs of the redcoat winter. Miss Franks,
indeed, found the change a melancholy one, though
there were not wanting American officers ready and
willing to fill the place of her English suitors. Her
exasperating wit was more piquant than gentle loyalty,
and the warmth of her impetuous heart won forgive-
ness for spirited sallies at which everybody laughed,
and for satiric verses at which nobody could have
laughed, — they were so exceedingly bad. New York
opened for her fresh scenes of gayety and dissipation
until she married a young English officer, Colonel
Johnson of the Seventeenth Regiment, and sailed for
England, never to return. Her husband served with
distinction in many campaigns, succeeded to a good
estate, and was made a baronet; yet Lady Johnson,
with the half tender, half whimsical perverseness of
so many clever women, cherished in old age a regret-
ful affection for the country she had abandoned, and

for the cause her foolish girlhood had scorned. "Would that I, too, had been a patriot," she said gently to General Winfield Scott, when he visited her many years afterwards at Bath. "I have gloried in my rebel countrymen."

Sir Henry Clinton, now in command of the English forces, was eager to take the field; but found it no easy matter to leave Philadelphia while Washington held himself ever in readiness to swoop down on the departing army, which was terribly hampered by the number of citizens who wished to go to New York under its protection, and, what was still more inconvenient, wished to carry their worldly possessions along with them. Three thousand prominent Tories had arranged, indeed, to sail with Admiral Howe's fleet. They dared not remain in the town after the protection of the troops had been withdrawn; so, with heavy hearts, they bade farewell to their birthplace, which few of them were destined to see again, and on the seventeenth of June, "the finest and the saddest night I ever knew," wrote one reluctant exile, they beheld for the last time the old familiar landmarks fade slowly in the deepening gloom. By far the greater number of the loyalists, however, placed themselves under the care of the army; and Clinton, having completed his preparations with the utmost secrecy, and disposed as best he could his wagons, artillery and stores, withdrew his forces so swiftly and so

silently during the night that followed the departure
of the fleet, that none knew his purpose until the early
morning showed the city streets silent and deserted.
"The English did not go away," it was said, "they vanished"; and Miss Wister records in her diary the astonishment that was felt at Gwynedd when the unexpected
news reached them. The word flew fast and far over
the country-side, and a few hours after Clinton's rear-
guard had left Gloucester Point, a regiment of American dragoons galloped past the quiet State House
yard. The fortunes of Philadelphia had reached
another turning-point; a new, and not altogether a
joyful life, awaited her.

It was one thing, however, for the Englishmen to
slip off on their perilous march, and quite another
for them to continue it in safety. Washington was
on their track: his forces outnumbered theirs, and
he was not impeded by a vast quantity of stores and
luggage. Whether it was pride, or kindness, or sheer
obstinacy that made Clinton hold fast to the manifold possessions of the flying Tories, would be hard
to say. At one moment he resolved to make a bonfire of all their encumbering wagons, and, at the next,
determined to keep his word, and guard them to the
end. An action was inevitable, and on the twenty-
eighth of June was fought the often discussed and indecisive battle of Monmouth. The heat was terrible,
— that sudden, ruthless, mortal heat which nature holds

in capricious reserve, and which is her chosen weapon when it pleases her to play a part in the futile struggles of men. Soldiers fell dead in their ranks without a wound. The Hessians roundly swore they could not and would not fight under such a pitiless sun. What the issue of the combat might have been, had General Charles Lee not retreated too soon over the dangerous morasses, and had Washington not advanced too soon to attack the only partially entangled enemy, is a point which still interests the student of military tactics. Ordinary readers are content to know that the action was without results, and that the lively satisfaction expressed on both sides probably meant that both sides were equally discontented. The Americans solaced themselves by court-martialling and disgracing General Lee. The English enjoyed the proud consciousness of having saved every wagon-load of stores, at the sacrifice of many lives. Sir Henry Clinton pursued his way to New York without further molestation, and Washington, turning back, took possession of Philadelphia.

CHAPTER XIV

LORDS OF MISRULE

A CITY which has been for nine months in the hands of a foreign enemy is always a pitiable sight. Armies are demoralizing things, and it is only after they have taken their departure that the full extent of the mischief they have wrought becomes apparent to every eye. Sober thrift and quiet rectitude have well-nigh vanished. The industrious artisan has become a midnight brawler; the once decent young housewife walks the streets, an outcast, with her bastard baby in her arms. Restlessness and discontent are in the very air, and the old, dull, decorous life has become distasteful, alike to men and women. Poor Philadelphia, bruised, and sore, and shaken, needed a firm and kindly rule to bring her back to health; but having suffered sadly from her foes, she found herself, on the return of friends, to be in a far worse case than ever. It is true there were not wanting men who, like Morris, and Wilson, and Dr. Rush, strove hard to stem the tide of violence, and to save their city from an ignoble reign of terror, which had not even the saving grace of mistaken

237

enthusiasm. But loud-voiced demagogues held the
public ear; and the mob, so long repressed by the
presence of an unsympathetic soldiery, was once more
happy and alert. There was a fierce demand for
vengeance upon Tories, and the selection of a few
victims to appease the people became a matter of
immediate necessity. The men picked out for this
purpose were well chosen, being too poor and humble
to have troublesome friends, yet not so absolutely
insignificant as to make their execution a matter of
no moment to anybody. They were both Quakers, a
happy stroke of diplomacy, and both were charged
with the same offence. Carlisle, a carpenter, had
kept one of the city gates during the English occupancy; and Roberts, a miller, though no such important post was ever assigned him, had enlisted under
General Howe's command, and would have been wiser
had he departed with the rest of the troops.

These two carefully selected malefactors were tried
in the criminal court for high treason, and condemned
to death. The jury that brought in the verdict of
guilty recommended them to mercy, and petitions for
their pardon were signed by many hundreds of citizens, including prominent Whigs. But the mob, like
the Minotaur, demanded its dole, and on the fourth
of November, Elizabeth Drinker writes sadly in her
diary : —

"They have actually put to death, Hang'd on ye

Commons, John Roberts and Abraham Carlisle, this morning. An awful day it has been."

General Arnold was placed by Washington in command of Philadelphia, and at once began that life of

MT. PLEASANT: ARNOLD'S HOME

costly and formal elegance which gave universal dissatisfaction, and to supply the money for which he plunged deeper and deeper into speculations. It is not always an easy matter to content civilians, who have ever been wont to complain loudly of the wantonness of soldiers; and we find the irascible Chris-

topher Marshall inveighing with much bitterness
against the officers of Washington's staff: "Careless
of us, but carefully consulting where they shall go to
spend the winter in jollity, gaming, and carousing;"
a reproach to which the wind-swept hills of Valley
Forge could have made answer true. Arnold's unpopularity, however, was a serious matter. In social
life he had many friends, and his marriage with Miss
Margaret Shippen allied him closely to the most
prominent families in Philadelphia; but the people in
general — not the rabble, but the respectable portion
of the community — were deeply angered by his
pride, and regarded his suddenly acquired wealth
with equal envy and mistrust. Joseph Reed, the
president of the Executive Council and the acknowledged leader of the Constitutionalists, was his
avowed enemy; and the quarrels between these two
opposing powers relieved Philadelphia of any oppressive dulness during the autumn and early winter
of 1779. Reed accused Arnold of gross venality;
Arnold accused Reed of inciting riots, and laid upon
his shoulders — unjustly — the blame for the shameful inertness which permitted a mob of only two
hundred men to destroy what property it pleased on
the fourth of October, and to shoot Captain Campbell at the window of his own house.

In truth, it was a time of reckless agitation, and
the spirit of revolt against all authority, public or

private, was rapidly undermining common safety and
domestic restraint. Elizabeth Drinker writes on one
page of her journal: "Our great men, or ye men in
Power, are quarrelling very much among themselves;"
and on the next, with a ludicrous appreciation of
her own personal discomfort in this fine, strange atmosphere of freedom: "Our new maid had a visitor
all day, and has invited her to lodge with her, without asking leave. Times are much changed, and
Maids have become Mistresses."

We hear a great deal during the next few years, both
in letters and journals, about the vexatious behaviour
of servants. Marshall grows eloquent on the subject,
and confesses that his wife has been made ill more
than once by sheer anxiety for a little lass who
has been bound to them, and who persists, notwithstanding many exhortations and corrections, in stay-
ing out all night. The streets of Philadelphia, once
so quiet and secure, were no longer safe for any
woman after the twilight hour. The country roads,
once peaceful as those of Arcady, were now infested
by prowling soldiers, deserters, and highwaymen.
The history of the Doans, five robber brothers,
"strong, handsome, generous, and humane,"—if we
may trust contemporary records,—affords a pleasing
illustration of the time. These famous and very
popular outlaws were Tory sympathizers who, in the
beginning of the war, hoped to preserve a strict neu-

R

trality; but who found themselves soon objects of
suspicion and attack. They were heavily fined for
non-attendance on militia duty, their stock was sold,
their farm was confiscated. They then resolved to
follow the memorable examples of Dick Turpin and
Claude Duval, and, taking the road, became a terror
to the whole country-side. Like their models, they
were capriciously generous, giving freely to the poor
what they stole from the rich; and the small farmers
of the neighbourhood, whose political principles were
of the vaguest order, had no fault to find with men
who never took so much as a turnip from their fields,
and who often assisted them in the profitable but perilous business of supplying food to the hungry English soldiers. Women, with their customary disregard
for dull integrity, looked upon the five brothers as
heroes of romance; and children, listening eagerly to
tales of their intrepid exploits, resolved to be highwaymen themselves as soon as ever they were grown.
"The Doans," we are told, "delighted to injure public property, but did no harm to the weak, the poor,
or the peaceful."

Even public property, however, deserves some sort
of protection, and even the rich weary in time of being
despoiled. When the depredations of these spirited outlaws became too heavy for endurance, a strong body of
militia was sent to assist the sheriff in tracking them
down. They were hunted day and night, were finally

brought to bay, and made a most desperate resistance. Two were shot dead by the soldiers, one escaped, and two were brought prisoners to Philadelphia, and hanged without delay. In the city they excited profound sympathy. "Many temperate people," says their historian, "expressed great commiseration for them"; and the memory of their courage and their kindness surviving the memory of their misdeeds, they grew in time to be considered as upholders of a lost cause, rather than criminals brought to justice, and expiating their offences against society upon the gallows-tree.

None of this sentimental regard was evinced for another class of law-breakers, whose transgressions were of the mildest order, and who sinned against the community, only that they might obey the troublesome dictates of their consciences. The Quakers could not and would not serve in the militia. Strict members of the Society held it unlawful to offer an armed resistance to any authority, however tyrannous and oppressive. This subjected them to heavy fines, which, unhappily, they thought it, not only inconvenient, but wrong, to pay. Certain taxes levied for military purposes were also regarded by them as iniquitous, and they opposed to all such measures their old weapon of passive, impregnable obstinacy. In colonial days, wise men like Benjamin Franklin had known how to circumvent these ill-timed scruples; and the Quakers had not always been averse to the diplomacy which wrested from them measures they could not openly concede, and saved them from a dangerous rupture with conflicting powers. But the men now holding authority were in no humour for dallying with the disaffected, or making allowances for perverse conscientiousness. The Friends, moreover, were exceedingly unpopular with the mob, which was sure to applaud any severe measures passed against them. Already many prominent members of the Society had suffered banishment and confiscation. Those who remained were liable at any time to have their houses searched for English goods, or their furniture dragged away to be sold for an unpaid fine. The entries in Elizabeth Drinker's diary show her to have lost in this manner so many of her household chattels, that the reader wonders she had pot or pan, chair or table, left in her pillaged home. There is something irresistibly pathetic in the sight of any woman despoiled of those belongings to which she clings with an affection man seldom understands; and our sympathy for this Quaker housewife is all the keener because she utters no word of complaint, but states as briefly as possible, and without comment, the losses she suffers day by day.

On the fourteenth of June, 1779, she writes : " George Pickering came this afternoon for ye Non-association fine, which came to thirteen pounds, which is thirteen shillings, as ye money now is exchanged twenty to one. He took a Looking-glass worth between forty and fifty shillings, six newfashioned Pewter plates, and a three quart Pewter Bason, little or nothing the worse for ye wear."

Again, in the early autumn, she makes a similar entry: "This morning, in meeting time, (myself at home) Jacob Franks and a son of Cling, ye Vendue Master, came to seize for ye Continental Tax. They took from us one Walnut Dining-Table, one Mahogany Tea-Table, six handsome Walnut Chairs with open backs, crow feet, a shell on ye back and on each knee," — how lovingly minute this description! — "a Mahogany-framed Sconce Looking-glass, and two large Pewter Dishes. They carried them off in a cart from ye door to Cling's."

Poor mistress of an empty house who watched her well-kept chairs dragged off in this ignominious way to public execution, and whose grief at losing them was heightened by the knowledge that the miserable sums for which they were to be sold bore no proportion to their value! There is real bitterness — though still no open outcry — in the brief note of May 1, 1780: "Jeremiah Baker took a Mahogany folding Card-Table from us this morning, for a Northern Liberty Tax amounting to about eighteen shillings. Ye Table was worth between three and four pounds."

How very much easier and more agreeable to have paid the eighteen shillings, we cannot help thinking; but there is no tyrant so oppressive.as an inexorable conscience, and it is plain that this alternative never even presented itself to the minds of the unfortunate Quakers, despoiled by the strong hand of the law.

All this time, the depreciation of the currency, the scarcity of provisions, the alarmingly high prices demanded for the bare necessities of life, and the growing unwillingness of merchants to sell at any price,

WOODFORD HOUSE

were fast bringing Philadelphia to a condition of absolute distress. The angry Constitutionalists clung to the notion that the remedy for these evils lay in stringent legislation, and they resolved to bully the State back into its old prosperity. It was not possible, indeed, for the Committee of Inspection to make butter, sorely though the butter was needed; but it *was* possible to pass a law, forbidding any man to pay

more than fifteen shillings a pound for it. Neither
could the members of the Committee grow wheat,
though the poor cried out for bread; but they could
devise another law, forbidding farmers and traders to
sell their grain privately, or to ask its full value in
the open markets.   Nothing is easier than this kind
of legislation, and nothing more purely inefficacious. —
"There shall be in England seven half-penny loaves
sold for a penny; the three-hooped pot shall have ten
hoops; and I will make it felony to drink small beer."
Rather than part with goods at a loss, the merchants
closed their shops, the importers concealed their stores,
the farmers brought no more provisions for the hungry
townsfolk to eat.

Congress, meanwhile, was helping liberally to lead
the country to financial dishonour and ruin by repeated issues of worthless paper, — five millions one
month, ten millions another, twenty millions the next,
until the currency became so absolutely valueless as
to pass into a familiar proverb, — "not worth a Continental."   By the close of the war, four hundred
dollars of American money would not bring four
English shillings; but as early as 1780, a man might
come perilously nigh starvation while his pockets were
lined with notes.   "I have more money than ever I
had, but I am poorer than ever I was," complained a
writer in Dunlap's *Packet;* and his state was the state
of all.   An apprentice lad named Leyham, having

served two months in the militia, received two hundred dollars for his pay. He bought a pair of shoes for one hundred dollars, invested another hundred in a sleigh-ride, and went empty-handed home. A Philadelphia barber of a humorous turn of mind papered the walls of his shop with the depreciated currency, to the huge delight of his customers. At the sale of Cornelius Land's household effects, a frying-pan brought one hundred and twenty-five dollars; a wood-saw, one hundred and eighty-five dollars; three steel forks, one hundred and twelve dollars, and an old clock, eleven hundred dollars. Silk sold in the Philadelphia shops at one hundred dollars a yard, tea at sixty dollars a pound. A bill of Colonel Allen's has come down to us from this happy period, and illustrates the formidable cost of articles which could never have been considered luxuries.

"1 Pair Boots	$600.00
6¾ yds. Calico, at $85 per Yard . .	752.00
6 yds. Chintz, at $150 do. . . .	900.00
4½ yds. Moreen, at $100 do. . . .	450.00
4 Handkerchiefs, at $100 each . . .	400.00
8 yds. Quality Binding, at $4 per Yard .	32.00
1 Skein Silk	10.00
	$3,144.00

"Jan. 5th, 1781."

Quite a little fortune for such a modest account. How many thousands of dollars must a woman have crowded into her purse, when she went forth to do a morning's shopping!

It seems incredible that men could be found willing
to play their parts in this financial farce, and to thrust
the dismal diversion upon others. But in the spring of
1781 a new issue of paper currency was ordered, and,
at the same time, stringent laws were passed to compel
the people to receive it. Any one who expressed a
preference for real money, when this make-believe
money was offered to him, should be taught by heavy
fines the wickedness of such unpatriotic discrimination.
A small minority of Anti-Constitutionalists, led by
Robert Morris and Thomas Mifflin, did, indeed, oppose
the measure with all their strength; and, knowing too
well such opposition was in vain, Morris prepared and
offered to the Assembly a protest, in which he expressed
in no unfaltering terms the contempt of a sane and
honourable man for such wanton destruction of the
public credit. The time was soon to come when the
finances of the country were to be in his capable
hands; but, even in the present chaotic confusion,
he laboured hard to bring about some semblance of
law and order. The Bank of Pennsylvania, which
was founded solely in the interest of Washington's
army, was due largely to his ability and munificence.
Without its help, the ragged and hungry troops
must have either disbanded or starved in their
quarters. The Bank of North America, chartered by
Congress as well as by the Assembly, was organized
upon his plans, and controlled by his policy. In the

days of our deepest humiliation it restored credit, quickened commerce, supplied some measure of integrity, and saved us from financial ruin. Its history, however, belongs to a later period, when foreign foes had yielded their place to domestic enemies, less easily reckoned with, and far less easily subdued.

In January, 1779, Congress celebrated with a great civic banquet the long desired and long delayed alliance with France. It had been no easy task for Franklin to cement this alliance, and to make of sentimental friendship a firm national bond. The French, indeed, had received him with effusive delight. He was the idol of the hour. His house at Passy was the resort of statesmen, scientists, and scholars. If he appeared in the streets, the mob shouted itself hoarse in his honour; when he went to court, fair ladies dropped wreaths upon his head, which must have been inex-

STAIRWAY IN STATE HOUSE

pressibly embarrassing. Wits praised his conversation, dandies, his dress, and poets dedicated to him verses that were fully as bad as his own. His benignant features were painted over and over again, and his portraits set in lockets, rings, and snuff-boxes. Learned Academicians shed tears of joy on seeing him embraced by Voltaire. The enthusiasm he aroused extended itself to the country he represented; and the cause of the colonists was pronounced to be the cause of justice, liberty, and humanity. Yet none the less, France hesitated long ere she sent her aid to these admirable patriots, the success of whose arms seemed then more than doubtful; and French capitalists prudently declined to lend a single franc to men whose courage and principles they ardently admired, but whose financiering was open to objections. From the universal admiration for all things pertaining to America, the American currency was most unkindly omitted.

It cannot be denied that the allurements of a brilliant society, and the still more congenial companionship of learned men, beguiled Franklin into an occasional neglect of his mission. He wrote some excellent pamphlets which few people read, and which convinced nobody; and he assured his friends at home that nothing but their own success would persuade France to become their ally. This was true. Burgoyne's surrender at Saratoga did more service than a year's hard talking. For the first time,

French strategists thought it worth while to lend aid to the colonies, in the hope of injuring Great Britain. The treaty which recognized the independence of the United States was signed February sixth, 1778; the following month, Franklin was formally received at court as an American commissioner; and, on the thirteenth of April, D'Estaing sailed with his fleet from Toulon.

The arrival in France of that clear-headed man of affairs, John Adams, brought order out of chaos, and gave a less sentimental basis to the friendship between the two nations. Franklin was appointed our minister; and, while Adams toiled like a clerk in the commissioner's office, the philosopher played chess with Mme. Brillon, or wrote his famous "Bagatelles" for the amusement of that vivacious slattern, Mme. Helvetius. He was now over seventy, and had merited a few years of trifling by a lifetime of arduous and useful labour. Leisure he enjoyed, as well as the lively and affectionate society of women. The enthusiasm manifested by France for himself, and for his work, awakened in his heart corresponding sentiments of cordiality; and he had no fault to find with this Arcadian and misrepresented nation, save that it took too much snuff, and wore too much powder on its hair, — offences so venial they could hardly have merited a revolution for their Nemesis. At times, amid the pleasures and honours of his official life, he sighed for his old home, and begged to be recalled; but his popularity was so great, and his name carried with it such weight and influence in diplomatic circles, that it was not deemed expedient to permit his return until 1785, when Thomas Jefferson was sent to fill his place.

The alliance with France infused fresh hope and courage into the hearts of the despondent Americans. On the twenty-fifth of August, 1780, the Chevalier de Luzerne gave a grand entertainment to the members of Congress and other prominent citizens, in honour of the French King's birthday. Our enthusiasm for our allies was mounting fast to fever heat, and, indeed, the country sorely needed any emotion which could enliven or sustain it. Confidence was lost. Our troops, ill-fed, ill-clad, unpaid, were sullen and mutinous, held in their ranks with difficulty, notwithstanding the brutal punishments inflicted on deserters, and accustomed to revenge their own hardships upon the farmers and country people whom they plundered without mercy. The feeble resources of the revenue had been taxed to the utmost. Political leaders, impotent for good, were quarrelling fiercely among themselves, and Philadelphia was the chosen arena for their disgraceful strife. "It is obvious," wrote Reed to Washington, "that the bulk of the people are weary of the war"; and Washington sadly confessed in return that never before had he seen the discontent so general and so alarming. The French officers were angry and aghast at the forlorn condition of our affairs, which seemed hopeless to men who could not understand what splendours of endurance and action still lay behind that "slough of Despond." "Send us ships, troops, and money," wrote Rochambeau to Vergennes; "but do not depend upon these people, nor upon their means."

When the skies were darkest, and brave hearts were heaviest, came the news of Arnold's proposed treachery, casting a taint of dishonour upon the whole country, and adding a burden of bitter humiliation to the accumulated disasters of the war. The plot, indeed, was discovered, West Point was saved, and André died a shameful death on the bleak hillside of Tappan.

> "He was not slain with the sword,
> Knight's axe, or the knightly spear;"

and the tragic sharpness of his fate has made imperishable the name of the blithe young soldier whose race was so swiftly run. He is truly the world's conqueror whose name the world holds dear. Not years of honourable work, well done and amply rewarded, win this capricious and undying regard; but rather the sudden snatching away of life full to the brim of gladness, and gay courage, and the promise of noble things. André's remains were carried over the sea in 1821, and interred in the south aisle of

Westminster Abbey, where sleep the best and bravest of England's soldier sons. The inscription on his monument states simply that he was beloved by his fellow officers, and that he died for his country and his King.

In Philadelphia, where Arnold was so well known, and where the proudest and happiest period of his life had been passed, the news of his treason awakened a fierce but easily allayed excitement. His estate was immediately confiscated, and everything that belonged to him was publicly sold. His wife entreated permission to remain under her father, Mr. Edward Shippen's, protection; but this grace was denied her, and she received orders from the Executive Council to leave Pennsylvania within two weeks. She joined her husband in New York, and subsequently went with him to London, where Sir Banastre Tarleton was wont to declare her the handsomest woman in Great Britain. The Philadelphia mob solaced itself by hanging Arnold in effigy, and expended much wit in devising a figure with two faces, which held a mask in its hand, and represented the traitor. This puppet was dragged in a cart through the streets, accompanied by a picturesque and, it was hoped, accurate facsimile of the devil, and preceded by a band of music making all the noise it could. The populace was so well amused by the procession, and by the hanging and burning of the effigy, that it neglected its usual pastimes. No

Tories were stoned, no doors nor windows broken, no property of any kind destroyed, though many citizens, as guiltless as the puppet, passed anxious hours before the peaceful rising of the sun.

In September, 1781, the French troops under Count Rochambeau passed through Philadelphia on their way south, where the repeated successes of the American arms had given a new aspect to the war, and filled despondent hearts with hope. The splendid appearance of these foreign allies, their martial bearing, their debonair gayety and good-humour won universal admiration. The regiment De Soissonnais especially, in its picturesque uniform with rose-coloured facings and white and rose-coloured plumes, lent a most welcome air of brightness and well-being to our forlorn, threadbare army, which had never been fine, and which was now pathetically shabby. The Frenchmen were reviewed by Chief Justice McKean, who wore on this occasion a brave suit of black velvet which must have cost at least five thousand dollars of Continental currency. General Washington, Count Rochambeau, and M. de Luzerne were present; and the universal satisfaction was vastly increased when it was made known that four hundred thousand crowns had come over from France, and that there was once more a prospect of our own troops wearing — not rose-coloured plumes, but sound shoes and decent breeches. So great was the public joy over this brighter outlook, that the mob in buoyant mood surrounded the residence of M. de Luzerne, and kept him awake all night by shouting lustily for King Louis XVI.

Before the allied armies left for the south, news of a still more important character was brought to cheer them on their way. The French fleet under the command of Count de Grasse had crossed the seas in safety, and lay awaiting further orders in the Chesapeake. It was this fleet which, closing in on the Virginia coast, cut off from the English army all chance of escape by water, and compelled Lord Cornwallis to surrender to General Washington at Yorktown, October 19, 1781. On the twenty-third of October, two hours before sunrise, the word was carried by an express rider into sleepy Philadelphia; and a German watchman, who was the first to hear the news, proceeded tranquilly on his rounds, announcing at intervals to such as lay awake to listen: "Past three o'clock, and Lord Cornwallis is taken."

s

CHAPTER XV

THE surrender at Yorktown practically closed the war, although the treaty of peace was not signed until two years later. A burden was lifted from the hearts of men, and every colony joined in the universal thanksgiving. Philadelphia expressed her lively satisfaction after her time-honoured methods; rang her bells with joyful ardour, fired salutes all day long, and sent off countless rockets at night. Weary of war and of politics, she longed to be a little gay and cheerful once again, albeit the State House walls still echoed the wrangling of her leaders. The Southwark Theatre, which had been closed since the English occupation, was opened with cautious courage under the euphonious title of "Academy of Polite Science," as the word theatre still stuck in the throats of the godly; and the first representation was given in honour of General Washington after his return from Virginia. Beaumarchais' "Eugénie" was the play, with "The Lying Valet" for an afterpiece; and there was moreover a fine patriotic prologue, designed to soften the hearts of the Presbyterians, and a grand transparency symbolizing the union of the States, to please all the distinguished officers who were present.

In point of fact, no one was more grateful for a little timely diversion than Washington, for on his shoulders had fallen burdens too heavy to be carried, and anxieties too keen to be endured. Relaxation of some kind was a supreme necessity; and he had, in addition, that love

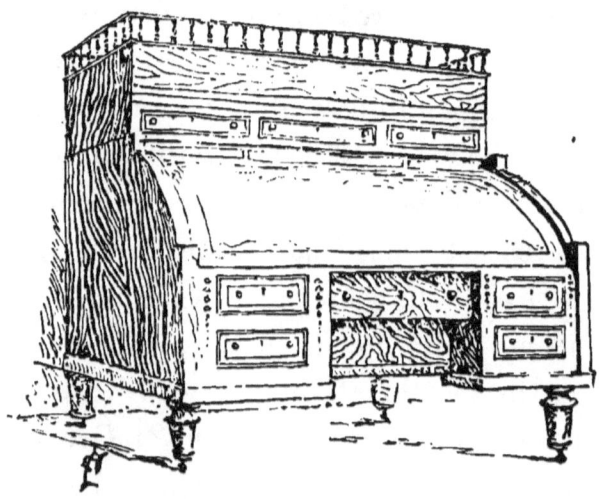

WASHINGTON'S DESK

of pleasure which was inherent in every Virginia gentleman. It was not the theatre alone which delighted him. but the circus, and every other show, including balloon ascensions, which were perhaps his supreme favourites, and cock-fights, which he relished as unblushingly as Christopher North. The minute record he kept of his expenses enables us to know how ardently he tried to amuse himself, and how little the country afforded in the way of entertainment. He gave nine shillings to a man "who brought an elk to exhibit"; and he went with impartial avidity to see an automaton, a dancing bear, a puppet show, waxworks, and a tiny menagerie, which consisted exclusively of a tiger and a lioness. He had a passion for lotteries and raffles, in both of which he was distinctly unlucky all his life. The money he invested in lottery tickets brought him in scant return, and he never drew one of the alluring things for which he purchased a chance. Whether it were a necklace, a coach, a watch, or a gun, he met with the same unfailing disappointment. "By profit and loss, in two chances in raffling for Encyclopædia Britannica, which I did not win, £1/4,"—is a characteristic entry in his account book.

On the thirteenth of May, 1781, M. de Luzerne formally announced to Congress the birth of the Dauphin of France, a child who escaped by an early death the bitter fate of his younger brother, the boy martyr of the Temple, the most pathetic figure in history's blood-stained page. A letter from the King was presented and read on this occasion, and much public interest was manifested. Indeed, our affection for our allies had by this time reached its height, and the little prince was the object of an enthusiasm as keen and as transient as if we had been his hereditary subjects. The general satisfaction was quickened into delight when, on the fifteenth of July, M. de Luzerne gave his celebrated *fête du Dauphin*, the most costly and beautiful entertainment Philadelphia had witnessed since the Mischianza. Fifteen hundred guests were invited, who arrived promptly at half-past seven. The gardens surrounding the minister's house were brilliantly illuminated, and a hall or pavilion, open to the air, was erected for the dancers. The contemporary descriptions of this garden and this hall sound like Aladdin's palace. It is difficult to read the glowing paragraphs, and imagine arches, colonnades, leafy bowers, glittering domes, and deep romantic groves as parts of the old Carpenter Mansion at Sixth and Chestnut Streets.

The interior of the dancing-hall, which had been built by a French architect in less than six weeks, was elaborately ornamented, and lit by hundreds of tapers. Four statues stood within four niches: Diana hurling her spear, Flora garlanded with roses, Hebe holding Jove's cup, and Mars leaning on his shield, upon which was appropriately engraved the cipher of General Washington. The entertainment, as generous as the Mischianza, began with a concert, after which came a display of fireworks, "of superior and unrivalled excellence." The ball was then formally opened, and at one o'clock supper was served. Thirty army cooks were engaged to prepare this supper, and, as they were French army cooks, it was probably good. The heat was oppressive, and although we are assured that "joy did not cease to sparkle in every eye." it is

evident that it sparkled languidly, and that even the
youngest and gayest of the guests felt dancing to be
a diversion ill-suited for such a tropical night.

Philadelphia was, indeed, singularly unfortunate in
having all her anniversaries and grand celebrations in
midsummer. George III. had been born, reasonably
enough, on the fourth of June; and in the old loyal
days it had required no great endurance to eat noon-
tide dinners in his honour on the Schuylkill's pleasant banks. But the French King's birthday, which
was now kept with amazing fervour, and made the
occasion of yearly banquets and rejoicings, came most
inopportunely on the twenty-third of August. Our
own national holiday left nothing to be desired in the
way of burning heat; and a ball on the fifteenth of
July must have been but a doubtful pleasure. Perhaps the people who enjoyed it most were the unbid-
den guests; for M. de Luzerne, mindful of the charms
of publicity as exemplified in the French court, had
thrown down the brick walls which encircled his
garden, so that the populace could enjoy the brilliant
scene, and some ten thousand spectators availed themselves cheerfully of the privilege. General Washington, Count Rochambeau, the Marquis de Chastellux,
Robert Morris, Dickinson, Mifflin, and a host of other
distinguished men were there to be stared at; while
an Indian chief or two lent variety and picturesqueness to the scene. A most unique feature of the

entertainment was an apartment fitted up by the thoughtful host for the reception of those Quaker ladies whose principles would not permit them to join in the gayety; but who watched the dancers through a gauze curtain, — themselves unseen, — just as the Moslem women of Cairo look down through the latticed screens of their opera boxes upon the singers on the stage, or, it may be, upon their husbands sitting with fair-haired English girls, at whose feet lie all the forbidden pleasures of the world.

The treaty of peace concluded in Paris was finally signed at Versailles. on the third of September, 1783; Franklin, John Adams, and John Jay acting as our representatives. The independence of the States, of such, at least, as lay between the Atlantic coast and the Mississippi River, was recognized by England; the English troops sailed from New York on the twenty-fifth of November, and General Washington, resigning his commission, went blithely to spend his Christmas at Mount Vernon.

Philadelphia had not lacked occupation or excitement during these last months of uncertainty, for to the fierce quarrels of her politicians had been added the riotous behaviour of the soldiers, who fancied themselves imperious legions ready to terrorize a second Rome. The city had borne upon her shoulders the heaviest burdens and responsibilities of the Revolutionary war. As the birthplace of the infant nation, as the centre of interest, and the scene of the most important movements and events, she had been weighted with obligations which she had striven hard to fulfil, though rent with wounds, and shamed by the violence of her sons. Now that peace was assured, she drew a great breath of joyous relief, and prepared to turn her attention to her long neglected industries and commerce. It was necessary also to do justice to the college she had so wantonly injured, to restore the rights of citizenship to many who had been unwarrantably disenfranchised, to satisfy her public creditors, and to reëstablish that sound financial basis which the Continental currency had hopelessly destroyed.

In none of these laudable ambitions was she destined to immediate success. The ancient charter of the college was given back, but vitality and the spirit of scholarship would not return at the Assembly's persuasive call. The rival university still struggled hard for precedence, albeit there were many in her faculty, who, if we may trust the biting sarcasm of Dr. Rush, " knew not whether Cicero plead in Latin or in Greek, or whether Horace was a Roman or a Scotchman." The Whigs still clamoured vehemently against any concessions to the Tories, and succeeded for years in keeping alive a purposeless spirit of hostility. The creditors were left to mourn their unwise liberality; and the fierce attack of the Constitutionalists, under

Reed, upon the Bank of North America, proves that party spirit was still strong enough, and bitter enough, to play havoc with matters of finance. Philadelphia's politicians were in the habit of regarding the charter granted to an institution very much as a mother regards the toy given to a child, — as something to be taken away, placed on a shelf out of reach, and returned again, according to the caprice of the donor, or the amiability of the recipient. This is not a method calculated to produce confidence and security in the public mind; it is difficult to lay strong foundations on the shifting sands of partisanship; and, had the bank not been chartered by Congress as well as by the Assembly, it must inevitably have been destroyed, and the splendid efforts of Robert Morris to remedy the financial weakness of the country would have been, to our lasting shame, frustrated by political animosity.

After Washington, and after Franklin, the man to whom the nation owed its heaviest debt, its deepest gratitude, was Morris. Born in England, and brought as a child to Philadelphia, he made his own way by sheer force of intelligence, without the help of a single outstretched hand. At thirteen, he was sweeping the floors of a counting-house; at thirty, he was a partner in the great mercantile firm of the Willings, and beginning to take an active part in the keen interests and anxieties of public life. Rich, hospitable, popular, with a sound understanding and a complication-proof mind,

he gave to the Continental Congress, during the three
years in which he sat as delegate, such efficient aid that
every emergency added to the burdens that he bore.
His personal credit was vast, his generosity knew no
bounds, his readiness of resource found a way to extri-
cate his allies from every fresh dilemma. He it was
who furnished Washington with artillery and ammunition when the treasury was exhausted. He it was who
borrowed on his own promissory notes over a million of
dollars, with which to buy necessary food and clothing
for the army at the most critical period of the war. He
it was who struggled, almost single-handed, for the
restoration of specie, and the reëstablishment of our
public credit. There is the ring of prophetic wisdom in
his speeches, deploring earnestly as he did the uneasy
fluctuations of a government torn by conflicting interests, and "changing its measures by the breath of
democracy."

When the return of peace gave us leisure to understand our desperate condition; when the Continental
currency had ceased to circulate, and there was no hard
money to take its place; when the public coffers were
empty, and the interest on the public debts unpaid,
—then Congress turned to Morris as the only man
who could be of any help in times so sadly out of
joint. The eminently undesirable post of Superinten-
dent of Finances was offered to him; and, with unflinching courage, he set about the difficult labour of bringing

order out of chaos. Face to face with bankruptcy and ruin, he went steadily to his appointed task, sparing neither himself nor his fortune, begrudging no toil and no sacrifice in his country's cause. The arduous nature of his duties, and the heavy responsibilities they involved, broke down his health in three years, so that he was unable to continue in office; but the work which that great financier, Alexander Hamilton, brought to a successful issue, was begun by Robert Morris and his able assistant, Gouverneur Morris, — founder of our system of national coinage, — when they strove to restore to the States some measure of prosperity and credit.

Pennsylvania recognized the obligation which rested upon her to indemnify the Penns for the loss of their quit-rents, and of the proprietary lands which had been confiscated during the Revolutionary war. It was impossible, or at least it was impracticable, to fully compensate them for such vast estates. Indeed, the modest sum of one hundred and thirty thousand pounds which the Assembly voted for this purpose, did not cover more than a tenth of their forfeiture. But the manors and some property of no great value, which had been settled on the children of the Founder, remained in the possession of his great-grandsons, and the English government granted them annuities amounting to four thousand pounds. Mr. Sydney Fisher tells us that, down to the present day, rents from the most closely populated parts

of Philadelphia go over the sea to the descendants of
William Penn, who have no other connection with, no
other interest in, the city of his heart and hopes.

There is little doubt that after Congress had been
frightened away by the riotous soldiery, taking refuge
in Princeton before migrating to New York, Philadelphia returned in some measure to her old sobriety and
decorum. It is true that the spirit of reckless speculation still ran wild, and that many of her citizens had
not yet exhausted the delights of living beyond their
means. General Lee, as we know, described her as a
place of amusement and debauch, by which he probably
had in mind the poor little " Academy of Polite Science,"
with its " moral dialogues," and transparencies. " No
other city," says Mr. MacMaster, " was so rich, so extravagant, so fashionable." On the other hand, it is plain
that foreigners thought her amazingly discreet, and
sometimes just a trifle dull. The Chevalier de Beau-
jour, for example, found little to amuse him in her
boasted gayety, little to please him in her boasted
charms. " Philadelphia," he wrote, " is cut, like a chess-
board, at right angles. All the streets and houses resemble each other, and nothing is so gloomy as this
uniformity, unless it be the sadness of the inhabitants,
the greater part of whom are of Quaker or Puritan
descent."

Brissot de Warville, who came over the seas — like
so many modern French journalists — with the avowed

intention of collecting "copy," considered Philadelphia
to be altogether admirable, but very far from gay. "The
men are grave," he said, "the women serious. There
are no finical airs to be found here, no libertine wives,
no coffee-houses, no agreeable walks." This is carrying criticism too far. Coffee-houses there were, and
walks in plenty, agreeable enough, though not profoundly interesting to the eager young Frenchman who,
although disposed as Washington asserted, "to receive
favourable impressions of America," was naturally de-
pressed and daunted by its painful dissimilarity to
France.

Perhaps the truest verdicts are to be found a little
nearer home. The vivacious Miss Franks, while sadly
acknowledging that the women of New York were
handsomer than the women of Philadelphia, sighed
vainly in her exile for the freedom and ease, the wit
and grace, which lent gayety to the drawing-rooms of
the Chews, and Oswalds, and Allens. Miss Vining, one
of the most brilliant and admired of Philadelphia's
daughters, admitted, in a letter to Governor Dickinson,
that the town had grown strangely quiet since the flight
of Congress; but added proudly, "You know that here
alone can be found a truly intellectual and refined
society, such as one naturally expects in the capital of
any country."

In truth, the city was occupied with matters of such
serious moment, that she might be pardoned for not

always finding the leisure to be gay. The time had now arrived when, to quote Washington's very moderate language, success in arms had given the United States " the opportunity to become a respectable nation." The framing of a constitution was a supreme necessity, and in May, 1787, the delegates chosen for this Herculean task assembled in Philadelphia, and went immediately to work. Washington was elected to preside over the convention, which debated within closed doors for four months. Its meeting-place was the old State House ; and the hall which had first echoed the Declaration of Independence now rang with the earnest eloquence of men whose work it was to make this independence worth preserving, and upon the success of whose measures depended the future welfare of their land. The duty assigned them was the moulding of thirteen provinces, widely separated, sparsely peopled, wholly dissimilar, into a united and " respectable nation." It was fitting that the venerable walls which had witnessed the birth of liberty should lend their hallowed associations and traditions to the sincere efforts of inexperienced states-men, who strove to complete the work begun by their predecessors in 1776.

By September the National Constitution, under which we now live, was framed, and submitted for ratification to the States, which, one by one, consented to adopt it, though never without a sharp struggle, and a bitter protest from the disaffected, — natural enough, when so many conflicting interests were forced into an uneasy alliance. Pennsylvania, having given her adherence

"THE OLD STATE HOUSE."

with unwonted promptness, watched these struggles impatiently; and when ten out of the thirteen States had consented to the inevitable, Philadelphia prepared to celebrate their acquiescence with a grand Federal procession on the fourth of July, 1788. It was an industrial rather than a military parade, the parent of many more to follow, and it could hardly have been a very gay or brilliant affair; though in a lofty car — shaped like an eagle, and representing the triumphant Constitution — sat Judge Atlee, Judge Rush and Chief Justice McKean, clad in their official robes, and making up in splendour what they lacked in comfort and safety. All the trades and all the industries were amply represented. Mr. Richard Willing, dressed as a farmer, guided a plough drawn by four oxen, — a pleasant sight to see, — and Mr. Charles Willing, in the character of a ploughboy, walked by the oxen's side. A ship of state riding proudly on a canvas sea, with a gallant crew, and four pretty little boys for midshipmen, was dragged through the streets on a float; patriotic addresses were delivered without stint; and an ode, admirable in sentiment if not in execution, was written for the occasion by Francis Hopkinson, and attributed, on general principles, to Franklin. Copies of this ode were scattered among the crowd, and sent by carrier pigeons to different parts of Pennsylvania. The bells of Christ Church rang all day long, the ships along the river front were gayly decorated, bonfires blazed merrily at night, and a grand supper was eaten at Bush Hill in honour of the accepted Constitution. It was emphatically a celebration by the people, who understood clearly what they were celebrating, and its most pleasing characteristic was sincerity. " Every countenance," says a contemporary writer, " wore an air of dignity as well as of delight. Every tradesman's boy in the procession seemed to consider himself as a principle in the business."

So keen was the general enthusiasm that the word " Federal," which stood for the party of success, became popular enough for universal misapplication. Federal stables were made ready for gentlemen's horses, Federal hats were sold in the shops, Federal punch was ladled out liberally in taverns, and an enterprising dancing-master, quick to glean profit out of patriotism, secured many pupils by promising to teach a Federal minuet. Pennsylvania rightly considered that this was a favourable moment to rid herself of the cumbrous and bungling laws — the work of Rittenhouse and Franklin — under which she had struggled to live since 1776. The Anti-Constitutionalists, the party of moderation, now ruled the city and the State. The voices of such men as Benjamin Rush, John Cadwalader, Thomas Mifflin and Robert Morris were listened to with some degree of deference, and they united in urging the necessity for a more practical and reasonable form of local government. A convention was summoned, and a new State Constitution, bearing a general resemblance to the National Constitution, was framed in 1790. Philadelphia was reincorporated, and even her old armorial bearings were

T

altered, and made emblematic of the progress and prosperity which it was ardently hoped lay waiting for her grasp.

On the thirtieth of April, 1789, Washington was inaugurated, and the United States possessed at last a settled government and a visible head. When the President passed through Philadelphia, on his way to New York, he was received with joyous and disconcerting enthusiasm. Triumphal arches were raised in the streets, the houses were hung with flags, soldiers and citizens accompanied him at every step, and young girls strewed flowers along his path. Perhaps the most severely trying moment of all was at Gray's Ferry, where a crown of laurel hung dangling from an arch, under which he was doomed to ride. A little boy, robed in white and garlanded with flowers, held a string attached to this laurel wreath, and, at the critical moment when the hero passed beneath, it was lowered precipitately "upon his brow," — he having presumably taken off his hat for its accommodation, — while the multitude shouted itself hoarse with delight. Such are the penalties of greatness, and the settled gravity of Washington's demeanour permitted no one to know how much or how little he suffered upon these occasions. He was at all times fully alive to the dignity of his position, and took an open interest in the controversy which raged so hotly anent a proper title for the President. Congress and the Senate were equally averse to granting him any; but the sentiment of Philadelphia was strongly in favour of some good high-sounding phrase, and Chief Justice McKean urged "Serene Highness," as the most elegant and appropriate that could be chosen. Washington, it is said, fancied the title of the Stadtholder, — "High Mightiness," — and was deeply offended at General Muhlenberg for his wanton jest on the subject, when asked for a serious opinion.

It was no easy task at this time to steer safely between the rival claims of aristocracy and democracy; to satisfy at once the demands of what has been called "The Republican Court," and the demands of a most uncourtly public, which voiced its sentiments shrilly. John Adams had already been abused with fervour for using the obnoxious word "well-born," when speaking of certain prominent citizens. All men, he was reminded, are equally well-born, and it was not for him to draw distinctions between classes. When Thomas Jefferson returned from France, he had acquired a not unpardonable weakness for fine clothes, and appeared, so Mrs. Deborah Logan tells us, in "a suit of silk, ruffles, and an elegant topaz ring." This gave offence, and was held to be hardly consistent with republican simplicity; so he obligingly adopted a plainer costume, and was immediately and bitterly reproached "with going to the other extreme, as a bait for popularity." People who served the public were beginning to realize how very hard the public was to please.

The death of Benjamin Franklin in 1790 severed the last great link between colonial Philadelphia and the arrogant, uneasy city, struggling to adjust herself to new and necessary conditions. "For my personal ease," he wrote sadly to Washington during his long illness, "I should have died two years ago." To the very close of his life there was work for him to do, but his influence and popularity waned with his waning powers. Mrs. Logan, who sincerely admired and reverenced him, and who was generous enough to forgive his wanton attack on the memory of that fine and faithful public servant, James Logan, tells us that even his preëminence could not escape depreciation amid the rush of new events, and the conflict of warring powers.

"I have often thought," she writes, "that Dr. Franklin must have sensibly felt the difference between the éclat which he enjoyed in France, and the reception he met with upon his final return to his native country. The elements of two parties were then fermenting themselves into the form which they afterwards assumed. The mass of Pennsylvania was, as it has ever since been, decidedly democratic; but there was a contrary spirit then dominant, and thinly diffused over the surface of society, which rejected the philosopher because it thought he was too much of that stamp. The first Constitution of our State after the Revolution, which was his work, though adopted by the great body of the people, was disliked;"—small wonder!—"and I well remember the remark of a Fool, though a fashionable party man, at the time, that it was by no means 'fashionable' to visit Franklin."

And this in little Philadelphia, which had been patted and moulded into shape by his tireless intelligence and activity! It was not for her to play the part of critic where there was much to criticise, nor to reject too sharply that spirit of utility which, as Sainte-Beuve admits, was Franklin's measure for all things, and which, its work once finished, has no further message for the restless generations to come. The city he served should have even now a keener recollection of his services. The city he loved should have now a more generous affection for his name. When he died, she awoke, indeed, to a transient glow of gratitude and reverence. Twenty thousand people followed him to his grave in the yard of Christ Church, where the plain stone that bears the inscription, "Benjamin and Deborah Franklin. 1790." is visible to all who pass in the noisy street outside. The oration preached some time afterwards by Provost Smith was as laudatory and as emotional as those pronounced by Mirabeau before l'Assemblée Nationale, by Condorcet before l'Académie des Sciences, and by

Fauchet before the Commune of Paris.   Congress wore
mourning badges for a month, the French Assembly
for three whole days.   What more could be asked in
return for a lifetime of labour?   What more could

FRANKLIN'S GRAVE

be given by the world to the memory of a man who
had lived long enough to finish his work, and whose
death at eighty-four left no tragic sense of incompleteness which could be recognized as a personal loss,
and as such sincerely deplored?

CHAPTER XVI

WITH the return of Congress to Philadelphia, a
new life of fleeting gayety and extravagance
came to the Quaker City. Robert Morris was held
to be so largely responsible for this return, that the
caricatures of the day represent him as carrying the
congressmen and senators away from New York on
his shoulders. Many of them were doubtless very
unwilling to go, and deep are the murmurs which
have come down to us in the letters of discontented
officials at the cost of living in Philadelphia, and at
the irritating complacency of Philadelphians. "The
city is large and elegant," writes Oliver Wolcott to
his wife, "but it did not strike me with the astonishment which the citizens predicted. Like the rest of
mankind, they judge favourably of their own place
of residence, and of themselves, and their representations are to be admitted with some deduction." A
few months later, he expresses an irritation natural
enough in a man from whom too many complimentary speeches have been wrung. "The people of this

279

State," he complains, "are very proud of their city,
their wealth, and their supposed knowledge. I have
seen many of their principal men, and discover nothing that tempts me to idolatry."

As a rule, women loved Philadelphia, and the
charm of its social life, and paid scant heed to the
lamentations of their husbands or fathers. Mrs.
Adams, indeed, found Bush Hill, which had no
bush nor scrub upon it, a somewhat inconvenient and
lonely neighbourhood, and vehemently objected to
the high prices demanded for all things needful.
"One would suppose," writes the Vice-President's
very practical wife, "that the people thought Mexico before them, and fancied the Congress to be
its possessors." Even Washington was not without
concern at the general extravagance, at the heavy
house-rent he was compelled to pay, and at the ever-
increasing cost of hospitality. His letters at this time
are studies in domestic economy. Apparently the cares
of housekeeping were added to the cares of government,
and there is a ring of anxiety in his minute directions
anent the servants and their wages, in his determination that the cook shall bake his cake, and that the
butler shall not drink his wine, and in the complaint
which has been so often echoed by less famous men:
"It is unaccountable to me how other families, on
twenty-five hundred or three thousand dollars a year,
should be enabled to entertain more company, or at

least entertain more frequently than I could do for twenty-five thousand."

It does not appear that Mrs. Washington lifted these vexatious burdens from her husband's shoulders. We know that she was both dignified and affable in society, and that, being by nature fond of gayety. she never quite forgave Philadelphia for having robbed her of a ball in the gloomy autumn of 1775. We know also that she had her old family plate melted, and "reproduced in more elegant and harmonious forms," which would seem to indicate a lack of taste, common enough in the years which were to follow. But when there was need of new curtains for the windows, new caps for the footmen, or even a new mangle for the kitchen, the President was compelled, or thought himself compelled, to give orders concerning them; though the mangle — it was really a second-hand mangle bought from Mrs. Robert Morris — puzzled him sorely. "I *think* that is what it is called," he writes to his secretary, Mr. Lear, who was trying to put the house in order; and refers him for further information to Mrs. Morris, "who is a notable lady in family arrangements."

Washington's formal receptions — and they were very formal — were held every second Tuesday, between three and four in the afternoon, his dining-room being turned into a reception hall by the simple process of carrying out the chairs. There was true republican simplicity, dignified, reserved, austere, in the President's mode of life, and in his attitude towards the public. The ardours of a stump-speaking, hand-shaking, joke-perpetrating democracy had not then warmed the country into an easy brotherhood, and melted away the barriers between the head of a nation and its subjects. Washington loved his jest as well as lesser men. His private letters are full of jocularities, robust rather than fastidious; and, like Pope and Byron, he was much in the habit of repeating his good things, word by word, to his different correspondents. But though he had probably never in his life read a line of Epictetus, — no man deplored more keenly than he the lack of early education, — he understood instinctively that "to move laughter by thy discourse is a slippery descent into vulgarity, and always relaxes thy neighbour's respect." "His manner in public," says William Sullivan, "was invariably grave. It was sobriety that stopped short of sadness." Slow and rather cumbrous in his motions, and with an indistinct utterance, — a blessed barrier to oratory, — he knew well how to mingle graciousness with dignity, so that none who were admitted to his presence ever felt arrogantly repelled, or wholly at their ease.

It is wonderful how much can be accomplished by simple propriety of demeanour. The letters of both Americans and foreigners teem with animated and reverential descriptions of this republican ruler. Mr.

Richard Rush assures us that when he stood on the steps of Congress Hall, every eye was fixed upon him "in mute, unutterable admiration. Not a word was heard, not a breath. Palpitations took the place of sounds." Mr. Henry Wansey, who crossed the seas to visit us in 1794, confesses he was overwhelmed with "awe and veneration" when permitted to breakfast with the President; though "two small plates of sliced tongue, dry toast, bread and butter," carried a painful sense of incompleteness to his hearty English appetite, and he lamented in a carnal spirit the absence of broiled fish. Mr. Thomas Twining, an Anglo-Indian, who spent the following winter in Philadelphia, never seems to know which he admires the most, — the conversation of Mr. John Adams, or the silence of Washington. He is rather taken back — being fresh from the splendours of India — to find the latter living in "a small brick house on High Street, next door to a hair-dresser"; but he admits with delight that "the moment when Washington entered the room, and Mrs. Washington said 'The President!' made an impression on my mind which no subsequent years can efface."

The equipage of our chief magistrate was more imposing than his modest mansion, which was not small, however, but the roomiest which could be found for him in the city. He drove abroad in a big cream-coloured coach, globular in shape, and or-

namented in the French style with scantily draped
cupids, and flowing wreaths of flowers.   A tall German
coachman, "possessing an aquiline nose," handled the
reins, and the long-tailed Virginia bays were as beautiful as those which drew the virtuous Pamela to her
wedding rites.   The President walked about town

MORRIS HOUSE, GERMANTOWN

with no nervous apprehension of lowering his dignity,
and was in the habit of strolling every day at noon
to set his watch by Clark's standard at Front and
High Streets, gravely saluting the porters who un-
covered as he passed.

According to Senator Maclay, the presidential dinners were painfully solemn and serious affairs; but
Mrs. Washington's receptions appear to have given

universal satisfaction. The ladies who attended were, we are told, "elegantly, if not superbly dressed." Mrs. Adams notes "the dazzling Mrs. Bingham and her sisters, the Misses Allen, the Misses Chew, and a constellation of beauties," among the ordinary guests. Miss Sally McKean, with sublime effrontery, writes, after the first of these entertainments, to a friend in New York,—poor New York, still smarting under a sense of loss:—" *You* never could have had such a drawing-room. It was brilliant beyond anything you can imagine. And though there was a great deal of extravagance, there was so much of Philadelphia taste in everything, that it must have been confessed the most delightful occasion of the kind ever known in this country."

The gayety and charm of the Philadelphia women, their Paris gowns, and lively conversation, form the theme of universal comment. Mrs. Adams, indeed, though well pleased with so much friendly hospitality, seems a trifle bored by meeting "at all places nearly the same company." Her daughter admits that the women of Boston were more highly educated, but finds the Philadelphians easier in their manners, more gracious, and more desirous of pleasing. The Duke de Lauzun, the Marquis de Chastellux, and Count Rochambeau unite in praising both the young girls and the matrons, though wondering a little at their devotion to dress, and to the Paris fashions.

The Abbé Robin has the unkindness to say that, in the absence of parks and promenades, these fair daughters of Eve went to church, less to pray than to show their pretty frocks; and Brissot, who was nothing if not serious, laments openly that this feminine weakness for finery extended itself to the Quaker women, who tried in many ways to escape from the rigid thraldom of the Society. "These youthful creatures," he writes, "whom nature has so well endowed, whose charms have so little need of art, wear the finest muslins and silks. Oriental luxury would not disdain the exquisite textures in which they take delight." "Ribbons," observes the astute Duke de la Rochefoucauld-Liancourt, "please the young Quakeresses as well as others, and are the great enemies of the sect." Sometimes, indeed, the vanities of the world proved too strong for early principles, and fair apostates, like Mrs. Madison, cast off the yoke with whole-hearted impetuosity, striving to compensate themselves for the enforced seclusion of girlhood by indulging in every gayety and dissipation.

Frivolity was the order of the day. In vain would-be economists expressed with Oliver Wolcott a reasonable hope that "the example of the President and his family will render parade and expense improper and disreputable." No such pleasing result ensued. In vain the more conservative Friends protested loudly against sinful luxury, and a prominent member of the Society refused to enter the house of an acquaintance, because a carpet was spread upon the hall. "Better," he said, "to clothe the poor than to clothe the earth." Reproaches were unheeded, and the careless city waxed more and more extravagant as the merry months ran on. If husbands and fathers looked grave, feeling, as they must have felt, the unsoundness of this apparent prosperity, wives and daughters listened to no forebodings, but made hay blithely while still the warm sun shone. Of the amusements they loved, and of the admiration they excited, none of them seem ever to have wearied. "The young women of Philadelphia," writes the Duke de la Rochefoucauld-Liancourt, "are accomplished in different degrees, but beauty is common to all. They lack the ease and grace of French women, but they are charming, and have singularly brilliant complexions."

The acknowledged leader in all the gayeties of these unwontedly gay winters was Mrs. William Bingham, of whom we hear so much in contemporary records. Beautiful, rich, pleasure-loving, gentle in speech and light of heart, she lent a vivacity of her own to the limited society of a little city, where, as Mrs. Adams said, the same people met each other day after day, and night after night. Up the broad marble stairway, which we are told gave "a truly Roman elegance" to

her spacious home, thronged the Willings, the Byrds,
the Powels, the Shippens, the McCalls, the Blackwells,
the Cadwaladers, the Chews and Oswalds, many of
whom were — in true Philadelphia fashion — cousins,
first, second, or third, of their hostess, and of whom
we can only trust she did not weary in these some-

TEA-ROOM IN MORRIS HOUSE

what monoto-
nous entertain-
ments. Mrs.
Robert Morris
also enjoyed a
distinguished
position, upheld
by her husband's
great wealth, his
important ser-
vices to the
country, and his
splendid hospi-
tality which
knew no limit
nor restraint. Washington, whose own household was
conducted simply and abstemiously, notes again and
again in his diary the elegance of the dinners at
which he was a guest. Indeed, his constant presence
on these occasions shows how rigidly he performed
the very fatiguing social duties which he deemed his
rank demanded. Nor were the privileges of any class

of people ignored. In 1792 the Dancing Assembly
gave a grand ball in honour of his birthday. A
society which called itself the New Dancing Assembly, and which was largely composed of tradespeople
excluded from the older association, determined to
celebrate the anniversary in the same fashion. The
President attended the two balls, remained for the
same space of time at each, and at each proposed
the same toast, — " The State of Pennsylvania."

In curious contrast to the brilliancy of Philadelphia's
social life, to which the constant presence of foreigners
like Chateaubriand, the Viscount de Noailles, M. Talleyrand and the Duke de la Rochefoucauld lent interest
and distinction, were the crudeness of her literary and
artistic developments, the badness of her roads, — always a test of civilization, — and the unutterable discomfort of travel. Men, indeed, still read the robust
English classics of the eighteenth century, and occasionally a woman who, like Elizabeth Drinker, possessed
both leisure and intelligence, confessed to an acquaintance with Fielding. But scholarship was on the wane,
carrying with it all real appreciation of letters; and
with the exception of Charles Brockden Brown, whose
novels are still sometimes talked about though seldom
read, the prose and verse of literary Philadelphians
were for many years equally and strikingly inadequate. Only in correspondence, and in diaries not
meant for publication, do we discern that intelli-

gence and acumen which promised possibilities for the future.

Portrait painting was exceedingly fashionable in all American cities, and Washington set an admirable example by being painted over and over again, — as often, though not so well, as that least vain of monarchs, Philip IV. of Spain. Pennsylvania sent Benjamin West to England, where, like Mrs. Jarley, he became the delight of the royal family, the nobility, and gentry. Naturally he stayed amid these powerful patrons; but in his place came Robert Pine, Gilbert Stuart of Rhode Island, John Trumbull of Connecticut, and afterwards, Thomas Sully, who crossed the sea when a child of nine, and spent most of his life in Philadelphia. Charles Wilson Peale was born, like West, in Pennsylvania. He expressed his reverence for art by naming his six children Raphael, Rembrandt, Vandyke, Titian, Rubens, and Angelica Kaufmann. It is pleasant to record that two, at least, out of the six acted on their father's suggestion, and followed in his footsteps. Peale and his fellow artists were kept hard at work painting Philadelphia's judges and doctors, her rich merchants, her politicians, and, above all, her handsome daughters, as lavish apparently with their charms as were their English great-grandmothers in the gay days of the second Charles.

Yet was the Quaker City deeply imbued with her own conceptions of propriety, and not without her own standard of taste. Her women might unveil their bosoms to the careless eyes of men; but when the English painter, Pine, brought over the ocean a plaster cast of the Venus de Medici, he was not permitted to keep it in his studio where it could be generally seen. The bronze statue of a nymph holding a swan upon her shoulder, which is now in the oldest corner of Fairmount Park, was originally carved in wood by Rush, and placed in Centre Square. But though amply and even prodigally draped, the poor thing's clinging petticoats shocked public modesty, and she was loudly denounced as indecorous, and unfit for the open street. Twenty years later, the infant Academy of the Fine Arts imported a number of

"A NYMPH HOLDING A SWAN"

casts, copies of the famous statues in the Louvre; and so great was the disedification which they gave that the managers were obliged to set apart one day in the week for female visitors, when the nude figures were swathed from head to feet in muslin sheets.

As for the difficulties of travel, they mattered little to people who habitually stayed at home. In the early days, when the city was still in her innocent childhood, she sought no easy communication with distant towns. Adventurous spirits from time to time gratified a thirst for novelty, or were summoned to neighbouring provinces by the urgent cares of business. Mrs. Joseph Shippen journeyed on horseback from Boston to Philadelphia in 1702, with her young baby lying in her lap, and the lodestar which drew her along this weary way was the desire to see again her family and her friends. The first coach that ran between Philadelphia and New York was started in 1756, and took three whole days to make the trip. When a swifter conveyance covered the distance in two days, it was boastfully christened the Flying Machine, and twenty shillings were demanded for a seat. By 1789 this time had been greatly reduced; and the Rev. Jeremy Belknap, author of the "History of New Hampshire," gives us an animated account of travelling from New York to Philadelphia in the "New Flying Diligence," which outsped all competitors. "Between three and four in the morning," he writes, "we set off in the stage, rode nine miles to Bergen Neck, and then crossed a ferry which brought us to Woodbridge. Just before we reached the second ferry we perceived the dawn of day, and, when we were two miles from it, the sun rose, so that we had ridden sixteen miles and crossed two ferries before sunrise, besides shifting horses twice. The third stage brought us to Brunswick, where we breakfasted. We here crossed the Raritan in a scow, open at both ends to receive and discharge the carriage without unharnessing or dismounting, and the scow was pulled across the river by a rope. We passed through Princeton about noon, and got to Trenton to dinner; then passed the Delaware in another scow which was navigated only by setting poles; drove thirty miles over a plain, level country at a great rate, and arrived in Philadelphia at sunset."

Brissot, who made this pleasant trip a few years later, describes the diligence as "a kind of open wagon, hung with double curtains of leather and wool"; in which jolting vehicle, he perceived the principle of equality to be well maintained. "The member of Congress rides in fraternal fashion beside the shoemaker who elected him."

Other cities, however, were less easy of access than New York. Mr. Thomas Twining, who desired to go from Philadelphia to Baltimore in 1795, found that the only public conveyance was the mail wagon, which, for the accommodation of travellers, held four rough benches, *without backs*. Under these benches the luggage was stowed, so that the wretched passengers, aching all over, and unable to gain a minute's rest, could not even thrust their feet a little way before

them. Heavy leather curtains were kept fastened
down the whole time, and no glimpse of the surrounding
country afforded a minute's distraction or relief. The
roads were uncompromisingly bad, and the wagon
jolted heavily over ruts and stones. Two entire days
were passed in this misery. At the midway inn where
the voyagers spent the night, they were all packed into
a single garret room, called up the second morning
at two-thirty A.M., and sent off breakfastless at three.
Mr. Twining appears to have been the most amiable
Englishman who ever visited our shores. He praises
everything in Philadelphia, from his very select board-
ing-house — "a private house for the reception of members of Congress" — to "the most esteemed article of
an American breakfast," buckwheat cakes. Even the
monotonous sameness of the streets, he considers per-
plexing rather than disagreeable. But the two days
in the mail wagon strained even his good-humour,
and he mildly insinuates in his diary that a leather
strap, on which passengers could rest their backs, would
be neither difficult nor expensive to adjust, and would
add immeasurably to the comfort of travellers. It
seems a moderate demand.

OLD MARKET-PLACE

CHAPTER XVII

TWO FORMS OF FEVER

THE French Revolution, which followed so swiftly upon our own, was watched in the United States with a breathless interest, in no wise lessened by the difficulty of obtaining news. Excitement, which is now alternately awakened and allayed by daily cablegrams, each contradicting the message of the previous morning, then burned with a steady intensity. The birth of the French Republic was hailed with joy, and its baptism in blood was passed over as lightly as such unpleasant details would permit. The gratitude which our country felt for the assistance France had given us in our sorest need, disposed the mass of people to forgive her the excesses which were committed across so many miles of ocean. Distance softens the direst horrors, and enables us to endure with tranquillity, evils too ghastly for a near acquaintance. The death of King Louis sent, indeed, a thrill of shame and sorrow through thousands of hearts that had not wholly forgotten his ancient friendship for the colonies, nor the times when his birthday was kept as a civic festival. But this temporary revulsion of feeling was, in turn, overcome by a sudden and keen enthusiasm when it was generally known that the young Republic, as brave as it was cruel, had declared war against England and Spain, and that Citizen Genet was on his way to the United States to demand succour and support.

The satisfaction, it must be admitted, was confined wholly to the people. The President and the Congress felt nothing but doubt, perplexity and chagrin. Genet landed at Charleston, and consumed four weeks in getting to Philadelphia. His journey was like a royal progress, impeded at every step by public and flattering ovations, well calculated to turn a stronger head. By the time he reached his destination, he was naturally convinced of his own supreme importance, and the reception given him by the city served to increase rather than to lessen this delusion. His coming was heralded by the French frigate, *l'Ambuscade*, which, on the second of May, sailed up the river, and anchored at the Market Street wharf, amid the wild acclamations of the crowd.

She was a self-assertive frigate, leaving no one in doubt of her intentions. A liberty cap adorned her foremast, from which floated a pennon, inscribed, "Enemies of equality, reform or tremble!" Her mainmast bore a similar legend: "Freemen, we are your friends and brothers;" and her mizzenmast proclaimed to the world: "We are armed to defend the rights of men." She fired a salute of fifteen guns, and was answered rapturously from the shore, while the bells of Christ Church pealed out their shrill and joyous welcome, and the throngs along the river front shouted their hoarse delight.

Two weeks later, Genet arrived, and was met at Gray's Ferry by a vast concourse of townspeople who brought him triumphantly into the city, presented him with a glowing address, and prepared a grand banquet for him at Oeller's Tavern. Among his ardent friends and partisans were Citizens Dallas, Rittenhouse, Duponçeau, Charles Biddle, Thomas Mifflin and Thomas Jefferson; for it is to be observed that "citizen" was now considered the only title fit for a son of freedom. Mr. Smith and Mr. Brown became Citizen Smith and Citizen Brown, and felt themselves much altered and purified by the transformation.

At the tavern dinner, vast enthusiasm was displayed. Duponçeau read a French ode, which might have been better enjoyed if it had been more generally understood. The Marseillaise was sung with fervour, and Genet treated the company to a "truly patriotic and

Republican song," which Mr. MacMaster quotes entire,
but of which one verse will suffice to show the merits.

> " Should France from her lofty station,
>   From the throne of fair Freedom be hurled,
>   'Tis done with every other nation,
>   And Liberty's lost to the world."

After this poetic outburst, the *bonnet rouge* was
solemnly placed upon the head of every guest, beginning
with the French minister, who was probably the only
man to feel at ease during the ceremony.

In sharp contrast to all this popular excitation was
the cold reception given by Washington to the unwelcome representative of the new Republic. Genet, who
was already deeply angered by the proclamation of
neutrality, felt himself outraged by the President's formal words and chilling demeanour, to say nothing of
the medallion of Louis XVI. which he perceived upon
the wall of the drawing-room, and which he resented as
an "insult" to his nation. His demand for the two
millions which the United States still owed to France
was not unreasonable, for the money was sorely needed;
but Hamilton reported the treasury to be empty, — its
chronic state, — and declared that to anticipate the date
fixed for the payment of the debt, which could only be
done by an act of Congress, would be to violate the
treaty of neutrality. As for the "fraternal compact"
which the envoy hoped to establish between the two
countries, nothing could have been less desired by the

THE SCHUYLKILL'S BANK

President, the Congress, the shipping merchants, whose trade with England was at stake, or the conservative citizens who mistrusted, not without reason, the methods and morals of our proposed ally.

On the other hand, the mass of the people were eager to support France in her tremendous struggle, and to them Genet made an open appeal for sympathy. The populace, as he knew, had ruled Paris, and, through Paris, France. Why should not the same power be absolute in the United States? Moreover, he had the sanction of the *National Gazette*, the organ of the extreme Republicans, and the mouthpiece of Mr. Jefferson, which habitually censured Washington and the administration, and spoke with fervid scorn of " Mr. Hamilton's myrmidons," by which it meant all holders of bank-stock or government bonds. To the people accordingly — sacred depositaries of wisdom and understanding — the French minister turned for aid ; and they responded with a cordial vehemence as pleasing as it was profitless. Revolutionary societies, in imitation of the Jacobin clubs, were founded in Philadelphia. Bands of Genatines, as they were called, paraded the streets, singing "*Ça ira*," when sober citizens were in bed, and swearing that the United States should be forced to fight Great Britain. "Ten thousand men," wrote John Adams, who was seriously alarmed at the crisis, " were in the streets of Philadelphia day after day, threatening to drag Washington out of his house, and effect a revolution in the

government, or compel it to declare in favour of the
French, and against England."

To give our Quaker town a still more lively resemblance to unshackled Paris, women and children took
part in these feverish demonstrations. Young people
of both sexes thronged the highways, all wearing tri-
coloured cockades, and singing the Marseillaise, or that
lurid chant,

> " Dansons la Carmagnole,
> Vive le son, vive le son,
> Dansons la Carmagnole,
> Vive le son du canon ! "

without having any very clear conception, owing to the
general ignorance of French, of just what the words
implied. In Girard Street, then an open square, un-
adorned by the spacious old houses and quiet gardens
which made it for years one of the most respectable of
thoroughfares, a liberty pole was erected, surmounted by
the *bonnet rouge ;* and around it danced, hand in hand,
boys of twelve and decent grey-haired men, all shrieking
revolutionary songs, and all mad with the fierce excitement of the hour. Even the better class of citizens who
favoured the cause of France were not restrained by
taste or judgment from acts of coarse brutality. At a
dinner presided over by Governor Mifflin, a roast pig
was brought in to personate King Louis, and its head,
severed from its body, was carried around the table,
amid triumphant jeers, and cries of " Tyrant ! Tyrant ! "

A Philadelphia tavern was suffered to display upon its sign-board a revolting picture of the bloody and mutilated corpse of Marie Antoinette. What wonder that Genet, reminded at every turn of Paris and its familiar delights, should have deemed his cause secure? What wonder that he grew bolder and bolder in his support of the French privateers, and more and more insolent in his tone towards the President and the administration? How could he suppose that this fever would fade away as swiftly and as unreasonably as it had come? A few more public dinners, a few more speeches, a few more songs and experiments with the *bonnet rouge*,— and even his friends wearied somewhat of the cause. Washington, who was at no time long-suffering where the dignity of his position was at stake, demanded and obtained the recall of a minister who had violated every principle of diplomacy. His successor, Citizen Fauchet, arrived in February, 1794; but by that time the Reign of Terror was nearing its end. Genet lingered in the United States until summer, and then the death of Robespierre convinced him that France was no longer a safe abode for too ardent Jacobins. He decided to remain where he could be sure of keeping his head upon his shoulders; and, selecting a home in New York, he made many friends, and won for himself two American wives before he died in 1834.

Even while the revolutionary craze was at its height, French émigrés, fleeing from the embraces of

the guillotine, found a hospitable retreat in Philadelphia, bringing with them gayety and grace which
lent their very poverty an air of distinction, and made
it seem a different thing from the sordid narrowness,
the troubled reticence of Anglo-Saxon penury. When,
a few years later, Louis Philippe sought shelter in the
same quiet haven, he lived in a single room over a
barber's shop. Here he gave one night a little dinner
to some very distinguished guests, and apologized with
serene good-humour for seating half of his visitors on
his bed. "I have myself been in much less comfortable places," he said cheerfully, "and without the
consolation of agreeable company."

In August, 1793, Philadelphia's enthusiasms and
animosities, her joys and follies, were stifled into one
common fear by the breaking out of the yellow fever.
Amid the terrible scenes that ensued no one had
leisure to cherish hysterical sentiment; no one remembered to say "Citizen Brown" or "Citess Robinson";
no one cared whether France was a republic, a mon-
archy, or an empire. There was an end to all caper-
ing about liberty poles, for Death was dancing grimly
in the desolate streets, and he shared his merriment
with none. Through the whole summer the disease
had been raging in the West Indies, and vessels from
the infected ports, being permitted to enter the city's
docks without inspection or quarantine, brought the
contagion swiftly to our doors. Its first stealthy

advances awakened little notice. A few stevedores, a sailor or two, died, and no one knew what ailed them. More sickened, and suddenly, without further warning, without pause for mere suspicion or uncertainty, the terrified city realized that she was in the grasp of the pestilence. On the twenty-first of August, Dr. Benjamin Rush writes the first of a long and deeply interesting series of letters to his absent wife. A malignant fever, he says, has broken out on the river front. Already he has been called on to treat a dozen patients, and three of them are dead. Two days later, Elizabeth Drinker notes with characteristic brevity in her diary: "A fever prevails in ye City, particularly on Water St., between Race and Arch Sts., of ye malignant kind; numbers have died of it."

From this time until the coming of the first keen frosts of November, the story of Philadelphia is like the oft-repeated story of the Plague. The fever swept as a whirlwind through Water Street, leaving none but dead behind it, and spread with horrible speed into every quarter of the town. In the panic that ensued, there was a mad rush for the safety of the open fields and the adjacent towns. Seventeen thousand people fled within a month. The mayor, Matthew Clarkson, stood stoutly at his post, and, with the help of a committee chiefly composed of Quakers, organized measures of relief, — measures which were necessarily inadequate, though they alleviated the untold misery

of the poor. People burned tar in the streets, and
carried sprigs of wormwood, — pitiful, impotent little
remedies, by which they hoped to stay the relentless
hand of death. The corpses were buried quietly at
night, as in plague-stricken London ; and through the

AN OLD STREET

scattered suburbs of the city, men and women, unable
to secure the services of undertakers, dug lonely graves
in fields and woods, and laid their lost to rest. Elizabeth Drinker's diary is filled with horrors that affect
us all the more powerfully because, Quaker-like, she
allows herself no license in narrating them. In that

vain frenzy of selfishness which stifles pity, those who
were yet untainted thrust their sick and dying into the
streets, or fled themselves from the squalid rooms where
Death was busy with his work. Amid so much brutality, so much callous indifference to ties of kinship
and affection, it is touching to read of the poor sailor,
haggard and heartbroken, who stopped Dr. Rush in
the street, and offered him twenty pounds — a sailor's
fortune — if he would pay but a single visit to his
infected wife.

Indeed, painful as are the details which Dr. Rush
is necessarily forced to relate, his letters breathe such
steadfastness of purpose, such fortitude, such unbroken, unostentatious heroism, that they invigorate
rather than depress the reader. " I enjoy good health
and uncommon tranquillity of mind," he writes in
the beginning of this terrible season ; and when, two
months later, his health is shattered by repeated attacks of the fever, his tranquillity is still unmarred.
Never once does the absent wife stoop to beg her husband to consider his own safety ; never once does the
physician remember with a selfish pang that every
risk he runs jeopardizes the welfare of his family.
The path of duty is so clearly and sharply defined
that there is no room in either heart for the consideration of side issues.

In justice to human nature, however, it must be
admitted that in this case duty received a splendid

x

stimulus from professional pride and professional hostility. Dr. Rush discovered a remedy for the fever, which he firmly believed and asserted to be infallible, if taken in time. He bled his patients as freely as though he had been a sixteenth century practitioner, and he dosed them with jalap and mercury instead of the quinine usually prescribed. The majority of Philadelphia's doctors repudiated this treatment, and the battle that raged around the bedsides of the sick and dying lent zest to the physicians' perilous labours. They risked their lives hourly, but they had the honour of science as well as the good of humanity to sustain them.

Dr. Rush's sentiments are never a matter for doubt. On the thirteenth of September he writes: "Yesterday was a day of triumph to mercury, jalap, and bleeding. I am satisfied that they saved in my hands nearly one hundred lives. . . . Scores are daily sacrificed to bark and wine." As the fever grew more deadly, the contest deepened and darkened. "The physicians murder by rule," he writes on September 21st. "Nor is this all; they have confederated against me in the most cruel manner, and are propagating calumnies against me in every part of the city. . . . Never before did I witness such a mass of ignorance and wickedness as our profession has exhibited in the course of the present calamity."

Life is not wholly a burden to any man who cher-

ishes such hearty antagonism as this, and it is plain
that wrath was a most excellent tonic to the good
doctor, and helped him materially to face the daily
perils that beset him. The city, he admits, was a
mass of contagion. The tainted air was loaded with
foul and nauseating odours. He himself was as deeply
poisoned as Rappaccini's daughter, and believed that,
like the maid, he was safe from all further infection.
"I ascribe my freedom from fatigue and my sleepless
nights wholly to the stimulus of the contagion in my
system," he writes; "for I am so full of it that it
has now become part of myself. It is not dangerous
unless excited into action by heat, cold, fatigue, or
high living."

This is the language of enthusiasm, and in this ex-
alted frame of mind he battled to the end. When at
last the cold weather checked the progress of the
fever, it had counted nearly five thousand victims, a
ghastly reckoning if we remember that the city, deserted by all who could escape, held less than thirty
thousand inhabitants during the greater part of these
terrible months. When the pestilence was at its
height, two hundred victims were buried in a single
day; and often the frightened housewife, opening her
door cautiously in the early morning, would see upon
her step the swollen corpse of some abandoned creature
who had crawled thither to perish, alone and unpitied,
in the night. Ten physicians and ten clergymen — two

of them Roman Catholic priests — died in the fulfil-
ment of their duties: and to the brave and tranquil
charity of the Quakers many stricken wretches owed
their lives.

The battle of the drugs, however, had not yet been
fought to the close. It was renewed with much spirit
and animosity when the yellow fever revisited Philadelphia, in a less virulent form, during several succeeding summers. Dr. Rush endured the attacks of
his brother practitioners with what slender patience
he could muster; but when, in 1797. William Cobbett
ridiculed him unmercifully in *Peter Porcupine's Gazette*, and likened his treatment to that of Dr. San-
grado, he promptly sued the Englishman for libel,
and was granted damages to the extent of five thousand dollars. It was an enormous sum for those days;
but the physician was beloved by the community he
had served, and the journalist was unpopular, both as
a foreigner, and as a satirist who habitually and un-
wisely hurled his shafts at the idols of the populace.
The verdict ruined him. His property was seized, and
sold at a sacrifice. He returned to England, and from
that day forth no man diverted himself at the expense
of mercury and jalap. The pastime was held to be
too costly.

With the approach of winter, the coming back of
the frightened exiles, and the comforting assurance
that the fever was at an end, Philadelphia felt herself

encouraged to take up once more, though in a modified form, her interrupted sansculottism. She began by holding a modest meeting in the State House yard to protest against the seizure of American vessels by British cruisers, and to urge the government to extend to France every favour which " friendship can dictate, and justice can allow." This was the little end of the wedge, and was followed in a few weeks by a public parade, and a public dinner, at which Citizen Fauchet received the "fraternal embraces" of his American sympathizers, "amid the animated joy and acclamations of the whole company." The vestry of Christ Church was at the same time bidden to remove from the east front of the edifice an ancient medallion, containing a bas-relief of George II.; and though the order emanated only from that dubious authority, " the people," it was promptly and patiently obeyed.

In early summer the city amused itself with a grand demonstration in honour of the French Republic. A statue of liberty was erected at Twelfth and Market Streets; and, on an altar at its base, young girls strewed offerings of flowers, while an oration in French was pronounced, and fraternal embraces were exchanged. The crowd, delighted with the spectacle, sang the Marseillaise, danced the Carmagnole, made a bonfire of the English flag, and rapturously applauded the sentiment, " May tyrants never be withheld from the guillotine's closest embraces."

It seemed like a repetition of the mad folly which a year before had supported Citizen Genet's insolent assumption of authority, but there was this difference between the two situations. Then the rabid Republicans really hoped to force the administration into an alliance with France; now they knew that all such hopes were futile. They were at liberty to be as picturesquely and sentimentally Gallic as they pleased; but while they were wearing tri-coloured cockades, and singing the Marseillaise in our once decorous Quaker streets, Chief Justice Jay was in England, negotiating a treaty in the interests of long-neglected commerce. It is true that this treaty was exceedingly hateful to the populace, which swore that the chief justice had sold his country to Great Britain, and which manifested its displeasure by burning his effigy at Kensington, breaking the windows of the English consul and of Mr. William Bingham, and bitterly maligning the government. It is true that at a town meeting which was attended by Stephen Girard and a number of prominent men, a resolution was adopted, stating briefly and angrily that "the citizens of Philadelphia do not approve of the treaty between Lord Grenville and Mr. Jay." Yet Washington's serenity was undisturbed. Perhaps he did not care whether the citizens of Philadelphia approved or disapproved. He had braved their displeasure before this, and they had vilified him — as he wrote to Mr. Jefferson —"in such exaggerated and indecent terms as could scarcely be applied to a Nero, a defaulter, or a common pick-pocket." Perhaps he was upheld by the knowledge that the merchants and shippers of the city were eager for their interrupted trade. The treaty was ratified on the eleventh of August, and the President listened unmoved to the echoes of the hostility it aroused.

And indeed it was high time that the authority of the administration should be asserted and maintained. The Scotch-Irish whiskey distillers of Pennsylvania had for years ignored or opposed the excise law, as a form of taxation of which they personally disapproved, and which they, in consequence, resolutely declined

JEFFERSON'S CHAIR

to pay. Advice, expostulation, reasoning, had all been tried in vain. They responded by tarring and feathering the collectors, and by threatening to burn Pittsburg, then a village of only twelve hundred inhabitants. A "second Sodom," the pious insurgents called this straggling township, and declared themselves ready to play the rôle of an avenging Providence, and destroy it. It was not until the patience of the government had been exhausted, and an army of fifteen thousand men had been sent into Pennsylvania, prepared to argue the matter "in platoons," that the distillers were convinced of their error, and realized that it was no longer their privilege to obey or reject at discretion the laws of the United States.

In Philadelphia, the same spirit of what was then termed liberty vented itself in reckless declamation, and in a lively sympathy for France, as the country which had assuredly presented to the world the most expansive theory of freedom. So exceedingly French had we become that Citizen Adet, who had in turn replaced Citizen Fauchet, requested the suppression of the town directory, because the English minister's name had been printed in it before his own, and the public supported him in this mild demand, with which the publishers stoutly declined to comply. Cobbett, who undertook to fight the battle of Great Britain in *Peter Porcupine's Gazette*, was the object of a deeper hostility than often falls to the lot of any one man, a relentless hostility which seemed to give him genuine satisfaction until it proved his ruin. Even the repeated seizures of American vessels by French privateers, though it sorely damped our enthusiasm, could not altogether subdue it; and Dr. George Logan, an ardent Republican and anti-Federalist, conceived the brilliant idea of going to France as a self-appointed "ambassador of the people," to obtain a redress of this grievance.

His mission, which was generally understood though not openly acknowledged, aroused profound excitement in Philadelphia. Friends and followers sang his praises loudly; conservative people asked themselves what would be the result if private citizens should often undertake to settle their country's difficulties, without the authority of the administration; and hostile Federal newspapers made the most of the situation by pretending to believe he had gone to obtain the help of a foreign power, and that his object was the destruction of our government, and the establishment of an American Reign of Terror. "Can any sensible man hesitate to suspect," piped the *Philadelphia Gazette*, "that Dr. Logan's infernal design can be anything less than the introduction of a French army, to teach us the value of true and essential liberty by reorganizing our government through the blessed operation of the bayonet and the guillotine? Let every American now gird on his sword. The demagogue has gone to the Directory for purposes of destruction to your lives, property, liberty, and holy religion."

It was all deeply interesting, though the concluding chapters seem a little tame. Dr. Logan returned home without an army at his heels, and without having softened the hearts of the Directory. He was coldly received by Mr. Adams who did not approve of self-appointed envoys. The official representatives of the United States met, however, with no greater success; and the aggressive attitude maintained by France made our unreciprocated admiration a trifle ridiculous, even in our own eyes. " Hail Columbia! " written by Hopkinson, and first sung in Philadelphia on the twenty-fifth of April, 1798, took the public fancy by storm, and gradually supplanted the Marseillaise, although denounced by the extreme Republicans as an " Anglo-monarchical " anthem. Amid so many cares, interests, and anxieties of our own, it became impossible to fix our attention permanently upon the triumphant career of a foreign nation, especially upon a foreign nation which seized our ships, and paid no attention to our continued remonstrances. Philadelphia was on the eve of a great change which was to materially alter her history and her character. She had long been the most important city of the colonies, and of the United States. She had been the centre and the heart of our national life. She had been the lawgiver, both of Pennsylvania and of the Republic. She had been proud, gay, quarrelsome, and wantonly extravagant. She had well-nigh forgotten the lessons of her Founder. Now her honours were about to be wrested from her, one by one. In 1799 the state Legislature was removed to Harrisburg, and Philadelphia, after a reign of one hundred and seventeen years, was no longer the capital of her province. In 1800 the Federal government was carried to Washington, and with it went political supremacy, and that

social distinction which was then its closest ally, and
which can never be wholly divorced from the centre
of political power.

The nation, too, was in a state of transition and
restless anxiety. Adams had succeeded to the presi-
dency, and in December, 1799, Washington died.
He was buried at Mount Vernon; but Philadelphia,
excited and sorrowful, decreed him funeral honours,
dragged his empty bier through her streets, and listened at night to a monody, delivered at her theatre
to the accompaniment of solemn dirges. The stage
was decorated with a huge catafalque, bearing the
hero's portrait encircled by an oak wreath. Above
was an eagle weeping tears of blood, and, underneath,
an inscription explaining with needless lucidity that
these were the nation's tears.

The diary of Elizabeth Drinker contains two long
entries, the unwonted details of which clearly show
that even tranquil Quaker households were deeply
interested in these mournful commemorations, in
which — as Friends — they could not conscientiously
take part, but which they were just as eager as other
people to see. On the twenty-fifth of December, she
writes: "There are to be great doings to-morrow by
way of respect to George Washington; a funeral
procession, and an oration or eulogium to be delivered by Henry Lee, a member of Congress from
Virginia. The members of Congress are to wear

deep mourning; the citizens generally are to wear
crape around their arms for six months. Congress-
hall is in mourning, and even the Play-house. There
has been, and is like to be, much said and done on the
occasion. I was sorry to hear of his death, and so are
many others who make no show. Those forms, to
be sure, are out of our way; but many will join
in ye form that cared little about him."

On the twenty-seventh of December, she writes
again: "The funeral procession in honour of ye late
Commander-in-chief of the Armies of the United
States, Lieut. Gen. Washington, yesterday took
place. They assembled at the State-house, and went
from thence in grand procession to ye Dutch church in
Fourth Street, called Zion church, where Major Gen.
Henry Lee delivered an oration to four thousand
persons, or near that number, who were, 'tis said,
within the church. Ye concourse of people in ye
streets and at ye windows was very numerous.
Nancy and Molly were at' their sister Sally's, to
gratify their curiosity.

So all is over with G. Washington."

CHAPTER XVIII

DEPRESSION

THE history of Philadelphia for the first half of the present century does not make vivacious reading. She had turned her page, and the long story of her struggles, her triumphs, her pride of place, her political power, her reckless dissipation, was at an end. In its stead, we have a dismal narrative, full of such familiar phrases as "dull times," "hard winters," "stagnant trade," "great suffering among the poor,"—all included in the inevitable reaction from a mad extravagance that had no sounder basis than speculation, and the allurements of an inflated currency. The embargo act of 1807, which

317

forbade vessels to set sail from the United States for
any foreign port, put the finishing touch to the commercial ruin of a city which had covered the sea
with her ships. The act may or may not have been
annoying to the foreign ports which it was meant to
injure; but the havoc it made at home was never a
matter for doubt. Philadelphia drooped pitifully
under this cruel hurt. "The grass grew on her
wharves, the ships rotted in their moorings." Hungry,
penniless sailors paraded the streets, and the sympathy of the people was strongly aroused for these
poor mariners who were so childishly incapable of
understanding the law which locked up their boats,
and bade them starve in peace. Help there was
none, however, and hundreds of them made their
way to Nova Scotia, and, entering the English service, regained their sea under an alien flag. Desperate efforts were made by ship-owners and captains
to elude the embargo; but Napoleon the ruthless
ordered the seizure of all American vessels, without
distinction or favour, cynically observing that, by the
commands of their own government, they were forbidden to sail, and that he was assisting the United
States to maintain her admirable restrictions.

The once prosperous Quaker City was now dull, dejected, and heavy with many cares. All classes shared
in the general anxiety; few men were rich enough to
help their poorer neighbours. Robert Morris, old,

bankrupt, and brokenhearted, had seen his noble fortune melt like mist, and his friends vanish away like
floating mist-wreaths. His beautiful home, which never
reached completion, was sold by the sheriff, and pulled
down stone by stone; his books and ornaments were
bought by fellow-townsmen; and he who had saved the
honour of his country, who had fed and clothed her
starved and ragged soldiers, who had deemed no labour
too great, no gift too generous when the welfare of the
Republic was at stake, was suffered to lie for four
years in a debtor's prison, while the people he had
served in their utmost need wagged their heads wisely,
and talked pious platitudes about the Tower of Babel
and inordinate ambition. Each summer the ravages of
the yellow fever emptied the jail where Philadelphia's
greatest citizen, forgotten or ignored, breathed the pestilential air, and waited patiently for the end. When
at last he was set at liberty, that end was near at hand;
but that it did not find him still in durance was a
matter for self-congratulation on the part of his countrymen. Something they felt was due in return for his
services, and Robert Morris was permitted to die under
a roof of his own, and in the arms of his wife. Who
shall say that republics are ungrateful!

The refusal of Congress to re-charter the Bank of the
United States in 1811, added another heavy load to the
financial distress of Philadelphia. In vain her merchants, her manufacturers, her carpenters, and house-

builders sent their deputations to plead for a new charter, and to lay their dire necessities before the House. Of what avail was the homely reasoning of mere business men and mechanics, when Henry Clay, master of rhetoric and flowing periods, denounced the towering pride of corporations, and scoffed at the utility of banks. So, on the eve of war, the city saw herself crippled and bound. France had swept away her ships, Congress had swept away her credit, and England stood ready to sweep away whatever might by any chance be left.

In these sad times, the old fighting instinct came to the rescue of the commonwealth. "National happiness," says the peace-loving Deborah Logan, "was suspended by the war of 1812"; but this is a more than doubtful statement. National prosperity was, indeed, sorely crippled, and no town outside of New England was more cruelly impoverished than Philadelphia, where all the necessaries of life had grown alarmingly dear, and where the stagnation of commerce threatened absolute ruin. But with the declaration of war, of an unpopular, but not inglorious war, came the excitement of combat, pushing sordid anxieties into the background, and filling men's minds with other and wider cares. The city sent forth her sons to fight, and some of them, like Lieutenant Biddle of the *Wasp*, brought back honours to lay proudly at her feet. She fitted up privateers, — her old diversion, — and she found, Heaven knows how! money for the government loan. The adventurous raid of Sir George Cockburn, who marched into Maryland with five hundred men, as with an invading army, and whom nobody took by the shoulders and turned out, thrilled her with wholesome shame. The capture of Washington aroused her to a sense of personal disgrace and personal danger. It even silenced for a time the quarrels of her contending factions, and sent every able-bodied man to drill at Camp Dupont, or to work at the defences which, being inadequate, were happily never needed. No citizen was permitted to shirk his manifest duty, the "State Cockade" was pinned upon every shoulder, and even the comfortable voice of conscience was unheeded in the din. Pious men, who could not endure the ungodly aspect of the camp, were requested to drill apart, and make up a corps of their own.

By this time the French fever was permanently cured. Napoleon's scornful treatment had proved wonderfully efficacious in healing the most desperate cases, and when the news of his downfall reached our shores, Philadelphia, exulting openly, set at once about the usual dinners, without which no public event could be properly commemorated. She toasted the Emperor Alexander and the King of Sweden; she toasted Holland and Germany, amid wild acclamations of delight; she toasted the "patriots" of Spain and Portugal. But England, whose great struggle with her great enemy

Y

was over at last, England, who had held together the
allies, paid their soldiers, and fought their battles, received no notice at these civic banquets. Her part in
the work was ignored, for she was still our foe, and the
dawn of peace upon the continent gave her a breathing
spell which could not fail to be disadvantageous to our
cause. All things considered, it might have been better for us if Napoleon had engaged her attention a
little longer.

But on Christmas Eve, 1814, the treaty of Ghent was
signed, and while General Jackson was fighting and
winning the battle of New Orleans, word was coming
slowly over the sea that the war was at an end, and that
the United States were once more free to turn their
attention to their own pressing needs. Philadelphia's
share of needs was plainly manifest. The foreign commerce, which had brought her prosperity for so many
years, had received a check from which it never wholly
recovered. Her shipping merchants, who had built up
noble fortunes in the past, strove, but strove in vain, to
regain their old ascendency. The opening of what was
then called " the West "; the network of canals, and
afterwards of railways, which made transportation possible and even easy, gave a tremendous impetus to New
York, now reached as readily as her sister city, — New
York proudly commanding her splendid harbour, and
the natural outlet for our grains. We laugh when we
read of the old Philadelphia newspapers gravely discuss-

ing the relative merits of canals and railways, and coming to the serious conclusion that the latter were "inex-
pedient" in Pennsylvania. Sleepy little town, we think,
which at the same time rejected the introduction of gas,
declaring it to be a public nuisance, unsafe, undesirable,
and with an "intolerable smell." Yet it was a long
time before the gas-pipes proved themselves blessings
to the community; and the immediate result of the
railways was to make Philadelphia a half-way house to
the great city of commerce, New York.

"But Linden saw another sight,"

when, very slowly, there dawned on Pennsylvania the
knowledge of the mineral wealth hidden beneath her
bosom, and with it came a dim revelation of the vast
industrialism of the future. The first successful experiments with our own anthracite coal were made in Philadelphia immediately after the declaration of peace, and
its superiority over the Virginia coal in heating and
rolling iron promised magnificent results, sure to be
long in coming, but sure to come at last. One fifth of
all gold or silver ore found in his province, had Penn
promised to send back to England's king; but here at
length were the mines whose inexhaustible riches should
fill the land with plenty. Four years later, we find Lehigh coal offered for sale in Philadelphia, "in quantities
not less than one ton," the price being eight dollars and
forty cents. It was such a novelty, and people were at

once so curious and so doubtful, that the clever agents kept what they called a "specimen fire" burning all day long at 172 Arch Street, that purchasers might see for themselves what an admirable fuel they were buying.

The year 1816 saw the second National Bank of the United States established in Philadelphia, a bank destined to be wrecked, like so many other institutions, by factious hostility and violence. Her mint — not the present marble pile with its Ionic columns, but a modest predecessor — was coining plenty of copper cents, and a few silver dollars, then highly esteemed, and all too insufficient for the country's needs. The rapid increase in population, with its corresponding decrease of grace and virtue, industry and thrift, had made the feeding of the poor and the suppression of crime more difficult and more inefficacious every year. It is true that so many benevolent associations were at work starting soup kitchens and kindred charities in the Quaker City, that for a long time she was known as the "emporium of beggars," and idle vagabonds flocked from neighbouring states to enjoy her hospitality. Yet destitution on the one hand, and viciousness on the other, kept pace with her daily growth. The almshouse and the prison were equally crowded, and equally mismanaged. Philadelphia, says Mr. MacMaster, was attempting to control a population of a hundred thousand by the same primitive methods she had used suc-

THE MINT

cessfully for twenty thousand. She had become a city, without ceasing to be a village.

While things were in this uncomfortable period of transition, La Fayette came to the United States, and twice visited the town, "the great and beautiful town

OLD HOUSES BY THE RIVER

of Philadelphia," as he politely said, "which first welcomed me as a recruit, and now welcomes me as a veteran." Of the warmth of this welcome there was no shadow of doubt. What other man could have borne the weight of such sustained enthusiasm! Six cream-coloured horses drew his carriage, and the First and Second City Troops escorted him proudly through the thronged streets. He was dined, and wined, and presented with unstinted addresses in French and English. The Free Masons, the Cincinnati, the school children, and all orders, societies, and bodies of citizens generally waited upon him, and were received with indefatigable courtesy. He amiably permitted himself to be taken to all the city's sights, from the penitentiary and the new waterworks at Fairmount, to Vauxhall Garden, where a band of little boys and girls met him with lighted torches, and surrounded him as a guard of honour while he listened to the music, or stared at the appropriate fireworks.

Philadelphia always delighted to show reverence to her distinguished guests. Kosciuszko, for whom "Freedom shrieked," had visited her hospitable homes, and had received unvarying kindness and respect. Kossuth was to prove in the future that her admiration for patriots and patriotism was still undimmed. But La Fayette she really loved. He had fought her battles, he had been wounded in her cause, he had given her and her sister cities the honest devotion of his youth. His career since those early days had not been a very dazzling one; but the breathless, blood-stained, terrible, glorious history of France had permitted only the strong and the unswerving to play memorable parts upon her shifting stage. It was not a time for well-meant futilities, or indecisive action; and men more resolute than La

Fayette had failed to steer their course amid such Titanic storms. It must have been to him an inexpressible pleasure to see once again the land of his boyish enthusiasm, the people who cherished for him nothing but affection and respect. Never did any man thirst more keenly for admiration; never did any nation admire more honestly, or with more fervid zeal. The visit of this well-loved Frenchman rekindled even the embers of a burned-out fire; and when the Bourbons were expelled from France after the revolution of 1830, Philadelphia awoke to a transitory glow, called meetings, passed resolutions, and sent her sober citizens marching through the streets to the airs which had once heated the city's blood to fever point, but which now produced only an afternoon's pleasurable excitement.

There were still links which bound this restless, fast-growing population to the past, still old habits and customs not easily relinquished. The social aspects of the town had altered less than her political and commercial life. She was quieter, more thrifty than in the first expansive years of freedom, but otherwise unchanged. She is unchanged to-day. When things are as good as they can possibly be, what consummate wisdom in leaving them alone! Before the present century had started on its course, before Washington died, or Congress was carried to New York, Dr. Caspar Wistar, author of the first American treatise on

anatomy, was gathering under his hospitable roof those
informal Sunday night assemblies which were destined
to grow into the celebrated Wistar Parties, as much
an institution of Philadelphia as the Mint. Like all
things fated to long life, they did not start ready
made, did not proceed from any definite plan of organization; but expanded slowly and comfortably from
a few guests to a large club, from the friendliness of
Sunday evenings to the more formal elegance of Sat-
urdays, from cakes and wine which nobody wanted to
oysters and terrapin which nobody pretended not to
want.

All this took time. In 1811, conviviality had extended no further than the introduction of ice-cream,
nuts and raisins, — strange food for hungry men;
but the meetings had grown regular, and many
strangers of distinction brought charm and variety
into the quiet nights. Among the early guests were
Baron von Humboldt, who, returning from Mexico
and the West Indies, lingered a little while in Philadelphia; and Captain Riley, the narrative of whose
long captivity among the Arabs was one of the treasures of every child's library. Children's libraries were
not then the plethoric bookcases of to-day, and Captain
Riley ranked as a second Sinbad for wonderful adventures and ill-luck.

After the death of Dr. Wistar in 1818, it was
resolved that his evenings should be perpetuated by

a club bearing his name, the members of which should be chosen from the Philosophical Society, thus securing "mutual improvement," as in Franklin's youthful days. The ice-cream was wisely abandoned in favour of hot dishes, which increased and multiplied as years went on, until they made a very pleasing impression upon so apt a judge as Thackeray, who was not wont to ignore the essentials of life. "If I had been in Philadelphia, I could scarcely have been more feasted," he was good enough to write, after a season of London and Paris dinners; and the gratified Philadelphian, reading this generous tribute to his birthplace, murmurs under his breath, "Praise from Sir Hubert Stanley," and feels justly proud of the Quaker City's hospitality.

In 1824 were founded the Franklin Institute for the promotion of mechanical and scientific studies, in which Philadelphia had always outranked her sister cities, and the Pennsylvania Historical Society, which had for its purpose "the elucidation of the history of the State." Both these institutions began life with characteristic modesty, and maintained the utmost discretion amid the vicissitudes of impecunious youth. The Franklin Institute, like the Academy of Natural Sciences, was the work of a dozen young men, who hardly knew how much they hoped to accomplish, when they banded together and devised their first unpretending schemes. A few lectures in the old Academy building, a few classes for architectural and mechanical drawing, a few more, later on, for mathematics and modern languages. This was all they could boast, save a few useful friends like Alexander Dallas Bache, great-grandson of Benjamin Franklin, who held the chairs of chemistry and natural philosophy in the University of Pennsylvania, and who was one of the most enthusiastic workers for the Institute which bore his great ancestor's name. There seemed no lack of pupils, however, ready and glad to avail themselves of these lectures and classes; and among the earliest was a young bricklayer named Thomas Walter, who learned thus the rudimentary principles of architecture, and who some years later designed Girard College and the Capitol at Washington.

Little doubt was felt at any time of the Institute's permanent success. It had among its historical relics the original electrical apparatus, and the clumsy printing-press of Benjamin Franklin, and it appealed to the spirit he had fostered, to the seed which had taken deep root in such congenial soil. Did not Philadelphia, in the days of her tender youth, prefer lectures on electricity to the graceless levity of the theatre? "Pennsylvania," says Mr. Sydney Fisher, "is overwhelmingly manufacturing, saturated with industrialism, — the result of tendencies that have been working for two hundred years." At the very time that Thomas Walter was learning other things than the laying of brick on brick, a young silversmith and tool-maker named

MASONIC TEMPLE

Matthias Baldwin was struggling with a problem so intricate, and of such absorbing interest, that all the former occupations and amusements of his days faded into dull nothingness by its side.

How curious are the chances that come into men's lives and make them what they are! The use of steam as a motor power for railways had by the year 1829 dawned as a splendid possibility upon the world; and it occurred to Mr. Franklin Peale, the enterprising manager of Philadelphia's flourishing museum, that a miniature locomotive in good working order would be a strong attraction to his patrons. He laid the matter before Matthias Baldwin, who undertook eagerly, yet with profound misgivings, to construct the ingenious toy, which was to be large enough to drag two carriages, each holding two people, around a track laid on the museum floor. The little engine when completed was wholly successful, both from a scientific and from a commercial point of view, — Peale well understood the temper of the Philadelphians whom he studied to please, — and seeing it run its appointed course faithfully hour after hour, the managers of the Germantown and Norristown Railway Company came to the conclusion that steam would be an improvement on horse power, even for their few miles of road. They directed Baldwin to build them a locomotive, equal in drawing power to an English engine recently imported by the Camden and Amboy Railway Company, and which he was at liberty to inspect and study. It was a tremendous undertaking for one so slenderly equipped; but labouring day and night with his own hands, improvising his own tools, training his own workmen, triumphing over obstacles and defeats, Matthias Baldwin toiled on, and Old Ironsides, parent of American engines, was put upon the road on the twenty-third of November, 1832.

Vast was the excitement it created, and vast the crowds that flocked to see it start, or — thrilling with conscious courage — take their places in the carriages it drew. Its utmost speed was thirty miles an hour, and such admirable care did the company take of this new possession that it was never permitted to run out carelessly in the rain. The following is the notice inserted in the *Daily Advertiser :* —

"The locomotive engine (built by M. W. Baldwin of this city) will depart daily, when the weather is fair, with a train of passenger cars. On rainy days, horses will be attached."

So much for being a petted only child!

The difficulties in the path of the early manufacturers were so great, their discouragement was often so profound, that Matthias Baldwin was wont to say decisively many times before the engine was completed, "That is our *last* locomotive"; futile words when destiny had shaped his appointed course. The

. . . "fairy-tales of science"

are the fairy-tales of modernity, and the mighty progeny of Old Ironsides have gone forth over the civilized world. To Canada, to South America, to Russia, to Austria, to Scandinavia, they have carried the story whose interest never flags, — the story of man's conquest over the elements, of his patient labour, his resolute perseverance, his unflinching courage, and final mastery.

For matters unconnected with steam and electricity, Philadelphia evinced but a languid and half-hearted regard. The Pennsylvania Historical Society, founded the same winter as the Franklin Institute, received scant support from a community which, having broken away from the past, was ready to bury it forever out of sight. The members met in one of the rooms of the Philosophical Society, elected Mr. William Rawle as their president, and limited their expenses for fire and candles during the first year to the modest sum of fifty dollars. Unhelped and unheeded, they set about their appointed task, — the collection of books, pamphlets and manuscripts, many of them of great value, yet in danger of being permanently lost through the general indifference to their safety. For more than twenty years they continued this useful work before aspiring to quarters of their own, and then rented a single room on Sixth Street, which they fitted up with a bookcase and other furniture, — "cost, not to exceed one hundred dollars." Here, and in the upper story of the Athenæum they remained for twenty-five years, and the success of their labours is shown by the size of the library they amassed. When, in 1872, they moved to the commodious "New Hall" on the grounds of the Pennsylvania Hospital, they carried with them twelve thousand volumes, eighty thousand pamphlets, — not much trouble to collect *these* in a State which never wearied of printing them, — and a vast array of unsorted manuscripts. They had worked very quietly for nearly half a century, but they had not worked in vain.

The present home of the Pennsylvania Historical Society contrasts pleasantly with the simplicity, not to say the indigence, of its youth. Thrice fortunate in having secured the fine old property of General Patterson on Locust Street, it is spared the evil fate common to most institutions, — the inhabiting of buildings glaringly new, and ostentatiously appropriate. From the spacious, beautiful rooms, with their ineffaceable air of elegance and hospitality, may be seen the leafy garden, narrower than of yore, but inexpressibly welcome to the tired eyes of the brick-dweller. In these rooms are stored away more than forty thousand books, — the pamphlets are now long past being counted, — and a number of interesting historical relics, from Philadelphia's first charter, 1691, and the wampum belt presented to Penn by the Indians, to "Poor Richard's" Almanacs, and the log-book and telescope of Dr. Kane. Here, too, is the charming portrait of young William Penn in the days of his martial boyhood, and the original despatch which brought the news of the battle of Lexington, and a collection of nine hundred medals of Washington, — a pleasant tribute to fame, — and Franklin's little punch-keg which rolled so smoothly from thirsty guest to guest, and the gold and white china presented to the philosopher by Madame Helvetius, which seems to have suffered no scath nor mutilation at the hands of ravaging housemaids. Those were not days when cups and saucers were made to illustrate the mutability of matter.

In 1831 Stephen Girard died, and the bulk of his estate was bequeathed to the school which bears his name. The millions he had amassed in the old prosperous days of foreign traffic made him the Rothschild of his age. He was known to be the richest man in the United States, and people who loved to talk about other men's money never wearied of reckoning up his fortune. He was solitary, austere, morose, a good citizen, a just master, but with few associates, and fewer friends. He was childless, his wife was mad, he lived alone, "exchanging no offices of courtesy or kindness with his neighbours." Yet in that dreadful summer when Philadelphia was desolated by the yellow fever, and afterwards, when cholera swept her slums free of their miserable inhabitants,

no one worked harder for his fellow townsmen than
Stephen Girard; no one gave more liberally than he,
time, money, and even sympathy, that rarest of bene-
factions from a millionnaire, and which is worth more
than all his millions multiplied. Girard was not by
nature kind; his was no bright, broad, genial outlook
on the world; yet there is not lacking evidence to
show that he helped again and again where help was
sorely needed, and where no one recognized the
helper's hand. Men called him — perhaps with truth
— an atheist, and atheism was distinctly unpopular
in the city which religious enthusiasm had founded
and sustained. The clause in his will which forbade
to clergymen of any creed the exercise of their sacred
functions within the precincts of his school, and
which refused them even the common privilege of
entering it as visitors, added to the uncanniness of
his reputation. The bequest was a magnificent one;
but why, it was asked, should orphan boys be denied
the ministrations of the faith which was their birthright? Why should this cold hostility to all tenets
and dogmas reach from the grave to influence the
lives of little children, uprooted by indigence from
the soil of home, and flung into the broad, bleak
arms of systematic, organized charity?

It was not possible, however, to disobey or to ignore
any injunction in Stephen Girard's will. No man
ever knew his own mind more accurately than he

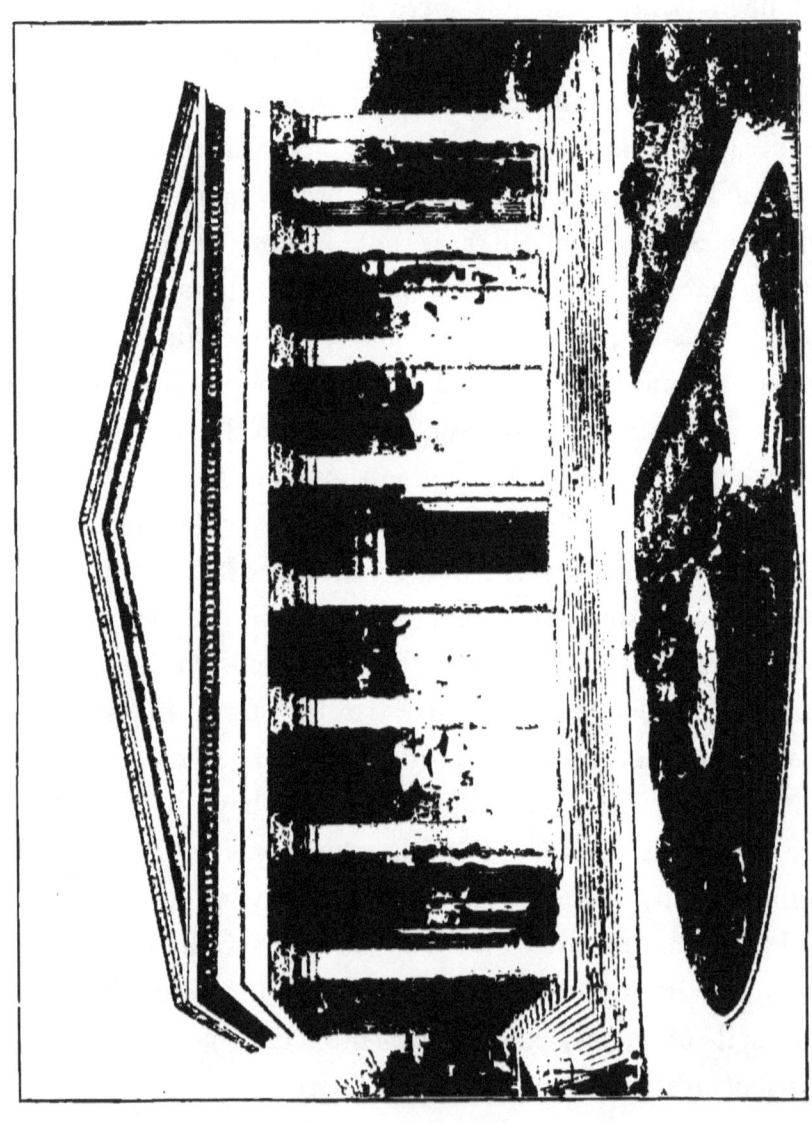

GIRARD COLLEGE.

did, nor left more minute directions, — even to the vaulting of the ceilings, which gave forth such reverberating echoes that they had to be covered over before master or boy could hear each other speak in the schoolrooms. The only matter in which the directors were permitted to use their discretion was the study of the classics. "I do not forbid, but I do not recommend the Greek and Latin Languages," is the wording of the will. It was Girard also who applied the term "college" to his great charity school, which is not a college in the correct and accepted sense of the term. The lads are admitted when they are from six to ten years old, and under no circumstances remain after they are eighteen, while by far the greater number leave at an earlier age. They are taught French and Spanish, — which were especially enjoined by the founder, — the common English branches, and the industrial arts, so that as many as possible may learn to labour deftly with their hands.

It is difficult to do justice to the size and scope of this remarkable institution. The trust fund for its support has, through the careful management of the directors, increased to the enormous sum of fifteen millions. The first beautiful building, with its stately columns, and its air of noble simplicity, has been reinforced by thirteen others, all pleasing to the eye, and all admirably constructed. They cover, with their lawns and playgrounds, an area of forty-one acres; and within them sixteen hundred boys are maintained and educated, forming a little city of their own; a community hemmed in by streets and houses, yet apart from the home life which surrounds them; bound by close kinship to toiling women and men, yet remote from common paths, from common cares, from the common pleasures and pains that make up the ordinary, every-day existence of Philadelphia's equally poor but less secluded sons.

The year that followed Girard's death was fraught with many evils. The intense and unusual heat of the summer lent a deadly malignity to the cholera, which by this time had returned again and again to exact its heavy tolls. So great was the mortality that, in the narrow Arch Street jail, seventy prisoners died within two months; and every evening, strollers who had come forth to breathe a little air, even the stifling, tainted air of the city by-ways, saw the corpses carried from the prison gates, and piled in the waiting carts. Then, too, the hostile attitude of President Jackson, who in July vetoed the bill to re-charter the Bank of the United States, awoke bitter but futile resentment, and was ominous of coming calamity. Philadelphia's banks had always led stormy lives; but she had hoped, and hoped in vain, that a national institution, well-ordered and beneficial, might win more gentle treatment. Valiant efforts were made by the directors to avert the threatened destruction; their official statements were pronounced satisfactory, and Mr. Nicholas Biddle, the bank's president, did all that lay in the power of mortal man to soften the animosity of its enemies. But Jackson, who was not easily turned from a set purpose, followed up his veto by removing the government deposits. Business was paralyzed, one failure followed another, and, in this desperate emergency, it was deemed possible to re-incorporate the stock in a state institution, which was chartered by the Pennsylvania Legislature in 1836. From that day until its final collapse in 1840, distress was keen and ruin imminent. All classes suffered from a blow that was aimed at all alike. The rich lost heavily through the rapid depreciation of stocks, the poor were rendered poorer by the inevitable reduction of wages. It was a melancholy period, which the historian is glad to pass swiftly and lightly by.

One incident of the time is worth narrating for the pleasant illustration it affords of our grandfathers' conservatism and piety. Only in 1830 did Philadelphia succeed in ridding herself of the chains which churches of all denominations were permitted to stretch across the streets during the hours of service, so that neither preacher nor congregation should be disturbed by passing vehicles. People were supposed to stay quietly at home, or to sit quietly in their pews, on the Sabbath day, and not to drive profanely through

"THE SILENT CITY"

the silent city. But necessity knows no Sunday, and it often happened that the doctor speeding to his patients, the engines speeding to a fire, were fatally delayed by these barriers which forced them to turn aside again and again before their destinations could be reached. Even the driver of the mail protested irreligiously against such devious and winding ways, and a strong effort was made to have the troublesome impediments removed. The churches, one and all, wrestled stoutly for their peculiar privilege, but public sentiment mastered their opposition. The chains fell, and sleepy citizens, dimly conscious of Philadelphia's progress, murmured softly like the obstinate Galileo, "Still it moves!"

CHAPTER XIX

RIOTS

FOR many years the City of Brotherly Love had been preëminent for the bitterness of her hostile factions, and for the unruly behaviour of her mob. The populace had learned its lawless lessons during the Revolution. It had sincerely enjoyed breaking the windows of Quaker citizens, or raiding the houses of Tories. These diversions coming to a close when the Republic was firmly established, were succeeded by other and no less lively demonstrations. Genet's heroic sympathizers had threatened Washington and the administration with open violence. Labour riots had become more and more common, as times grew harder and harder. The weavers in Kensington defied the sheriff, routed the police, and destroyed the hated machinery. The volunteer fire companies, "brigand firemen," as Mr. Fisher calls them, added a powerful element of disorder to the city they were supposed to serve. Rival companies fought desperately for the possession of plugs, while houses burned to the ground, and favoured thieves, to whom the firemen had granted their patronage and protection, pillaged the property of all that could be swiftly seized. If a mob fired a building, — no unusual occurrence, — and the hose companies sympathized with the mob, they refused to extinguish the flames. If their sympathies were on the other side, they naturally preferred fighting their opponents to bothering about the conflagration. In either case, householders suffered, and so powerful had these ruffians become, so influential were they in city politics, that no man dared to protest openly against their evil doing.

The anti-slavery agitation, which grew more violent after 1830, awoke such passionate resentment and opposition in the hearts of the masses that riot followed riot. Negroes were pelted in the streets, white men, who pleaded their cause, were pelted on the platform. Houses occupied by negroes were burned to the ground, and their inmates fled in abject terror beyond the city limits. In May, 1838, the Abolitionists held their meetings in Pennsylvania Hall, on Sixth Street, and many prominent agitators denounced the accumulated evils of slavery. Among the rest, John Greenleaf Whittier, then editing the *Pennsylvania Freeman*, read a poetical address, in which he rejoiced — prematurely — over the consecration of the hall to the noble cause of emancipation.

"One door is open, and one temple free,
A resting-place for hunted Liberty."

It was not open long. Two nights later, the mob burned it to the ground, and Whittier, disguised in a wig and a white overcoat, — like the detective of melodrama, — watched the work of destruction, and sighed over the non-prophetic character of his verse.

A NEGRO ALLEY

All this sustained defiance of law and order paved the way for the serious riots of 1844, the "Native American Riots" as they were called, because they arose from the clamorous opposition offered by the Native American Association to the equally vehement demand of the Roman Catholics that children belonging to their church should, when attending religious instruction in the public schools, be permitted to use the Douai instead of the King James Bible. This controversy being well established, and a consecrated character given to the impending struggle between two nationalities, the outbreak began, as most outbreaks do begin, through the inordinate desire of one faction to hold meetings and denounce their opponents, and the irresistible impulse of the other faction to break up the meeting with brickbats.

That the Native Americans should have selected to gather together and expound their views in the immediate vicinity of the Hibernia Hose Company, showed either a readiness for the strife, or a painful lack of perspicuity. The habit, long acquired, of holding pitched battles over disputed fire-plugs had made mighty fighters of all the volunteer companies. That the Hibernians should have sallied forth and attacked the meeting evangelical, was, while neither wise nor right, hardly a matter of surprise to those who knew the Irish temperament, and the pure joy it feels in breaking heads. A lively combat ensued, in which guns were fired, some of them from the windows of the Hibernia Hose House, many people were injured, and one lad killed. At seven in the evening the sheriff, Mr. Morton McMichael, arrived on the scene, but was powerless to check the rioting, which grew fiercer and fiercer under cover of the darkness. An attempt was made by the Native Americans and their upholders to burn a schoolhouse occupied by the Sisters of Charity and their pupils, — helpless creatures who had been guilty of no violence, and who could not even avoid being in danger's way. They were stanchly defended, however, by the Irishmen; and, as the battle deepened, a number of "innocent spectators," who should have been at home, were severely wounded, and houses tenanted by Roman Catholics had all their windows broken.

It was a bad night's work. Several injured men died after being carried to the hospital, and the general excitement was fast reaching fever heat. The Native Americans held another meeting the following day, passed resolutions, denounced the Catholics, and, growing angrier and angrier under the spur of their own eloquence, marched in a body to attack the Hibernia Hose House. The Irishmen were there to meet them, and a fierce struggle followed, in which six of the invaders were killed. They succeeded at length in firing the house, and the flames spread with appalling rapidity to all the neighbouring properties. Alarm was given, and a number of engines came to the rescue; but the mob, now blind with fury, and unable to distinguish between friend and foe, refused to allow any of the firemen to approach the burning buildings. It was only the arrival of the First

Brigade, commanded by General Cadwalader, which calmed their emotions, and persuaded them to sullenly disperse. The conflagration was checked, but not before thirty houses and the old "nanny-goat market" were reduced to smouldering ruins.

Up to this point there had been little to choose between the lawlessness of either faction. Honours were easy, and upon all shoulders rested the burden of blame. But the passions of the mob had been heated to danger-point, and it was pleased to side with the Native Americans, and to profess the same religious enthusiasm which lent zest to the Gordon riots in London. The torch has ever been the favourite weapon of the populace, and it was used with terrible efficacy and good-will. The Catholics were no longer able to defend their property. Bishop Kenrick issued a manifesto, entreating and commanding them to offer no violence under provocation, but to trust to the protection of their country's laws. The struggle did not lie now, as in the beginning, between the Native American Association and the Irishmen, but between the mob and the military, between open outlawry and the authority of the State.

One day of quiet lulled the city into a false sense of security, and on the next, a maddened crowd, rising like locusts from the ground, swept through the streets of Kensington, and at broad noon applied the torch to St. Michael's Roman Catholic Church, and to the schoolhouse, the "nunnery" as it was called, which had so narrowly escaped destruction three days before. Both buildings were burned to the ground, and the rioters decided to prolong the entertainment by firing the rectory and some adjacent houses. They were sincerely anxious, or so they affirmed, to confine their attentions to members of the erring creed; but unluckily the flames recognized no polemical distinctions, and spread straight on, consuming two rows of humble residences, and filling all hearts with consternation and dismay. It was five o'clock before the arrival of the soldiers dispersed the mob, and saved the entire quarter from destruction; and in the meantime another body of rioters had gathered in front of St. Augustine's Catholic Church, at Fourth and Vine Streets. This was in the heart of the city, far from the scene of the previous disturbances, far from the offending hose company, and the homes of the Irish weavers. The City Troop was stationed near; Philadelphia's mayor was present on the spot. Apparently, mayor and military were alike disregarded. The incendiaries broke open the church, and set it on fire. The flames, mounting rapidly and without hindrance, licked the roof and the wooden cupola, surmounted by a gilded cross. When this cross fell crashing to the ground, cheer after cheer burst from the throats of the surrounding mob. While men shrieked their approval and delight, the City Troop rode by at full gallop, their brilliant trappings lit by the glare of the conflagration. The rioters defied them doggedly, and went on with their work of destruction.

Adjoining the church was the schoolhouse. It had been turned into a hospital during the dreadful summer of 1832, and in it the Sisters of Charity had nursed the sick and dying cholera patients through those long months of burning heat and pestilence. Now it was once more a school, and contained the valuable library of the Augustinian priests. There were over a thousand books, many of them rare old editions of the classics, which could not be duplicated in the United States. The mob flung these books out of the windows, kicked them into heaps, and made bonfires of them in the street. A few were saved, many were stolen, before the flames spread to the schoolhouse, and consumed all the rest in one swift, hopeless destruction. By morning nothing was left save a mass of ruins, and the blackened walls of the church, on one of which, high over the spot where the desecrated altar had stood, might still be deciphered the prophetic words, "The Lord Seeth." Men looked at them and wondered, as they look to-day at the dim figure of Christ with outstretched arms, which, whitewashed rudely over by Moslem hands, still stands faintly but ineffaceably portrayed above the apse of St. Sophia.

The city began to realize the gravity of the situation, and the extent of its own danger. Mayor Scott called a meeting, enrolled a number of citizens in the "peace police," and divided them into patrols for the protection of life and property. Bishop Kenrick ordered all Catholic churches to be closed the following Sunday, lest fresh provocation should lead to fresh disorder; and for the first time, since the early history of Philadelphia, men stayed in their homes because they dared not assemble for service. St. John's, then the Catholic cathedral, and St. Mary's had both been threatened by hostile mobs; and St. John's had been saved from the torch by the timely appearance of General Cadwalader, who found the rioters ready for their work, and gave them five minutes in which to disperse. So great, however, was the feeling of insecurity, so menacing the attitude of the populace, that the sacred vessels and the vestments were removed from the churches, and concealed in private houses. Even the Catholic orphans were not permitted to remain in the asylums which no longer afforded them a safe shelter.

The grand jury, then in session, presented a long and feeble statement, "regretted" the extent of the violence, intimated that it was really time the disturbances should cease, and charged the beginning of the outbreak to " the efforts of a portion of the community to exclude the Bible from the public schools"; — hardly a fair assertion, inasmuch as the Douai version of the Scriptures, while less beautiful as English literature than the translation authorized by King James, is still "the Bible,"

INTERIOR OF ROMAN CATHOLIC CATHEDRAL

and to read it is not to exclude Holy Writ from education. Nevertheless a sentiment prevailed that the street riots were in some sort religious and devotional, a nineteenth century crusade, unduly zealous perhaps, but stimulated — like the Gordon riots — by pious fervour. The Native American Association grew rapidly from a few hundreds to many thousands; and, conscious of its own strength and of the weakness of its opponents, it prepared for a grand demonstration on the Fourth of July, a demonstration which should effectually but peacefully reveal its imposing size and majesty.

For provoking quarrels and for disseminating contagion, nothing is so preëminently successful as a parade. The Catholics were, indeed, more impressed than was altogether desirable by the mighty preparations for the Fourth. They were thoroughly alarmed for the safety of their churches, and the congregation of St. Philip Neri's applied to the arsenal for arms, with which a volunteer company under a commissioned officer could protect the property, if attacked. Twenty-five muskets were furnished on an order from Governor Porter. These were never used, because no assault was made on the day of the great procession; but when it was generally known that guns and powder had been stored in the church, a strong feeling of hostility was aroused. If people were to be permitted to defend their possessions after this martial fashion, there would be an end to all the pleasant pastimes of the last fortnight. The sheriff accordingly removed the objectionable arms the following morning, but the excitement did not subside ; and, on the sixth of July, the slow gathering of the mob, which grew denser and denser as night approached, gave ominous warning of the trouble still to come. General Cadwalader, who by this time had grown pardonably weary of the populace and its diversions, strove hard to clear the streets ; and the soldiers, though taunted and insulted by the rioters, succeeded by midnight in dispersing them for a few hours, — the lull before the storm. Day had not dawned before they were back again, sullen, resolute, ripe for any form of violence, a force not easily reckoned with nor subdued. In a few hours they had broken the windows and battered down the door of St. Philip Neri's, forced the militia who were guarding it to withdraw, and established themselves triumphantly in the church, as in a fortress that had been carried by storm.

Once more General Cadwalader prepared to dislodge them, and this time he realized the nature of the impending strife. The troops were ordered to clear Queen Street. It was no facile task. The mob, well-armed, and well supplied with ammunition, fought fiercely in the narrow highways. Through the long summer afternoon, and far into the night, the battle raged. From windows and from pointed roofs the rioters fired down upon the soldiers. They dragged three cannons from a ship lying at the wharf, loaded

OLD MARKET-PLACE

them with bolts, chains and spikes, and discharged them
again and again, the result being as fatal to the crowd
as to their opponents.   They stretched ropes across the
darkening streets to obstruct the passage of the cavalry.
It was picturesque, and exceedingly like Perugia in the
Middle Ages, when the Baglioni and their rivals fought
in the great square of the Cathedral : but it was not
at all like Penn's City of Peace, which he had founded
as an asylum for the oppressed, where no sword was to
be drawn, and no man persecuted for his creed.

The soldiers, hemmed in on every side, were well-
nigh exhausted.   They also had two cannons, brought

2 A

from the battery at Second and Queen Streets; but
their ammunition was nearly gone when the arrival of
the First State Troop forced the mob to give way.
By midnight the firing ceased, and by dawn, twenty-
four hours after the rioters had assembled in front of
St. Philip's Church, the streets were clear, and peace
restored to Philadelphia. Only the wounded and the
dead were left to tell the price she paid.

This was ·the last mad outbreak of the populace.
Governor Porter, now fully awake to the public
peril, called together all the troops that could be
spared from Pennsylvania's more tranquil towns, and
the presence of five thousand soldiers calmed the angry
passions, and chilled the religious enthusiasm of the
mob. Nor had the city learned her lesson without
profit therefrom. It was clearly evident that the old
system of boroughs and townships no longer afforded
a safe or strong municipal government, and that some
closer bond was necessary to draw together the different parts of one great whole, and unite them in a
single corporation. In 1849 a meeting of prominent
citizens, under the leadership of Eli K. Price, began
the work of reform, which was so successfully concluded by the Consolidation Act of 1854. Philadelphia, instead of being divided and subdivided in a
fashion which lent itself to perpetual strife and a dangerous weakening of responsibility, became one united,
consolidated city. The pernicious system of taxation,

which was all cost and no returns, disappeared in favour
of more practical methods. The volunteer fire companies were shorn of their political power, compelled to
modify their methods, and finally abolished altogether,
when many dry eyes witnessed their departure. The
police corps was reorganized, and bands of ruffians, like
the "Bouncers" and the "Schuylkill Rangers," no
longer found themselves at liberty to terrorize one district, and retreat safely to another, where the arm of the
law could not reach them. The common schools were
securely established, and education took a great leap
forward, — a leap in the dark, said the discontented,
but anything seemed better than standing perfectly still.
In fact, the city had grown weary of immobility; weary
of the torpor which had bound her for the past forty
years, and had reduced her to a dead level of mediocrity;
weary of narrow ways, of insignificance, and provincial-
ism. New life was tingling in her veins, new hopes and
fears were beating in her heart. Already the shadow
of strife was darkening over the land, and drowsy
Philadelphia awoke to play her part in the coming
struggle. The voice to which she had ever responded
had been the voice of war.

CHAPTER XX

IT is the irony of fate that the province Penn founded to be the home of peace should have gained distinction as a fighting state. He had planned a refuge from the din of contention, the wickedness of bloodshed; and the colony he loved cast aside the traditions which had nourished her. Pennsylvania, as Mr. Sydney Fisher observes, has, in the course of her history, " produced more distinguished military men, manufactured more war material, and had more important battles in more different wars fought on her soil, than any other State in the Union." It is the old story of destiny and the plough overturning the plans of men and mice.

Theoretically, Philadelphia had always been opposed to slavery. Germantown protested against the holding of slaves in Penn's lifetime, when the custom was universal. The Friends had ceaselessly combated what they believed to be a deadly evil; and the keen desire of the southern congressmen to remove the seat of government to Washington arose from a not unnatural anxiety to escape the endless protests of the Quaker Abolitionists. It is true that the populace, largely composed of foreign elements, grew more and more hostile to the anti-slavery agitators, until its anger culminated in negro riots, and the burning of Pennsylvania Hall. But Philadelphia and Philadelphia's mob were never in accord. It is true also that the city's trade was largely with the South, that she had always been on terms of especial friendship with southern towns and states, and that she was unwilling to see this cordial understanding weakened, and her commerce injured, by reckless agitation on the part of those who had no interests at stake. The abolition movement had never wholly won her favour, and, though the Fugitive Slave Law was little more to her liking, she strove for years to enforce it, to keep faith with her neighbours, and to respect their legal rights. It was a conflict of emotions, the end of which might have been easily foreseen by those who witnessed the joyous welcome given to Abraham Lincoln before his inauguration, and the enthusiasm evoked when the President-elect raised the new flag with its thirty-four stars — the last star for the recently adopted state of Kansas — over the roof of Independence Hall. The lessons taught by those historic walls had not been learned in vain. Philadelphia may have regarded with cold aversion the New England orators who stirred the animosity she was most anxious to allay; but there was neither doubt in her

mind nor hesitation in her actions when the safety
of the Union was imperilled.   Of speeches in the
market-place she had grown weary and mistrustful;

"OVER THE ROOF OF INDEPENDENCE HALL"

but, if the call came, she was ready as of old to argue
the matter stolidly in platoons.

The call did come with the attack on Fort Sumter,
and with the President's demand for seventy-five
thousand volunteers to quell the rebellion.   The first

State to respond was Quaker Pennsylvania, the first soldiers sent to Washington were five companies of Pennsylvania militia, under the command of General Robert Patterson and General William Keim. General Patterson was at this time in his seventieth year. He had served in the war of 1812, and in the war with Mexico; but an Irishman from county Tyrone is seldom too old to fight, and General Scott, then commanding the United States army, entrusted to the care of this Philadelphia veteran the "Department of Washington," and the protection of the Capitol.

Twenty-five regiments were exacted as Pennsylvania's first quota of men. They were raised immediately, and thirty more were offered, but, at the time, refused. The Pennsylvania Reserves were organized the same year for the defence of the State, — fifteen thousand men, serving three years, and holding themselves in readiness for any emergency. The emergency came quick enough after the Confederate victory at Bull Run. The President instantly called the Reserves to Washington, and from that time to the close of the struggle they fought with great distinction, never being permitted to return to the service of their State.

Meanwhile the industries of war changed Philadelphia into a great hive, where men and women toiled like bees to manufacture much that the country needed, and needed instantly. In the arsenal, men laboured day and night; in the Southwark Navy Yard, the force was gradually increased from six hundred to seventeen hundred, and yet the work could not be done in time. Cannons were cast in the foundries, thousands of wagons were made for the service of the artillery and of the commissariat. Countless throngs of women were employed in cutting out and sewing the blue-grey uniforms of the soldiers, now hastening from every township in the State, from every home in the city, to bear their parts in the bloody strife.

Yet even while Pennsylvania's sons went forth to join the ranks, even while Meade, McClellan, Reynolds, and many more were heaping up honours for her name, she was, none the less, the home of the "Copperhead," of the Democrat whose heart was not in the war, and who ardently desired peace. He was a force to be reckoned with, an opponent not easily subdued. The ceaseless cry for more men, more men, and ever more men to fill up the places of the dead; the terrible carnage in each succeeding battle; the overflowing hospitals; the desolate homes; the flinging away of human lives without stint, without mercy, without reckoning, — these things embittered the soul of the Copperhead, and lent weight to his vehement denunciations. His unwelcome presence, his unsilenced tongue, evoked endless complications; not the least of which was the deciding where freedom of speech ended, and disloyalty began. This was a point on which zealous patriots and conservative lawyers naturally failed to agree. Judge Cadwalader and his brothers on the bench were kept busy defining the exact nature of treason and misprision of treason; but their verdicts awakened little enthusiasm in the hearts of jurymen or the crowd. If a man sold firearms to the Confederates, that was treasonable, and he could — when caught — be promptly punished. But the editor of an evening paper might disparage President Lincoln, and praise President Davis, and the angry people were told this was the privilege of citizenship. They called it treason, though the judges wouldn't, and they broke windows and battered doors to emphasize their opinions; demanding indignantly, when arrested, if traitors were to be coddled, and loyal men punished, in the City of Brotherly Love.

When, in the summer of 1863, came the news of General Lee's advance to the Shenandoah Valley, the wildest excitement reigned throughout the Middle States, and centred itself in Philadelphia. Once more was heard the oft-repeated call for volunteers. A hundred thousand men the President demanded, to meet this sudden danger, and half of them were to be raised in Pennsylvania. The harvests were ripening with few hands to reap them; the dead lay uncounted in the trenches of every battlefield; but there was no holding back when the summons came. Governor

Curtin issued his proclamation, asking for soldiers to defend the State, and young and old responded swiftly to the appeal. Councils granted five hundred thousand dollars for home defences, and all Philadelphia citizens, exempt from active service, were bidden to enlist in a corps organized for the protection of the town. The ordinary business of life stood still. Shops were closed, and anxious crowds thronged Chestnut Street, and pressed about the State House, eager for tidings, yet fearful lest it should be evil tidings that they heard, lest word should come that Lee was even then advancing into the heart of Pennsylvania, and would stand at the city's doors.

General George G. Meade was at this time in command of the Army of the Potomac, whose leaders had succeeded each other with bewildering and disheartening rapidity. The battle that decided the fortunes of the State was fought at Gettysburg on the first, second, and third of July; a pitiless, glorious battle, where both armies contended with desperate valour for three awful days, and where the loss of life was too appalling to be calmly considered. In Philadelphia, wild and contradictory rumours filled all hearts with suspense until the morning of the fifth, when Meade's official despatches announced that Lee's advance had been checked; and, immediately after, the sick and wounded came pouring into the city. General Hancock, with a shattered leg, and five hundred unfortunate

CHESTNUT STREET

companions arrived on the fifth, and, by the twelfth, over four thousand injured soldiers lay in our hospitals, bearing witness to the cost of deliverance. Three thousand Confederate prisoners were at the same time carried to Fort Delaware. It was not easy to rejoice with so much suffering on every side, and when the long lists of the dead carried mourning to countless homes.

The news of the capture of Vicksburg by General Grant pointed clearly to the end of the unequal combat, and men began to ask themselves how much longer these ragged, unpaid, undaunted southern soldiers intended to hold out against fate. The feeble resources of the South were waning fast; those of the North were practically inexhaustible. Immediately after the battles of Gettysburg and Vicksburg, President Lincoln issued a proclamation, demanding three hundred thousand men to serve three years. They were to be raised by conscription, for it was no longer an easy task to find that number of volunteers; and, by the middle of July, the drafting — bitter work — began in Philadelphia. Before seven months had passed, two hundred thousand more men were needed to fill the gaps made by Grant's bloody conquests. In these two conscriptions, Philadelphia's quota was thirteen thousand men; yet she stood stanchly by her Republican governor, and by the great Republican President, though General

McClellan was deeply beloved in the city of his birth, and the anger aroused when he was superseded in command by General Burnside added immeasurably to the strength of the Copperheads, and to the disquiet of the whole population. The emancipation of the slaves had been gladly welcomed, even by the majority of the Democrats, and all classes united in one great effort to soften the sufferings of the wounded soldiers, whose numbers had now risen to dreadful proportions, notwithstanding the ceaseless thinning of their ranks by fever.

From the beginning of the war, Philadelphia had taxed her energies to the utmost in the unceasing effort to provide accommodation for the sick and injured. After the second battle of Bull Run, seventeen hundred of these unfortunates arrived within twenty-four hours; and, after Grant's battles in Virginia, five thousand were sent in an incredibly short time from the South, to be crowded into the already overflowing hospitals. It was well-nigh impossible to obtain trained and competent nurses; and the city gladly accepted the aid offered by the Sisters of Charity, at whose head was a woman of singular capacity and strength of character, Sister Gonzaga, well known for the work she did during those trying years. In the summer of 1864 the great Sanitary Fair was opened in Logan Square, where a number of buildings had been hastily erected for the purpose. It was like a little " World's Fair," brilliant, beautiful, varied, — everything but gay, — gayety being hard to grasp after more than three years of civil war. President Lincoln came from Washington to do it honour, and the proceeds, amounting to over a million of dollars, were devoted to the purchase of hospital supplies for the wounded soldiers in Pennsylvania, New Jersey and Delaware.

In December, 1864, there was still another call for three hundred thousand men, and the proclamation of the President allowed less than four weeks for the drafting of this new army, to which Philadelphia's contribution was eleven thousand, five hundred soldiers. It was, however, the last conscription of the war. The South lay devastated, drained of every resource, without money, without food, without ammunition. Boys of fifteen and old grey-haired men were fighting in her enfeebled ranks. The fertile lands were barren of their harvests, and, in the broad track of Sherman's destroying army, women and children starved by their desolate hearths. The end, so long deferred, had come at last; and on the tenth of April, 1865, word was carried to waiting Philadelphia that the remnant of Lee's forces, a pitiful remnant of twenty-six thousand men, had surrendered to Grant, and that the war was over. From her old State House roof rang out the joyful tidings, and every heart responded with rapture to the message of the bell. The war was over. It was hard to believe the truth, hard to feel sure that the pitiless drafting and the pitiless slaughter were already things of the past, and that men of one nation, brothers of one parent stem, were no longer marching to kill each other in the open field. Pennsylvania had sent over three hundred and sixty-six thousand of her sons to do this deadly work. One out of every eight inhabitants — a ghastly proportion — had gone forth to fight. What wonder that Pennsylvania's great city should draw a deep breath of relief when this pressure was lifted from her heart! Out of the handful of soldiers who had left the State during the war with Mexico, only one half returned. Out of the vast army who departed for the Civil War, so many perished that the universal joy was subdued by almost universal mourning.

The news of President Lincoln's assassination came like a bolt from the blue, and turned the public content into sorrow and ominous gloom. His body was brought to Philadelphia on the twenty-second of April, and lay in state for two days in Independence Hall, where four years before he had raised the new flag amid the joyous enthusiasm of the crowd. Now the people came in thousands to gaze sadly at his bier, and thousands more were turned from the doors when the two short days were over. It was a tragic ending to the story of the war, and it robbed peace of its gladness and its triumph.

CITY HALL

FAIRMOUNT PARK

CHAPTER XXI

THE QUAKER CITY OF TO-DAY

THE great wave of emotion which swept over the country with the strife which rent her apart, and with the slow reconciliation which bound her once more in unity, left its traces upon national life. War, the stern foster-mother of arts and letters, wakened the dormant spirit of the people, who responded, as all people do respond, to impulses borne of that strange quickening discord. Even to the South, bearing its heavy burden of humiliation and distress, came the thrill of this tingling renaissance, while the North and West sprang forward with giant bounds. Philadelphia, roused thor-

oughly from her long sleep, felt no disposition to drowse
again. The nation was fast approaching her hundredth
birthday. She was

"growing a great girl now,"

as Father *Punch* genially observed, and it was but fitting
that the town which had the honour of being her birthplace should joyously celebrate this auspicious anniversary. The Centennial Exhibition has been so far
surpassed by the glories of Chicago's exhibition that
people speak of it now with patronizing kindness, as of
something well-meant, but indifferently executed. It is
a point of honour for each world's fair to eclipse the
fair before it; and when a summit of splendour is
reached which cannot be outclimbed, the diversion must
come to an end, and even Paris find another plaything.
Philadelphia, always a pioneer, has been almost always
excelled by those who followed in her footsteps. She
it was, among American cities, who printed the first
daily newspaper, and the first magazine. She established
the first circulating library, the first corporate bank,
and the first medical college. She laid the keel of the
first American warship, and unfurled the first American
flag. She was the home of the first National Congress,
and of the first Supreme Court of the United States.
Finally, she organized the first World's Fair that this
country had ever seen, — no facile task, as those who
bore a part in it can testify.

HORTICULTURAL HALL

Perhaps the most cheering token that the Fair was at least a possibility lay in the success of the Franklin Institute, which in 1874 gave a very brilliant exhibition of the mechanical arts. But the difficulties in the path of the vaster enterprise were well-nigh insurmountable. Lack of money, lack of precedent, lack of knowledge, lack of skill, held back the eager hands. The national government promptly and firmly declined to grant any assistance, save the cost of its own exhibits, and a loan of one million, five hundred thousand dollars, which was repaid in full to the treasury when the Fair was closed. The city did not lend, but gave a similar sum ·for the erection of Machinery Hall, and the highly ornate Horticultural Hall, which commended itself to the taste of those who liked plenty of colour for their money. The State of Pennsylvania appropriated one million of dollars, which were ruthlessly expended upon Memorial Hall, a squat, clumsy building, sadly destitute of distinction or beauty, and which stands to-day in Fairmount Park, an abiding but unnecessary proof of our boundless waste, and limited artistic development. All the other expenses were borne by the board of finance which, under the able leadership of Mr. John Welsh, struggled and struggled successfully to raise the necessary funds.

Of the interest aroused by the Fair, of the wonder it excited, and of the impetus it gave, not to Pennsylvania alone, but to the whole nation, it is unne-

cessary to speak. Nature, indeed, with that grim
humour which is so scantily appreciated by her victims, exerted herself to play a part in the festivities;
and provided a season of such sustained and unprece-
dented heat that Philadelphia's reputation as a daughter of the tropics was forever established in the land.
From the tenth of May, when the Exhibition opened,
to the tenth of November, when it closed, there was
little escape from this baleful temperature; and, in
the summer days, the thermometer under the spreading trees of the Park, or in the shaded city streets,
ranged from ninety to one hundred and two degrees,
with a persistence which cost many lives, and can
never be forgotten by the survivors. Well did they
realize in those dreadful months the meaning of
Penn's proud assertion that his province lay "six
hundred miles nearer the sun" than England.

One of the immediate results of the Exhibition was
the arousing of a patriotic interest in centenaries,
which came thick and fast, and afforded plenty of
opportunities for demonstrations. In 1882 Philadelphia celebrated the two hundredth anniversary of
her Founder's arrival. A little ship resembling the
Welcome was towed to the Dock Street wharf on the
morning of October 24th, and William Penn's representative, stepping ashore, was duly welcomed, and
compelled to play his part in a merciless civic procession which took four hours to pass a given point,

and was as hopelessly uninteresting as only a civic procession can be. A nation without an army is — unless she wastes her money in less useful and honourable fashion — greatly to be envied on the score of economy; but her parades are seldom things of beauty. Yet, strange to say, the Quaker City has ever dearly loved these dismal diversions. She will now contentedly see her traffic stopped, and her impatient citizens wedged in waiting crowds, while hundreds of policemen and firemen walk stolidly and mournfully through the streets, the effect given being that of a gigantic funeral. At the bi-Centennial there were four whole days devoted to parades. Three thousand Knights Templar, twenty-four thousand tradesmen and artisans, and many companies of militia took turns in honouring the memory of Penn, and commemorating his journey over the sea to the colony he founded and loved.

In 1887 came the centenary of the adoption of the National Constitution, and three days were given over to the customary celebrations. One hundred years before, when the States wheeled into line and accepted the code of laws under which they were to live, Philadelphia expressed her joy by organizing the first great industrial procession that ever marched through her streets, a procession in which her leading citizens masqueraded amiably and picturesquely as cultivators of the soil. She now repeated this enter-

tainment without the masqueraders, but on such a
gigantic scale that the wagons and floats took seven
hours to pass the State House, and imprisoned spectators felt the glow of enthusiasm slowly chill before
the pitiless autocracy of hunger and fatigue.

Meanwhile the progress of the city outstripped the
ambition of her sons. Burdened by municipal blun-
ders, tainted by municipal corruption, she yet pushed
onward, freeing herself now and then from some of
the barnacles that clung, and still cling, about her
civic skirts. The Bullitt Bill, as the new charter
was called, did for her in 1885 what the Consolidation Act did in 1854, — cleared and simplified the
complicated machinery of her laws, reduced her
twenty-five departments to nine, corrected some star-
ing and unabashed abuses, and made of her mayor —
hitherto a figurehead — a very important and authoritative official, upon whose fitness or unfitness for his
post depends much of the city's weal. The enlarge-
ment of the harbour, the deepening of the river bed,
the establishment of the Bourse, the increase of manufacturing interests, the building of many ships and
many locomotives, — sisters and brothers of progres-
sion, — all have abundantly proved the power of the
people to move onward in certain well-defined directions. Whatever remains — and there is much remaining — of inefficiency and faithlessness in office,
of discomforts long endured, and dangers unaverted,

is due to that curious, apathetic good-nature which all Americans share in common, and of which Philadelphians have no more than their even allowance. Good-nature is a dangerous virtue for a nation. Our keen sense of the ridiculous helps us to endure much that should never be endured; and the easy laugh with which an American citizen recognizes the rascality of the men whom he permits to rule him, is a death-blow to the reforms which are essential alike to his well-being and to his self-respect.

The artistic growth of Philadelphia has been a fitful and feverish expansion. When she lost the quiet beauty, the exquisite sense of appropriateness and proportion which lent distinction to her colonial architecture, she wandered through devious paths, now clinging desperately to white marble and Grecian columns, — seeking safety in the definite and ascertained, — now giving free scope to much original and depressing ugliness. Squat, clumsy buildings, presenting a dead level of hopeless, but not actively offensive, mediocrity, gave place slowly to more ornate structures, which revealed both the riotous possibilities of unbridled decoration, and an almost superhuman grasp of whatever was inherently unfitted for its purpose. Nothing is more remarkable than the tireless ingenuity with which an architect will go far out of his way to illustrate the meretricious. Only in late years has there come a change, and now men, masters of their craft, have begun to adorn the old

Quaker town with graceful homes, and with public
edifices, stately, strong and simple, harmonizing as
far as possible with their surroundings, and reflecting that fine self-restraint which was the distinguish-
ing characteristic of the early colony.

It must ever be a matter for regret that the City Hall,
commonly called the Public Buildings, should represent
the most hopeless period in the history of Philadelphia's
architecture, and that its only claim to distinction should
be the marvellous manner in which it combines bulk
with sterling insignificance. Size alone, we are brought
up to believe, insures some degree of majesty. It is the
bigness of the Pyramids which overawes the puny traveller in Egypt. But the City Hall is very, very large.
It covers a wider area than any other municipal building in the United States. It is four hundred and
eighty-six feet long, and four hundred and seventy
feet broad. It has a courtyard two hundred feet
square, and a tower five hundred and ten feet high,
as tall nearly as the fair white shaft in Washington.
It ought to be reasonably impressive, even though it
were not beautiful. Yet the only effect it gives is that
of an almost squalid paltriness. The dingy and monotonous façade refuses resolutely to look vast; the
tower of marble and lumpy metal-work is equally
determined not to appear its proper height. The
surmounting statue of William Penn gives to the
whole a final, but needless touch of incongruity. On

every side the decorations are either mediocre or painfully grotesque; and in murky corridors, that look as if they ought to lead to prisons hidden from the light of day, ugly twisted forms writhe in unseemly attitudes, as though struggling to escape from such depressing and melancholy gloom. The thin slabs of marble that form the outer skin of the walls have crumbled here and there in premature decay, and have been replaced by fresh ones, the startling whiteness of which, contrasting with their blackened neighbours, gives the effect of a great patchwork quilt. New windows, not in the original plan, have been pierced where least expected, but where — presumably — the wretched inmates have begged for light and air. Of the millions expended upon this monument of inefficiency, and of the length of years it must stand in the very heart of Philadelphia to bear witness against the people who erected it, even those who profess a truly American unconcern endeavour not to think. As an illustration of what can be accomplished by an irresponsible building commission, the City Hall is not without interest nor without a moral; but if Experience be the best of teachers, she asks terribly high prices for her tutelage, and unambitious citizens are wont to wish that their own town had not selected to take such an expensive course of instruction.

Yet even while Philadelphia was learning bitter lessons, she was also acquiring rich gifts, — gifts, artistic,

scientific, educational, which were to enable her to com-
pete with other great cities in the race for all that makes
life pleasant, and of value. The Pennsylvania Academy
of the Fine Arts is the oldest institution of its kind in
the United States. Founded and chartered in 1805,
it had its birth in still earlier days, when Charles
Wilson Peale and Guiseppe Ceracchi struggled to
maintain their school of painting and modelling, and
when modest exhibitions were held in the State House,
exciting scant interest in the community. The first
Academy building stood back from Chestnut Street,
with a courtyard and green trees between its portico
and the grime of the city's highway. Old Philadelphians who associate it lovingly with their childhood's
days; who, when they were little boys and girls, walked
round and round the group of " Centaurs and Lapithæ,"
trying vainly to disentangle the combatants; who stood,
thrilling with terror, before West's vast canvas, " Death
on the Pale Horse," and wakened at midnight from
awful dreams wherein that ghastly rider followed them,
cannot well criticise the merits of these familiar objects. Perhaps decorous and inartistic citizens were
a long while escaping from the mental attitude which
bade them cover up the antique casts from women's
curious eyes. Perhaps they have not laid it wholly
aside even now, being pardonably perplexed by the
contentiousness of their many teachers, and by the variance in the lessons taught.

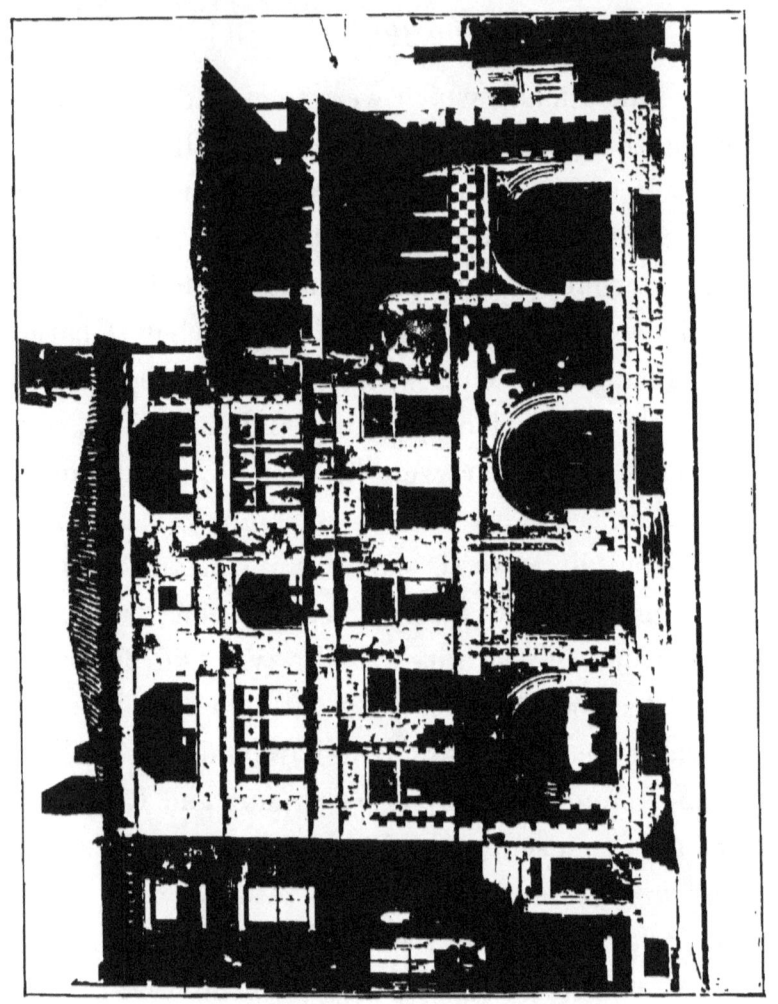

ART CLUB

But that we have grown in knowledge and in wealth since those primitive days, who shall be found to question? The little white edifice, with its Ionic columns and its graceful air of detachment, has been replaced by the present structure on Broad Street; the small museum of paintings, which included, however, valuable specimens of early American art, has expanded into a gallery of which the city may be justly proud. Private collections, containing pictures of exquisite beauty, have been acquired by bequest or by purchase. A generous endowment enables the Academy to buy year by year works of recognized merit; and the wisdom of the directors has saved these pictures from being covered with glass, a barbarous fashion, necessary only in soot-stricken England, and inexcusable in clearer, cleaner air. The exhibitions of early winter have grown from insignificance into a wide repute which promises even greater results in the future. It is a striking characteristic of Americans that, the profoundly discouraging attitude of the government they sustain cannot wholly stifle their love of art. They are willing to look upon her merely as an industry, and to hold that she can be regulated, like other industries, by the law of supply and demand, and by an adroitly repellent system of taxation. They still believe that "money makes masters," and that it lies in the power of wealth to quicken the genius it is prepared to patronize. But to covet pictures, and good

pictures, to covet even a sight of them if possession
be denied, is the first step to a wider knowledge ; and
it would be hard to overestimate the artistic education derived by Philadelphia from her yearly exhibitions, when from east and west and over the seas come
the canvases which hang for two short months upon
her spacious walls.

If the development of the Academy of the Fine Arts
be a matter for wonder and delight, what shall be
said of the development of the University of Pennsylvania, which, within a score of years, has expanded
in so marvellous a manner that none can now limit
her future ambitions and achievements. A century
and a half have passed since Franklin's " Proposals "
went the round of sedate little Philadelphia, and found
favour in many eyes. The college established by the
Philosopher has led a checkered life during these hundred and fifty years, with much of honour and much of
shame to give it light and shade. The high resolves
and brilliant promises of its impetuous youth were
chilled after the Revolution into ashes, which barely
kept alive a tiny spark of fire. Through long periods
of degrading inertia, when the blight of mediocrity
lay upon Penn's city and all within her walls, the
University — its very title a reproach — drowsed with
its somnolent neighbours. When the town awakened,
the old college awakened too, and wholesome humiliation
pricked it into action. Seventeen years ago the first

buildings were erected in West Philadelphia, a modest
quartette, substantial, but far from beautiful, and with
only fifteen acres they could call their own. From this
new birth came swift and steady growth. The spirit of
strenuous, insatiable progress moved forward with over-
mastering zeal. Even placid self-satisfaction, which
wanted to feel that it had done enough, was rudely
undeceived, and structure after structure rose to give
outward and visible sign of the restless power within.

LIBRARY OF THE UNIVERSITY OF PENNSYLVANIA

To-day the University covers upwards of sixty
acres, and finds this space too small. A library,
where the twenty thousand books carried over the
river have increased to nearly a hundred and fifty
thousand; a museum under the same roof containing
valuable collections of Egyptian, Babylonian, and
American antiquities; hospitals for men, women, dogs,

and cats, — for the medical school, which formerly outstripped its rivals, still stands abreast with all competitors; an unequalled institute of anatomy; a
botanical garden; dormitories, which have even the
grace of beauty to recommend them; halls, labora-
tories, buildings wherein all things may be taught
and learned, are grouped around the earlier foundation. The students have doubled and trebled in
these years of advancement, the faculty has been
proportionately enlarged. Better than all, the Graduate School, made adequate by liberal endowments,
raises the University to a higher educational plane
than seemed attainable a few years ago, and enables
her to give her sons benefits they have hitherto sought
from afar. When, in the future, the " Free Museum
of Art and Science " stands fair and complete, it will
be the crowning glory of a college, old as we count
age in this young land, and a connecting link with
that colonial period whose work we reverence, and
whose influence and importance we realize more
keenly day by day.

Other institutions of learning has Philadelphia,
though of less paramount importance. The venerable
Academy of Natural Sciences bears the weight of
many years and of past honours. The Drexel Institute, the School of Industrial Art, and the School of
Design for Women, open their doors to give what
practical aid they can to the great unanswered prob-

lem of education. Within a dozen miles from the
city's gates stand the Quaker colleges of Haverford and
Swarthmore, built and endowed by members of that
religious body which has laboured so successfully for
the material and intellectual welfare of Pennsylvania.
And near at hand is Bryn Mawr College, founded by

PEMBROKE HALL, BRYN MAWR COLLEGE

a Friend, Dr. Joseph W. Taylor, in 1880, for the advanced education of women.

If old age, with its traditions, and its curious record
of right and wrong, attracts us keenly to an institution, youth, brave, unabashed, triumphant, dazzles us a
little by its splendour. Bryn Mawr was opened for
scholars in 1885. It is thirteen years old, — a child
among colleges; yet its group of buildings with their

adjacent lawns, courts, and athletic grounds, cover fifty acres. The infant library — a lusty babe — has already twenty-five thousand books, and three thousand dollars are spent annually in enlarging it. Over three hundred students are accommodated in the four halls of residence, — Merion, Radnor, Denbigh and Pembroke. The Graduate School offers admirable advantages, and has been enriched with eleven resident and three European fellowships. Were Philadelphia wont to boast, even as much as a wise city should, she would vaunt long and loud the achievements of this young college, which in a few years has attained so fine a record, and set so high a standard of scholarship before the world.

But Philadelphia does not boast. She occasionally remembers that she might do so if she pleased, and she remarks now and then, half apologetically, that her Park is the largest in the United States, and the most beautiful in the world. Only the Prater of Vienna excels it in size, and no other approaches it in loveliness. Nearly two hundred years ago, when the little Quaker colony never dreamed of possessing a great pleasure-ground of its own, Mr. Richard Castelman, who spent the winter and spring of 1710 in Penn's town, records the delight he felt in walking with friends on clear afternoons to Faire Mount, in looking at the river, and breathing the wholesome country air. It was not, however, until a century later that the city made

its first modest purchase of Morris Hill, five acres in
extent, as a site for the proposed waterworks. A
little garden shaded by trees, with grass plots, gravelled walks, and a fountain, lay at the feet of the
steep incline. Rush's denounced statue of the "Nymph
and Swan" was placed picturesquely on the rocks,
where the tall jet of water from the bird's slender
throat fell into the pool beneath, and where the
maid's clinging draperies, wet with spray, no longer
offended the decorum of Centre Square. The same
sculptor executed two reclining figures, which were
placed over the doorways of the wheel-houses where
they still remain. One of them, a venerable and dejected old man, symbolizes the Schuylkill, fettered
by human ingenuity, and chained in locks and dams.
The other, a square, severe female of the Roman
empress order, typifies water, and was broadly and
comprehensively described by enthusiastic critics of
the day as "unequalled in its kind throughout the
world." The only exception taken to the work was
that the vase against which the figure leans, and
which represents the reservoir, is so full it overflows,
the little lumpy streams falling over the sides with
painful regularity, and hanging suspended in mid
air. This was held to be "picturesque, but not appropriate, as a reservoir should never overflow." It was
certainly far from veracious. A vase half full of
liquid mud would have been nearer truth.

The little Park became in 1825 a great favourite with the public, and all strangers visiting the city were taken to sit under the trees, and to examine the waterworks, which were not then, as now, a mass of complicated machinery, propelled by steam, and of interest only to the initiated. In the old days, when an afternoon at Fairmount was the keen and crowning pleasure of childhood, huge wheels revolved slowly

LILY POND IN FAIRMOUNT PARK

in the black water; awful, mysterious wheels, terrifying beyond measure to infant Philadelphians who peered down trembling from the rickety wooden causeway into the abyss below. The vibrations shook the slender balustrade against which they leaned; in the semi-darkness the swirling eddies were churned into foam; their hearts throbbed with a delicious ecstasy of fear; the world seemed turning, turning, with those mighty wheels down into the rushing waters; and then — when they could bear no more — came the swift revulsion from terror to exquisite delight, as they climbed back into the sunshine and the warm, soft air, and saw the staid, familiar grass plots, and heard the fountain splashing cheerfully in its marble cup. All is changed in that little old corner of Fairmount, which has been long abandoned for the more beautiful walks and drives beyond. The hall which had such a delightful echo, and in which stood Rush's wooden figures of Justice and Wisdom, has been dismantled. The marble boy, whose shameless nakedness was half hidden by the spouting fountain jets, has disappeared. The Nymph, who seems destined, poor thing, never to find a permanent home, has been lifted from her rocks, and placed in the centre of the garden. Even the children have broader playgrounds now, and no longer run ceaselessly up and down the steep reservoir hill. The world moves on its way, and every city holds spots like this, once prized, and now neglected, once full of life, now empty and forlorn.

The Park grew slowly until it counted its first twenty-four acres. Then Philadelphia began to taste the sweets of proprietorship, and coveted wider lands. Lemon Hill, Sedgeley, Lansdowne, and adjacent estates were added from time to time. Some care was taken to improve the grounds, and keep the roads in order. The beautiful Wissahickon Glen,

2 c

where, in the days of the Founder, the German
mystics had built their huts, to await, amid the fairest
scenery they could find, the coming of the millennium,
was purchased in 1868. George's Hill was presented
to the city by its aged owners, Mr. Jesse George and
his sister Rebecca, in whose family
it had remained for generations.
Many ancient landmarks
and historic man-
sions were in
cluded in the
boundaries
of Fair-

THE "SOLITUDE"

mount; some carried thither, like the little Letitia
House, built by William Penn for his discontented
daughter; some standing where they had stood for
a century or more, like Mt. Pleasant, the home of
Benedict Arnold, Belmont, the home of Judge Peters,
and the "Solitude," that Liliputian dwelling-place
erected by John Penn the younger, when some whim

for isolation possessed his restless soul. Even the "Castle," the time-honoured abode of the Fishing Company, which is the oldest club of its kind in the United States, was enclosed in the wide confines of the Park.

The Zoölogical Garden was opened in 1874, a handsome, well-appointed garden, perhaps a shade less melancholy than most of these sad prisons for beast and bird; — where the polar bear gasps in our torrid heat; where the caged eagle, motionless as stone, gazes with sombre eyes into the forbidden blue; and the lion paces hour after hour its narrow den, unutterable longing, unutterable weariness in every languid step. The day must come, though it seems far distant yet, when an advanced civilization will question its own right to condemn wild creatures to lifelong captivity, for the amusement which we call complacently instruction.

In Fairmount Park, the crowning glory of Philadelphia, the city has realized in her own way, and as best she could, her Founder's desire for green fields and spreading boughs. Closer and closer creep the houses, even in the suburbs which once had breathing space; higher and higher tower the great business buildings, lifting their stone walls against the sky; fouler and fouler grows the poisoned earth, until the trees, which once lent grateful shade to the hot, glaring streets, wither and die. But near at hand — a recompense for all such evils — lies this vast civic demesne, these broad acres that belong to all; with wooded tracts and deep ravines, with hills and dales, and brown streams rippling into shallow pools, and the river winding its leisurely way through the heart of the people's playground. The possession of this park illustrates the temper of the town whose English colonists brought

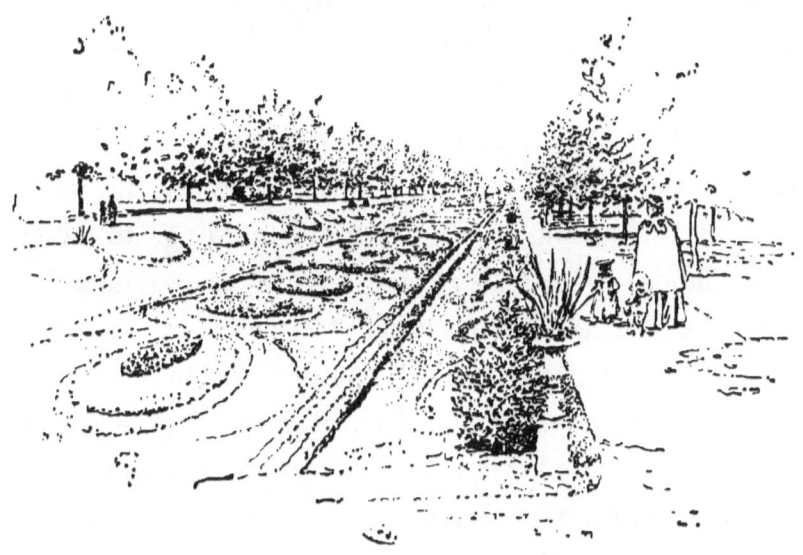

FLOWER BEDS, FAIRMOUNT PARK

over the sea a love for the country, and country life; and whose rich citizens built themselves suburban homes, considering, like true Britons, that the great pleasure of prosperity lay in the acquisition of landed estates.

They think so still, for, indeed, the city built by Penn has retained many of the characteristics which first distinguished her. It is not so easy as the careless believe to relinquish a birthright, to escape from an inheritance. Onward we must move, but our finest development lies along the lines marked out for our first footsteps. The debt Philadelphia owes to her Quaker colonists is no less apparent because she has put aside fashions of speech, and dress, and public worship. It is true that only for a few weeks in the year may the drab bonnets and broad-brimmed hats be seen in the crowded highways, and that they grow less marked with each succeeding spring. Yet, nevertheless, the impress of the Quaker hand lingers still; not only in the simple, dignified old buildings to which time lends an added charm, but in the ineffaceable spirit of the town. A quiet town always, at which noisier communities point fingers of derision, mistaking bustle for advancement. To pass from a great sister city to Philadelphia is like leaving Paris, where every one conscientiously strives to make as much noise as he can, and entering London, where every one conscientiously strives to make as little as he can, the result being a grateful silence, healthy for mind, and soul, and body. Even wealth wears a strange air of modesty in the old streets, where once the prosperous Friends gave little outward token of the fortunes they amassed and enjoyed. Money is the same great power all the world over, but there is ever a limit to its autocracy; and in Philadelphia it is expected to show as little arrogance as it can, which is a virtue that must be acquired in the beginning, but becomes a gracious instinct by inheritance.

A strong attachment to whatever has been, an equally strong, and often well-founded dislike for innovations, characterize Penn's city, which has seldom thirsted after novelties. Her prejudices are ancient, deeply venerated, and unconquerable. Strangers within her gates protest vehemently against these prejudices, and explain their absurdity in the clearest and most convincing manner. They waste a great deal of valuable time in this way, and are never quite sure whether they have been listened to or not. If the day ever comes when logic will persuade as easily as it preaches and proves, the face of the earth will be altered, and Philadelphia may change with the changing world.

Above all, the Quaker City lacks that discriminating enthusiasm for her own children, and the work of their hands, which enables more zealous towns to rend the skies with shrill pæans of applause, and to crown their favoured citizens with bays. Philadelphia, like Marjorie Fleming's stoical turkey, is "more than usual calm," when her sons and daughters win distinction in any field. She takes the matter quietly, as she takes most other matters, preserving with ease her mental balance, and listening unmoved to the plaudits of the outside world. This attitude is not wholly wise nor commendable, inasmuch as cities, like

men, are often received at their own valuation, and
some degree of self-assertion converts many a wavering mind. If the mistaking of geese for swans
produces sad confusion, and a lamentable lack of perspective, the mistaking of swans for geese may also
be a dangerous error. The birds either languish, or
fly away to keener air, and something which cannot
be replaced is lost. Yet anything is better than having
two standards of merit, one for use at home, and one
for use abroad; and the sharp discipline of quiet
neglect is healthier for a worker than that loud local
praise which wakes no echo from the wider world.

A quiet town. Her mobs which once went mad
with joy over the Revolution in France, or mad with
zeal for a religion, ill-understood and ill-obeyed, have
been calmed by age, or by the influence of a community
which never, even in moments of folly and degradation,
lost the saving grace of sanity. It is true that much
that is new and much that is bad have vulgarized and
vitiated the old tranquil life; but something that was
given to the infant city as she lay cradled between
her two rivers remains with her still, some leaven of
modesty, some legacy of soberness and self-restraint.
Still the tender, pathetic appeal of William Penn,
when he bade farewell to the colony he had founded
and cherished, rings in our ears, and finds an answer
in our hearts: —

"And thou, Philadelphia, the virgin settlement

of this province, named before thou wert born, what care, what service, and what travail has there been to bring thee forth, and preserve thee from such as would abuse and defile thee. Oh, that thou mayest be kept from the evil that would overwhelm thee; that, faithful to the God of thy mercies, in the life of righteousness, thou mayest be preserved to the end."